The Network Press QuickPath to NetWare® 4.11 Networks

Second Edition

The Network Press QuickPath to NetWare® 4.11 Networks

Second Edition

Jeffrey Hughes and Blair Thomas

NETWORK PRESS
SYBEX

San Francisco ■ Paris ■ Düsseldorf ■ Soest

Associate Publisher: Steve Sayre
Acquisitions Manager: Kristine Plachy
Acquisitions and Developmental Editor: Guy Hart-Davis
Associate Developmental Editor: Neil Edde
Editors: Vivian Perry, Peter Weverka, Marilyn Smith
Project Editors: Linda Good, Bonnie Bills, Shelby Zimmerman
Technical Editor: Deeanne Higley
Book Designer: Seventeenth Street Studios
Graphic Illustrator: Inbar Berman
Electronic Publishing Specialist: Bill Gibson
Production Coordinator: Anton Reut
Indexer: Nancy Guenther
Cover Designer: Archer Design
Cover Photographer: FPG International

Library of Congress Card Number: 96-68706
ISBN: 0-7821-1883-6

Manufactured in the United States of America

10 9 8 7 6 5 4 3 2 1

This book is dedicated to Wendy, Laurin, and McKenna, who very patiently supported this endeavor.

JFH

This book is dedicated to Pam and Jessa.

BWT

Acknowledgements

N O LITERARY WORK is due solely to the efforts of one or two persons, and this book is no exception. This project is a culmination of experience and information gathered from the outstanding members of Novell's Consulting Services group.

First, we recognize the contribution of James D. Sorenson, with his expertise in NetWare 4 installations and migrations. He has been generous with advice and suggestions on many technical aspects of this book. We appreciate his contribution to the migration chapters. His knowledge of NetWare is astounding.

Second, our appreciation to our technical reviewer Deeanne Higley, for her meticulous review of this book and her objective and insightful comments.

Third, our thanks to the many Novell consultants who have contributed directly or indirectly to this project: Gary Hein, Kyrt Nay, Dean Payne, Paul Reiner, Carl Seaver, and J. Orland Seaver.

We also wish to thank all those involved at Sybex, in particular Neil Edde, Linda Good, Bill Gibson, and Anton Reut for their support and valuable contributions during this project.

Many thanks to our editors, Vivian Perry, Peter Weverka, and Marilyn Smith, for their incredible insight and editing abilities. They have been an enormous help. Their contributions have far exceeded our expectations.

For their continuous support over the years, we thank our families and friends, among those Lorne 'Brad' Braddock, who is a great leader and role model for putting the customer first! Keep up the good work.

Finally, we wish to thank all our NetWare customers whom we have visited around the world. Our experience with you has provided the basis for this book.

Jeffrey F. Hughes
Blair W. Thomas

Contents at a Glance

Table of Contents

Introduction

A S A LAN PROFESSIONAL, you understand that the key to successfully implementing any hardware or software product is to identify the tasks you need to carry out and the order in which to perform those tasks. By following a specific task order, you learn a process that you can apply successfully every time.

Because NetWare 4.11 requires design steps along with the installation, you need to know the order in which to undertake these steps. The order is the key to success.

The QuickPath Process is a complete, easy-to-follow process for designing, implementing, and using NetWare 4.11 to its fullest capabilities in any size environment. The QuickPath Process is based on Novell Consulting Services' experience at scores of customer locations.

The relative brevity of the book should not be mistaken for incompleteness. Each chapter provides all the necessary information to ensure a successful installation of NetWare 4.11. Whether your network has only one server located in a single location or many servers connected over wide-area links, this book is for you.

Who Should Read This Book?

This book is designed for all LAN administrators, network engineers, consultants, resellers, and anyone who is setting up a new NetWare 4 network, migrating a network to NetWare 4.11, or considering such an installation or migration. *The Network Press QuickPath to NetWare® 4.11 Networks* provides timely and accurate information about all crucial aspects of NetWare 4.11.

If you are a consultant or reseller, you'll find this book a rich source of information for you and your clients. It will guide you in the planning, design, and implementation of NetWare 4.11.

What You'll Learn from This Book

In this book, you will learn the QuickPath Process for implementing NetWare 4.11, the foundation of IntranetWare, in simple or complex network environments. You will be presented with a proven process and strategy for deploying NetWare 4.11 at your site.

This book will provide you with detailed information on how to design an NDS (NetWare Directory Services) tree, with flexibility for future modifications as your needs change, and with stability, which your users require.

Once you have designed an NDS tree to meet your needs, you will be ready to install or upgrade to NetWare 4.11. The book clearly explains the steps required for installing a new NetWare 4.11 operating system or migrating from an existing network operating system to NetWare 4.11.

You will also learn how to handle day-to-day operations once you have NetWare 4.11 up and running. The book includes details about setting up printing, using NetWare 4.11 utilities, administering security, and managing your network, as well as troubleshooting problems.

How This Book Is Organized

This book contains three parts, covering NetWare 4.11 implementation, from preliminary design to daily operations.

Part 1, NetWare Directory Services Design, provides the information you need to produce an effective NDS tree design. The chapters in this part cover how to use NDS objects, how to create an appropriate naming standard for your network, how to arrange users and resources at suitable levels of the NDS tree, and how to design partitioning and replication. Part 1 also explains the rules of thumb for time synchronization within a network of virtually any size.

Part 2, Installation and Migration to NetWare 4.11, details the actual steps you need to take to install or migrate to NetWare 4.11 successfully. You will learn how to prepare for NetWare 4.11 by creating a migration and implementation schedule and designing a lab for testing your NDS design. The other chapters in this part provide details on installing NetWare 4 client software on your workstations and installing or migrating your NetWare servers.

Part 3, Day-to-Day Operations, covers the activities involved in maintaining a NetWare 4.11 network, including setting up for printing and using the NetWare 4.11 utilities. You'll also learn how to determine and implement the appropriate security for your particular network environment. The final chapter in this part deals with monitoring and maintaining NetWare Directory Services, including backup and recovery procedures and diagnosing problems.

The five appendices contain specialized and reference material that you will find helpful. Appendix A covers troubleshooting and includes a complete listing of error codes, their meanings, and suggestions for corrective actions. Appendix B provides tips for tuning your workstations.

If you are migrating from another network operating system, such as LAN Server, LAN Manager, or Banyan VINES, turn to Appendix C for complete instructions. For details on setting up specific network-direct printing devices, turn to Appendix D. And, finally, if you need to find the definition of a particular term, you can look it up in the glossary provided in Appendix E.

Get There Fast with QuickTips

This book includes a special QuickTips feature. Each chapter (except Chapter 1) begins with a QuickTips section, which provides important hints and tips that will get you through the task if you don't need the details. The QuickTips are based on numerous successful implementations of NetWare 4.11 at sites across the world.

You can turn to the first few pages of each chapter and skim the QuickTips, leaving the other portions for later reading. Along with each QuickTip item, you'll find a page number, which leads you to the in-depth discussion of that particular point. This way, you can easily find just the information you need.

Sources

As part of our research for this book, we have referred to the following *NetWare Application Notes,* published by Novell:

- "Understanding and Using NDS Alias Objects" (September 1993)

- "Time Synchronization in NetWare 4.*x*" (November 1993)

- "NET.CFG Parameters for the NetWare DOS Requester 1.1" (June 1994)

- "The Across-the-Wire Migration Utility" (September 1993)

- "Using Network-Direct Print Devices in NetWare 4" (June 1994)

- "Management Procedures for Directory Services in NetWare 4.01" (March 1994)

NetWare
Directory
Services Design

PART

The QuickPath
Process

CHAPTER

PROCESS IS DEFINED as a particular method of doing some task in a specified order. After extensive experience working with the NetWare 4 product, we recognized the need to define and order the steps involved in designing and implementing a NetWare 4 network.

From countless consulting visits at small and large network sites around the world, we have developed a process for design and installation that will virtually guarantee your success with NetWare 4. The QuickPath Process goes beyond providing design and installation information and actually orders every step.

This chapter presents an overview of the QuickPath Process. At the end of this chapter, you'll find a summary of what is new in NetWare 4.11.

After reading this chapter, you'll be ready to begin the QuickPath Process. The chapters that follow describe the steps in detail.

What Are the QuickPath Process and NetWare?

THE QUICKPATH PROCESS is an order and method for designing and installing a NetWare 4 network. You could compare the QuickPath Process to a recipe that requires a certain ordering of the steps for a successful result.

IntranetWare is a new intranet platform that offers all the advantages of NetWare 4 and also provides advanced intranet and Internet capabilities from your servers. These features include Directory Services, security, routing, messaging, management, Web publishing, and file and print services. IntranetWare also offers the Netscape Navigator Browser, FTP Services for NetWare 4.11,

Novell's IPX/IP gateway, and a multiprotocol router for wide area network (WAN) and Internet connections.

Unlike the single-server environment of NetWare 3, NetWare 4 organizes your resources in a network-wide group. For your NetWare 4.11 installation, you need to consider many factors that were not important in NetWare 3 or other server-centric installations.

You need to apply these considerations at specific points during the design of your NDS tree. The QuickPath Process shows you where in your design to consider each factor.

The term NDS tree *refers to the logical and hierarchical tree structure created when you install a NetWare 4.11 network. This structure is also known as the* Directory tree. *The tree organizes the objects in NDS. Its shape is inverted, with the root at the top and branches beneath. We will use the term NDS tree throughout the book.*

Keep in mind that you may need to modify some of the tasks presented here to suit the specific needs of your company or client. However, to get the best results, we recommend that you follow the order in which we present this material. Remember, the order of these tasks will make your implementation much smoother.

The Objective of the QuickPath Process

THE OBJECTIVE OF the QuickPath Process is to supply an easy method for understanding and implementing NetWare 4.11. To accomplish that goal, the QuickPath Process provides you with a blueprint for designing and installing your NetWare 4.11 network. Your blueprint encompasses guidelines for installing and migrating to NetWare 4.11. Once you customize the process to suit your organization, you can repeat the process at other locations within your company.

Additionally, the QuickPath Process will provide you with the confidence and skills you need to install or migrate a network to NetWare 4.11. With the clear guidelines presented in this book, you will gain confidence in NetWare 4.11 and in your ability to use it. You will find that many of the concepts within NetWare 4.11 are not difficult to master with proper explanation and clear guidelines.

The third and last objective of the QuickPath Process is to show you how to quickly perform the previous two objectives. The steps discussed in this book need not take months and months to bring you to a successful installation of a NetWare 4.11 server. Naturally, the more servers you have, the longer your complete migration will take. However, you can install NetWare 4.11 in a gradual process if necessary for your implementation.

The QuickPath Process Step by Step

THE QUICKPATH PROCESS consists of the following eight steps:

1. Organize and educate the NetWare 4 project team.

2. Understand the use of NetWare Directory Services (NDS) objects.

3. Create a naming standard for NDS.

4. Design your NDS tree.

5. Create a migration and implementation schedule.

6. Introduce a lab testing and pilot system.

7. Migrate clients and servers to NetWare 4.11.

8. Perform day-to-day operations and maintenance.

Each of these steps is described in the following sections.

1. Organize and Educate the Project Team

The NetWare 4 project team may consist of you and a few others if you're dealing with a small site, or of seven to ten people in a larger company. The project team will be responsible for the design and implementation tasks related to NetWare 4.11. The following responsibilities should be assigned to members of the project team:

NetWare Directory Services (NDS)	Creating a naming standard, the NDS tree, and partitioning/replication placement.
Training	Providing the network administrators and user community with the necessary training opportunities, which include a lab environment for hands-on training.
Servers	Managing the implementation of NetWare 4.11 to the company's designated servers. This includes the lab pilot staging and migration of your existing NetWare 3 servers.
Workstations	Configuring, optimizing, and updating the workstations to the client software for NetWare 4.11.
Applications	Testing compatibility for all production applications that will be run on the new operating system.
Printing	Designing the printing strategies and testing them in NetWare 4.11.

For your training program, consider what experience your administrators have with NetWare 3 and with NetWare 4.11. Administrators with a good understanding of NetWare 3 can concentrate their learning on the NDS aspect of NetWare 4.11. Their training should include design and installation of NetWare 4.11 and administration of NetWare 4.11.

If your administrators do not have much experience with any version of NetWare, they may need to attend courses for more basic training. All participants in your NetWare 4 project should have lab exposure.

Also consider what training should be given to end users. Because your end users will be shielded from the complexities of the network operating system, they should require very little training in using NetWare 4.11. You may want to consider training them to use NetWare's NWUser utility, which allows users to map drives and capture printers. All other activities for your users should be fairly automated. You can also train your users to operate Novell's Application Launcher Utility.

We have not devoted a chapter to educating your project team because your educational needs will vary depending on the personnel and the requirements of your company. We encourage you to seek training from Novell Authorized Education Centers and provide your administrators with on-site lab exposure. Hands-on training can be extremely valuable for your network administrators.

2. Understand the Use of NDS Objects

A basic prerequisite for designing an NDS tree is to understand the use of the NDS objects. This is similar to an artist understanding the use of color and brushes before starting a painting. The more you know about the use and function of the NDS objects, the more effectively you'll be able to place them in the NDS tree. Chapter 2 describes how to use NDS objects.

3. Understand NDS Naming Conventions

The next step in the QuickPath Process is to design an effective naming standard that will allow for any changes to your network structure as it grows. This standard should be informative and useful for users and administrators alike.

In order to create a standard, you need to know some of the basics of NDS naming conventions. Chapter 3 explains NDS naming conventions and provides guidelines for creating your naming standard.

4. Design the NDS Tree

With the basic groundwork in place, you will be ready to begin the actual design of your NDS tree. You approach this design in two phases: first, the top layer of the tree, and then the bottom layer. The top layer of the tree takes into account your network infrastructure and wide-area links based on geographic locations. The bottom layer of the tree structures your departments and organizations based on your company's organization chart.

After you've roughed out a tree design, you apply the extenuating factors that influence the design of your tree. For example, you will need to consider partitioning and replication. Chapter 4 describes an efficient approach to NDS tree design. The design factors are described in detail in Chapters 5 through 7, which cover partitioning and replication, time synchronization, and NDS access.

5. Create a Migration and Implementation Schedule

With a preliminary tree design in hand, you are ready to create a migration and implementation schedule for NetWare 4.11. This schedule provides a timeline for accomplishing the various design and installation tasks. Having such a document helps you to keep the process moving and gives focus to the remaining tasks.

The migration and implementation schedule will identify which users and servers you will initially migrate to NetWare 4.11 after completing your scheduled lab activities. Preparing for NetWare 4.11 migration is discussed in Chapter 8.

6. Introduce a Lab Testing and Pilot System

Lab testing is a vital part of the QuickPath Process. In the test environment, you can make mistakes and familiarize yourself with the NetWare 4.11 utilities and configuration parameters. You will test the operating system, as well as its features.

Set aside a definite time period in which you will perform and complete your lab activities. You should iron out all the kinks in the system in terms of migration scenarios, partitioning, backup and restoration procedures, and so on. You should also use the lab time to test the applications that you'll be using on the network for compatibility and performance with NetWare 4.11. You'll find that your time spent in the lab will return dividends when you move NetWare 4.11 into a production environment. Chapter 9 describes how to develop a lab testing and pilot system.

7. Migrate Clients and Servers to NetWare 4.11

Once you've accomplished the previous six steps, you'll be ready to migrate your network to NetWare 4.11. You will have drawn up a blueprint that will be your guide to the first and subsequent production installations of NetWare 4.11.

If you complete each step following the details provided in this book, you will be able to install and use NetWare 4.11 quickly and successfully. Once you have mastered the QuickPath Process, the installation and migration will become easier with each subsequent installation or migration you perform. Chapters 10 and 11 cover NetWare 4.11 migration to servers and workstations. Chapter 12 describes how to migrate to NetWare 4.11 from other operating systems.

8. Conduct Day-to-Day Operations

This final and ongoing step in the QuickPath Process deals with the daily activities of maintaining a NetWare 4.11 network. Once you have designed a tree and have successfully migrated a few servers, you need to understand what it takes to maintain the new environment. These tasks include NDS backup and restoration procedures, tree partitioning and modifications, and upgrading clients and servers with future revisions of NetWare 4.11. Chapters 13 through 15 describe these tasks.

These are the eight steps to successfully designing, implementing, and using NetWare 4.11. Regardless of the size of your network, the QuickPath Process will work quickly and successfully.

Features of NetWare 4.11

AMONG THE MANY features of NetWare 4.11 is NDS. NDS, or the Directory (spelled with a capital *D*), is a special-purpose database that effectively allows all the resources of a network to be managed and grouped together through the use of objects. These objects represent users, servers, print queues, and groups, just as they did in NetWare 3 versions.

In addition, NDS has expanded the number of objects to 32, including many more resource types, such as server volumes and organizational roles. You can now assign various attributes (properties) and security access to these resources, giving your network enormous flexibility as it expands and changes.

NDS Replaces the Bindery

In NetWare 4.11, NDS replaces the bindery in NetWare 3 with a global and distributed naming service database of all the resources contained on your network. (The bindery in NetWare 3 is based on a flat file system, in which the resource information is stored in a bindery file on each file server.) This distributed directory can be replicated on multiple servers for increased fault tolerance and performance.

NDS is based on the 1988 CCITT X.500 standard. NDS groups resources hierarchically in a tree-like fashion, beginning with a Root object at the top and branching downward to form what appears to be an inverted tree.

Because some areas of the X.500 standard were not clearly defined at the time Net-Ware 4.11 was created, Novell's X.500 implementation is slightly different from the X.500 standard. These differences mainly involve the access controls for objects.

NDS is a naming service that associates an object's name with a physical or logical entity on the network. As a user, you do not need to know where a resource (a printer, for example) physically resides. You only need to find the object that represents that printer resource. If you have been granted rights to that resource, you can use it to the extent that your rights allow. (See Chapter 14 for more information about user rights in NetWare 4.11.)

NDS Provides a Single Point of Login

NDS also provides a single point of login, a feature that has several important benefits. First, it allows your users to log in once to the network and have the background authentication process of NDS handle the subsequent connections to other servers.

Single-user login also makes things much easier for you as an administrator, because you create a user only once for the entire network. You don't need to deal with multiple user accounts on multiple servers. Multiple servers may contain the user's account information in NDS through the replication process, but as an administrator, you maintain only a single account. You'll be amazed to discover how much time you'll save.

NDS Is Scalable

Because NDS is scalable, your environment can easily grow from one server to a thousand or more servers, and your initial NDS design will grow with you. You won't need to start over from scratch and make major modifications whenever resources are added to the network. The partitioning process, which is discussed in Chapter 5, allows your NDS database to be distributed in accordance with your network growth. Because the NDS database is distributed, you are only limited to disk space on each file server. The size of your NDS database is not an issue as your network grows.

Third-party developers and Novell are currently developing more tools for managing the NDS tree as your needs and network environment change.

The NDS schema is also extensible through the use of Novell's API (Application Program Interface) set for NetWare 4.11, which will allow you to create other objects that do not exist in the current schema.

NetWare 4.11 Allows You to Manage Multiple Servers from a Distance

With NetWare 4.11, you can manage many servers from one central utility. As an administrator, you can manage multiple servers and resources easily and quickly from any Windows workstation. You can choose to have your network administered from one central location or you can distribute the administration over several people, with access to their own part of the tree.

NetWare 4.11 Provides Enhanced File and Memory Management

For enhanced file and memory management, NetWare 4.11 provides for disk block suballocation, data compression, and data migration.

Disk Block Suballocation

One of the greatest cost benefits to migrating to NetWare 4.11 is the use of disk block suballocation. Suballocation is a file system process unique to NetWare 4.11. This process allocates a disk block in increments of 512 bytes, regardless of your block size setting.

Disk block suballocation ensures that you will never waste more than 511 bytes when saving any file. You now have the flexibility to set your block size to the recommended maximum of 64 kilobytes without sacrificing valuable hard disk space.

Data Compression

NetWare 4.11 provides the capability to compress any files on your file system after a period of no activity. Data compression is not a mandatory feature, and you can determine which servers can benefit from its use.

New file attributes allow you to define which files to compress and how often they should be compressed. The FAT (file allocation table) entry for a compressed file remains in the directory structure, so you can locate and uncompress the file at any time.

Data Migration

Data migration is another NetWare 4.11 mechanism for managing files and their storage within your network. Companies that have huge numbers of records that must be stored for several years find data migration very useful.

You can move files that are accessed infrequently off your hard drive and onto a tape backup or disk jukebox media. After migration, the file is erased from your server's hard drive, but the file entry remains on your server. If you ever need to access those files, you can retrieve the file from your external media and copy it back onto the server.

NetWare 4.11 Improves Client Performance

Novell has improved its workstation client through its VLM (Virtual Loadable Module) architecture. The VLM.EXE client can be loaded into upper memory to provide more conventional memory. The VLM client acts as a multiplexer for loading other VLM modules.

Other features of VLMs include the following:

- Auto-reconnect feature if the server should become disconnected

- Maximum of 50 connections to different file servers

- Large Internet Packets (LIP) as part of the VLM client

- Packet Burst feature as part of the VLM client

The VLM client is versatile in the adjustments it can make for improving performance and workstation memory. (See Chapter 7 for more information about the VLM client.)

NetWare 4.11 Includes Enhanced Security Features

NetWare 4.11 provides more functions for administering security and defining access to your users. In addition to file system security, NetWare 4.11 provides NDS object level security.

The VLM client handles users' passwords so that they are never sent across the network, thus increasing the level of security on your network. (See Chapter 14 for more information about NDS security features.)

NetWare 4.11 Provides Auditing Capabilities

Novell provides an auditing capability that allows an auditor to record a number of server events, which can be stored in an audit log file. Some of these audit events include the following:

- Any file creations and deletions

- Any access rights granted to a user or other object

These auditing features are useful when audit trails are required by law or by some other industry governing body.

Now that you have an overview of the QuickPath Process and the new features in NetWare 4.11, you're ready to learn the details of each step. Read on.

Understanding and Using NDS Objects

QuickTips: NDS Objects

Use two main types of container objects 19

in your NDS tree: Organization (O=) and Organization Unit (OU=) objects. Container objects can contain other objects. The O object generally represents your company name. The OU objects represent geographic locations and departments. The other type of objects you will use are noncontainer (or leaf) objects. Noncontainer objects do not contain other objects. They represent users, ncp servers, printers, and so on.

Protect the Admin user object 22

so you don't lose access to your NDS tree. You can provide a backup by creating a second Admin organizational role object (use the NWAdmin utility to do this). Assign explicit Supervisor rights for this new organizational role at object [Root]. Do *not* make this organizational role object security equivalent to the original Admin user.

Use Alias objects to provide access to other 23
NDS objects

such as printers in other OU objects. An Alias object is simply a pointer to another object, which can be a container or noncontainer object in the tree. Aliasing is a method of giving an object more than one name. The object being pointed to is the primary (or aliased) object.

Assign users to Profiles for 25
special-purpose scripts

that execute after the container login script. A Profile script executes only for the users who have that Profile assigned as an attribute. Profile scripts can be used to create three varieties of login scripts:

- Global login scripts, which may encompass multiple containers in your tree.

- Location login scripts, which define a specific set of users that use a particular resource.

- Special-function login scripts, which are useful for special administrators and specific tasks.

Use Group objects to group users   27

according to a particular resource need. The Group object is usually activity-based. For example, engineers who needs access to two different software compilers on the same server volume might be grouped together with a Group object. Members of a group do not need to exist within the same OU object, but this is recommended for the best performance. Use Group objects within OU objects to further differentiate rights within an OU object.

Use Organizational Role objects to assign   28
rights to roles

instead of to a particular person. This object defines a position (or role) within an organization. You can move users into and out of the Organizational Role (OR) object as needed for assignment to that position. The rights assigned to the OR are received by users for as long as they are occupants of that role.

Use Directory Map objects in login scripts   30

to represent directory paths in the file system. These objects point to file system directories that contain applications. They are assigned to a specific volume and directory when created, and can be changed at any time to point to another file system volume or path. If you want to manage access to an application, you can use the IF MEMBER OF GROUP expression followed by the Directory Map in the login script.

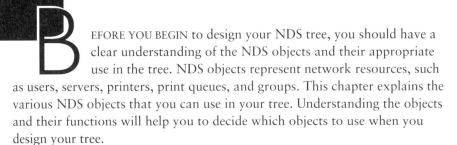

EFORE YOU BEGIN to design your NDS tree, you should have a clear understanding of the NDS objects and their appropriate use in the tree. NDS objects represent network resources, such as users, servers, printers, print queues, and groups. This chapter explains the various NDS objects that you can use in your tree. Understanding the objects and their functions will help you to decide which objects to use when you design your tree.

Of course, if you feel that you already understand NDS objects sufficiently, you can skip this chapter and move on to the next one, which covers NDS naming conventions (or the one after that, which provides guidelines for designing your NDS tree).

NDS Object Terminology

DS DEFINES A base set of object types that can exist in the Directory. These object types and their rules form what is called the *NDS base schema*. The NDS schema structure is automatically stored on every NetWare 4 server you install, even if actual objects are not defined and stored on that server. The NetWare 4 installation procedure places the schema on that server so that the database rules are in existence before you add objects to it.

By definition, objects are either *container* objects or *noncontainer* objects. Container objects are those that can contain other objects. Noncontainer objects, also known as *leaf objects*, are those that cannot have subordinate objects. For example, users, printers, and ncp servers are leaf objects.

Each object type is defined by a set of rules known as the *object class*. Each class includes a set of *properties*, also known as *attributes*. A user object, for example, describes an actual user on your network. The user object contains a list of properties associated with it. The information contained in the properties is referred to as *values*.

The terms attributes and properties are used interchangeably.

The properties are defined in terms of data types. The object's properties contain object information, access control information, and management data to maintain and control the actual network entity that the object represents.

One very common type of object is a user. The user object represents a particular network user and has particular properties associated with it. Users can be granted access rights to manage their own object properties. For example, users are granted by default the Read and Write rights to their Login Script property, which allows them to modify or create a personal login script.

In most cases, the default rights assigned to objects provide the access and flexibility that users require. Administrators need to add file access for specific applications and create the necessary groups and subadministrators as their trees expand.

Structuring Organization and Organizational Unit Container Objects

CURRENTLY, THE MAIN types of container objects you use are the Organization (O) and Organizational Unit (OU) objects. The O object represents the name of your company and is generally the first object on your tree underneath the [Root] object. (In some cases, your first container might be a Country (C) object, which is discussed in the next section.) For example, the object designation O=WWW is used to represent the company World Wide Widgets, Inc. A tree can include more than one O object to represent multiple organizations.

Below the O object are the OU objects that represent geographic locations and departments within your organization. For example, an OU could represent the Atlanta office (OU=ATL) or the Engineering department (OU=Eng).

Generally, the OU objects are nested to break down your company's locations and departments even further. For example, if you have ten regions in your company, you can create ten OU container objects to represent those regions. You can further break down the locations under these regions by creating OU objects to represent specific cities.

Each OU object may contain leaf objects (also known as noncontainer objects) that provide a one-to-one representation of network resources. For the most part, you place resources and users in the lowest levels of OU containers. However, you may also consider using a structure based on the "superserver" concept, which places servers at a regional (higher) OU level followed by OU objects that designate cities within the region. This method gives file servers easier access to multiple subordinate containers. Figure 2.1 shows a tree structure that follows the "superserver" organization concept.

FIGURE 2.1

An NDS tree structure with regional, city, department container objects, and leaf objects

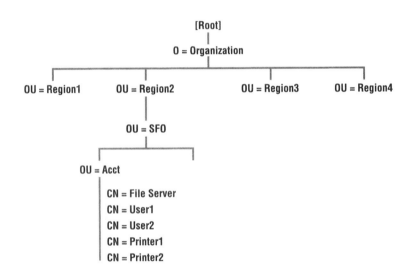

As you will see in Chapter 4, the locational approach to tree design is preferred at the upper levels. The top layers (O and first-level OU objects) of the tree are based on your network infrastructure and, therefore, relate to geographic locations in your company.

Using Other Types of Container Objects

NOVELL'S NETWARE 4.11 utilities also allow you to create a Country (C=) object. The Country object is directly below the [Root] object in your NetWare 4.11 tree.

Novell is working with other third-party providers to introduce NDS as a global operating system, so the use of the Country object may become necessary for corporations that provide services on a global network. Companies not acting as service providers of global directories do not need to use the Country object in their trees.

Another type of object that is defined in the X.500 specification and included in the NDS schema is the Locality (L=) object, which can be defined as (S) State or (L) Locality. Some third-party products allow you to enable the State and Locality containers as needed in your NDS tree. Except for providing a more descriptive name for a state or locality, these containers do not provide any benefit beyond what is found in the OU container.

Using Special-Purpose Objects

MOST OF THE questions regarding NetWare 4 objects are about creating and using the Admin user and other specialized objects. The following sections explain how, why, and when to use Admin, Alias, Organizational Role, Group, Profile, and Directory Map objects.

Understanding the Admin User Object

The Admin user object (as it's usually named by the administrator) is created automatically when you first install a NetWare 4 server. Initially, this user object has rights to the entire tree, as well as Supervisor rights to the file system of every server added to the tree. The Admin user is the first administrator of the tree. This user object not only has complete access to the file system (just as the Supervisor does in NetWare 3), but full access to NDS as well.

NDS grants the Admin user so much power in order to initially install the tree and establish rights for the file system on your first NetWare 4 server. As time goes on, you may want to distribute the management tasks for NDS and the file systems to other administrators.

Unlike Supervisor, Admin is not a reserved name for an object. You can rename the Admin to something less descriptive for security purposes after your server install.

Securing the Admin User

The importance of maintaining the Admin user cannot be overemphasized. When you first install NetWare 4.11, the Admin user is created at the Organization (O=) level. The Admin user has all rights (NDS and file system) at the [Root] object and, at this point in the installation, is the only user with such complete and extensive access to the network.

If you accidentally delete the Admin user, your access to the tree is effectively removed from the tree. Restoring access to the tree is a difficult process and can only be accomplished with assistance from Novell Technical Support.

After you have installed the first couple of NetWare 4 servers, make sure that the Admin user password is protected. Follow these steps to diminish the likelihood of losing access to your tree:

1. While you are creating the first NetWare 4 server, you are prompted for a password. Choose a password that is easy to remember and yet not common to people in your environment. Don't use the name of a friend, a child, your spouse, or the local football team, for example.

2. Create a second administration organizational role as a backup by using the NWAdmin utility. Do not make this object security the equivalent to that of the original Admin user. If the original Admin user were to be deleted, your Admin organizational role equivalent user would have no access to the tree because the security equivalency would be lost. Instead, assign explicit Supervisor rights for this organizational role at the [Root] object. After you create this secondary administrative role with its password, you will have another Admin role in case of emergency. Better yet, you will be able to use the secondary administrative role as your primary administrative source, if necessary.

3. Consider changing the password periodically so that fewer people know it and distribute it. Initially, a group of people may need to know the Admin password. Eventually, you should be able to reduce the number of people who have access to the Admin user account.

If you are installing a new NetWare 4.11 system, rather than upgrading from NetWare 3, the Admin user password is also assigned to the bindery supervisor.

Using Alias Objects

An *Alias* is a special object that points to another object you specify in the NDS tree. An Alias can point to either a container object or a noncontainer object. The object being "aliased" is known as the *primary*, or *aliased*, *object*.

For example, you may want to allow users to access a particular resource contained in another OU object. Figure 2.2 shows a tree structure in which an Alias references a printer in a particular OU. The Alias points to the primary object—the printer. You can consider the Alias object as a relay to another object in a different part of the tree.

FIGURE 2.2

An NDS tree structure with an Alias object used to provide access to a printer that resides in another OU

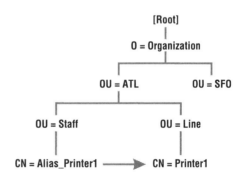

You can also use an Alias in one OU to reference another OU, thereby giving one OU a reference to the aliased OU's resources. For example, suppose you have created a Workgroups OU object that contains a series of workgroup servers. However, users in other OU objects also need access to those servers in the Workgroups OU. To solve this problem, you can set up an

Alias for users from several OUs to the Workgroups OU so that they can obtain access (based on security assignments) to those servers. Figure 2.3 illustrates this use of an Alias object.

Using an Alias can create additional NDS traffic on your network. Use the Alias object to specify print queues and a limited number of aliased users whenever possible.

Naming Alias Objects

You may want to give an Alias object a name that indicates that it is a pointer to another object. For example, the name might include the word *Alias*, as in Alias_Bob. In the example in Figure 2.3, the Alias object is named Alias_Workgroups. The object represented in NWAdmin is an Alias as well. NetWare 4.11 requires the use of different object names in the same container regardless of the object class. For example, CN=Joe and OU=Joe are not acceptable in the same container.

FIGURE 2.3

Including Alias objects in two OUs pointing to a Workgroups OU to provide access to its servers

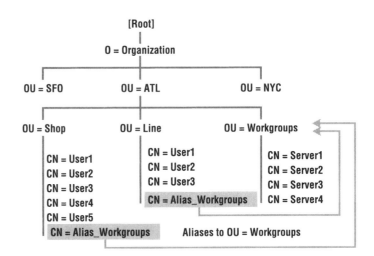

Granting and Administering Alias Rights

It is important to understand how rights are granted and administered to an Alias. The Alias has two states: dereferenced and non-dereferenced.

Dereferenced means that the Alias points to the properties of the primary object. When you effect a change to the Alias object, you are actually changing the primary object.

Non-dereferenced means that you are pointing to the properties of the Alias itself. If you change the Alias when it is non-dereferenced, you are changing just the Alias object itself, not the primary object.

Some operations that use the Alias automatically are non-dereferenced. When you modify the properties of the Alias (in the default state), you are modifying the properties of the primary object. However, if you perform a rename, move, or delete operation on the Alias, you are modifying the Alias itself and not the primary object.

If you delete the primary object, you delete the Alias object in the same operation, whether it is dereferenced or non-dereferenced.

Because the Alias object is only a pointer to the primary object, your rights assignments are still on the primary object itself. The Alias object has whatever rights were granted to the primary OU or user object.

Using Profile Objects

The Profile object is a special-purpose scripting object that executes a login script after the container login script. The Profile script can contain special drive mappings or environment settings that you want a specific group of people to receive. The Profile script executes only for users whose profile attributes specify a Profile object for execution.

When you first set up a user with the NWAdmin utility, you can specify that the user execute a particular Profile object. You can also add a Profile to a user at any time by modifying the user's property.

There are three main uses for a Profile script:

- To create a global login script

- To create a location login script

- To create a special-function login script

Creating Global Login Scripts

Netware 4 does not use a global system login script. Each OU object you create has its own login script, referred to as the *container login script*. The order of execution of login scripts is as follows:

1. Container login script, if present

2. Profile login script, if used

3. User login script (or the default login script if no other script is available)

Therefore, if you want to create a more global login script and include users from multiple OUs, you can employ the Profile login script to set up a specific environment for a group of users. A Profile login script can be used to provide an additional set of drive mappings to those specified in a container login script. Keep in mind that using a Profile object for large numbers of users across a large network is not recommended from a performance standpoint. A profile script, however, is ideally suited for a specific site and its containers.

Creating Location Login Scripts

A Profile object can also be used for determining resource allocations based on location. For example, suppose that each floor of your company has three printers and three print queues and you want to be able to assign a particular group of users to a specific print queue. You can use a Profile login script to automatically assign users with the profile attribute defined to specific print queues.

Creating Special-Function Scripts

You can create a Profile object for a special-function script, such as one to assign access for applications. For example, you can create a Profile script to be used by administrators only that gives users a specific drive assignment to an administrative utility.

In this scenario, you would move the administrative utility from perhaps the SYS:PUBLIC directory into a new subdirectory you create called ADMIN. When an administrative user logs on to the network, the administrator Profile script executes and assigns that user a drive mapping to the ADMIN directory. Only users executing the Profile script will be mapped a drive to the administrative utility. You can then grant rights to run the utility to administrators only.

Using Group Objects

Because of security equivalence, all members of a container object receive whatever rights the container possesses. Users inside Group objects also receive whatever rights the group possesses.

Group objects in NetWare 4 serve the same function as they do in NetWare 3. For more information on security equivalence, see Chapter 14.

You can use Group objects to give users within an OU or multiple OUs specialized rights assignments. Figure 2.4 shows an OU object called OU=MKTG that is populated with users and resources. Within this OU are two marketing staffs, Staff1 and Staff2, working on different projects.

FIGURE 2.4

Using Groups objects within an OU object to differentiate rights assignments

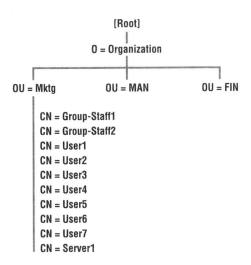

Each group is accessing different software on the server and needs different rights assignments. We created two Group objects called Staff1 and Staff2 and granted specific rights to each.

Within the container login script (known as the *system login script* in Net-Ware 3), the IF MEMBER OF GROUP statements are used to determine which users are part of Staff1 and Staff2. When each user logs in to the network, the login script determines which group the user belongs to, and then the appropriate drive mappings are assigned for the file system.

Another, less desirable way to accomplish this same goal is to create two more OU objects under OU=MKTG called Staff1 and Staff2. This method adds more layers of containers to your tree and requires you to create and administer two or more container login scripts—one for each marketing group. With the first example, the groups' assignments would be executed in the OU=MKTG login script.

Keep in mind that each OU object can have its own container login script. The user's login procedure looks to its own OU for a login script and does not search any higher in the tree for a container script. See Chapter 7 for more information about login scripts.

As explained in the previous section, the order of script execution is the container login script, the profile script (in addition to the container login script if it is available), and the user script (in addition to the container and profile scripts if they are available). If no user script is available, the default login script is executed. This means that one login script—the default script—will be executed at minimum. At maximum, three scripts—a container script, profile script, and user script—can be executed if they all exist.

Using Organizational Role Objects

The Organizational Role object is an extremely versatile object. It is similar to a Group object. The basic difference between the two is that a Group object is generally used in a login script (as in IF MEMBER OF GROUP) and is activity-oriented (it can be used for accessing a word-processing application on your server), whereas an OR object is not used in login scripts and is better suited for creating subadministrator objects that contain a small number of occupants.

The OR object has an attribute called *role occupant*. An occupant (user) can be moved in and out of the OR object quickly to facilitate short-term assignments. For example, if the regular administrator is out of town or absent for any length of time, another user can be moved into the Administrative OR temporarily to manage the network.

You create the OR object and assign specific rights depending on the characteristics needed for the role. You then assign users to the OR as occupants through the NWAdmin utility.

For example, if you wanted to assign a user the OU administrator role, you would create an OR object called OU_Admin and assign it explicit object rights based on the needs of that role.

The next step is to make a user an occupant of that OR. Through security equivalency to the OU_Admin object, the occupant gains the rights that the OR has been assigned. These can be Supervisor rights or less powerful rights, if appropriate. For example, if you would prefer that the OR occupant only be able to create objects in the OU, you can simply assign the Create Right to the OU_Admin object.

For more information about security equivalency, see Chapters 7 and 14, which cover access to NetWare Directory Services. Security equivalence is a very powerful feature. Anyone who is security equivalent to an object has all the rights granted to that object. Be careful which rights you grant to OU objects when you plan to add users to those OUs.

In the example shown in Figure 2.5, we have created an Organization Role object for OU=ENG. This OR is to be used by a subadministrator in the Engineering department. After creating this OR, we can grant Supervisor rights to the OR at the OU=ENG level. This means that we are granting rights on the object OU=Eng to OR_Eng. Next, we can specify Bob and Sally as occupants of the OR object. Through the mechanism of security equivalence, Bob and Sally receive all rights granted to the OR_Eng and have the rights necessary to be subadministrators for the Engineering department.

FIGURE 2.5

An Organizational Role object for the Engineering department, with Bob and Sally as occupants so they can function as subadministrators

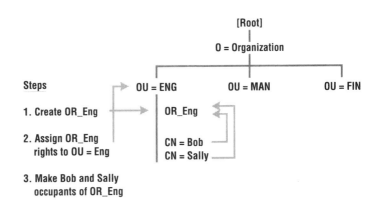

Assigning rights is discussed in detail in Chapter 14. That chapter includes in-depth examples of creating subadministrators.

Using Directory Map Objects

The Directory Map object is a special-purpose object that is used for pointing to a specific volume and directory path on a NetWare server. By using the Directory Map object name, you can map a drive letter to the Directory Map object name in your container (or any) login scripts.

For example, suppose that you have just installed a new WordPerfect application on your server and five container objects in your tree need access to the WordPerfect application. You can give each container its own login script with a reference to the WordPerfect application by mapping a drive assignment such as:

```
MAP S16:= .WordPerfect.ESP.NOVELL
```

If the WordPerfect version were updated later on, the drive assignment within the Directory Map object named WordPerfect would be changed to reflect the path of the new version of WordPerfect. In one step, all the users in five container objects would automatically be redirected to the newer application version. You would not need to change five separate login scripts. The only change would be to the Directory Map object. The Directory Map object can be a real time-saver in large network environments.

In this example, you need to assign the Directory Map object a path to the file(s) that you are referencing. The second step is to assign each user Read and File Scan rights to the file(s) you want them to execute. One approach to doing this is to assign Read and File Scan rights to the five container objects involved. This way, each user will receive those rights. Alternatively, you can grant Read and File Scan rights to the Directory Map object and make each user security equivalent to the Directory Map. The first method is easier to manage.

Extending the NDS Schema

THE NUMBER OF objects and properties currently in NDS is quite comprehensive. However, eventually you may want to create new objects. You can extend the NDS base schema by using Novell's Directory Application Programming Interfaces (APIs) to create new objects, class definitions, and attributes. Another way to extend the NDS schema is by adding existing attributes to existing class definitions. For example, you may need a special object to represent a group of compact discs that could be controlled through NDS or a special object to represent e-mail servers in your enterprise environment. You can also use other products, including those from Novell, to make extensions to the NDS schema by adding a new object class during installation.

Any changes to the schema will be reflected on all NDS servers in the tree. If a "snap-in" has been created for NWAdmin, however, the current NetWare 4.11 utilities will allow you to add or modify objects in your new object classification. If no "snap-in" has been provided, you may need to create utilities that can manage new object classes along with the currently defined NDS objects.

Once you understand how NDS objects are used, you will have greater flexibility in managing and designing your NDS tree. This is only the beginning. Novell and third-party developers will produce many more new objects in the months and years ahead.

Naming Conventions for NetWare Directory Services

QuickTips: NDS Naming Conventions

Create a consistent naming standard 37

for the objects in your NDS tree before you implement your first NetWare 4 server. A good naming standard gives users easier access to resources, minimizes user training, allows the NDS tree to grow, and makes NDS searches easier and more efficient.

For simplicity, use typeless names for your objects 40

rather than typeful names. In NetWare 4, you don't need to include the object's name type when you are entering names. Instead, just use periods to separate the elements of the name. For example, rather than the distinguished name CN=TANDERSO.OU=ENG.OU=SFO.O=WWW, you can use TANDERSO.ENG.SFO.WWW.

Produce an effective naming standard document 44

by providing a definition of objects to be implemented and supported in your Directory. The naming standard document should describe the required objects (and the reasons they are required) and the required attributes (and the reasons they are required) in detail. You should also provide an example of the naming standard for each object. Once administrators understand the definition and use of each object and its attributes, they will make fewer errors.

Follow guidelines for good naming conventions 47

including the following suggestions:

- Consider current naming standards and the improvements that are necessary to make them global.

- Use short and descriptive names.

- Avoid reserved characters (such as +, the period, =, and \) in names.

- Limit user names to eight characters so you can use each user name as the DOS home directory name.

- Identify printers by their location, department, and printer number. For print queue names, you can add the letters *PQ* to the printer name.

Use a system for your basic naming standard 48

such as this one:

File servers	*YYYZXXX##*
Print servers	*YYYZXXX##*
Volume names	SYS, APPS, DATA, USERS, SHARE

where:

YYY	Company or Department (e.g., FIN, ENG, or WWW)
XXX	Location (e.g., ATL, LON, or SFO)
Z	Server Type (e.g., F for File Server, T for Test Server, P for Print Server, C for Comm Server, or S for SAA)
##	Server Number (e.g., 01, 02, and 03 for three servers in a department)

N YOUR NDS tree, every object must have a unique name. The uniqueness of the name is based on its context or location within your tree.

You should create a naming standard before implementing your first NetWare 4 server. The standard you devise will serve as a basis for naming all your current resources, as well as the resources you add in the future.

This chapter explains the NDS naming conventions and provides guidelines for setting up your own naming standard.

Why Bother to Create a Naming Standard?

HERE ARE FOUR reasons for creating and using an effective, consistent naming standard:

- A consistent naming standard gives end users easier access to resources.

- A consistent naming standard minimizes user training when users move to a new container object.

- A naming standard allows for easier growth of the tree during merges or expansion.

- NDS searches are much easier when you search across a consistent naming standard. Consistent names also make NDS a better resource for doing searches.

NDS *Naming Basics*

THIS SECTION DESCRIBES some of the basics of naming NDS objects and how an object's name is determined when you are searching an NDS tree. We also explain the concepts behind an object's distinguished name, relative distinguished name, and context.

Name Types

Each segment of an object's name consists of the object name type and a name value. The name type and the value are separated by an equal sign (=).

Three object types are used most often:

- O=Organization

- OU=Organizational Unit

- CN=Common Name

The first two name types, O= and OU=, include all the container objects except Country and Locality. The name type CN= includes all Novell-defined noncontainer (leaf) objects. For example, if the leaf object is a user, a printer, or an ncp server, it is named by the type CN.

How Distinguished Names Are Derived

Each object in the tree is given a *distinguished name*, a complete name that is unique in the NDS tree. An object's distinguished name consists of the names of each object between itself and the [Root] object of the tree. Figure 3.1 shows how Todd Anderson's distinguished name is derived.

User Todd Anderson's distinguished name begins with his Common Name, TAnderso, followed by the name of his Organizational Unit, OU=Eng (for the Engineering department), followed by the Organizational Unit that the Engineering department belongs to, OU=SFO (for the San Francisco office), followed by the Organization object, O=WWW (for the company World Wide Widgets, Inc.). His distinguished name is written as follows:

```
CN=Tanderso.OU=Eng.OU=SFO.O=WWW
```

FIGURE 3.1

Each object in the tree has a unique distinguished name.

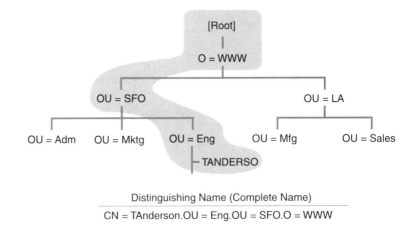

Distinguishing Name (Complete Name)

CN = TAnderson.OU = Eng.OU = SFO.O = WWW

For each element, the name type and the name value are separated by an equal sign, as in CN (for Common Name) = TANDERSO. The segments of the object's name are separated by periods.

In practice, you don't need to include the object name types to specify distinguished names. However, object name types are usually included in documentation for clarity. See "Typeful Names versus Typeless Names" later in this chapter.

In Figure 3.1, notice that the [Root] object—the topmost object in the tree—is not included in the object name. The [Root] object, which is always part of the user's fully distinguished name, is implied and is not written out. Another name for the [Root] object is the name of the tree you assign at the first server installation.

Distinguished names are not case-sensitive, so the names are resolved by the system no matter which case is used to enter the name. For example, the following two distinguished names are the same:

```
cn=tanderso.ou=eng.ou=sfo.o=www

CN=TAnderso.OU=Eng.OU=SFO.O=WWW
```

Contexts and Relative Distinguished Names

An object's *context* is its position or location in the NDS tree. If two objects are in the same container, they have the same context. Figure 3.2 shows user Todd Anderson's context in the tree. Todd is part of the Engineering Organizational Unit (OU=ENG), in the San Francisco office (OU=SFO), under World Wide Widgets Inc. (O=WWW).

FIGURE 3.2

A sample tree and user
Todd Anderson's context
in that tree

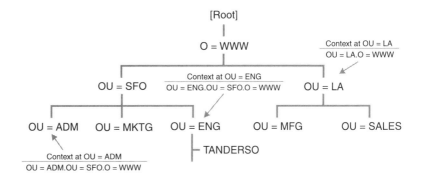

A *relative distinguished name* (RDN) is the leftmost name of the object relative to the current context that has been set for the user. The relative distinguished name combined with the proper context equals the distinguished name for the object.

Our sample distinguished name is:

    CN=TANDERSO.OU=ENG.OU=SFO.O=WWW

The relative distinguished name is:

    CN=TANDERSO

where the context is:

    OU=ENG.OU=SFO.O=WWW

If a user's context is in the same context as the object you are referencing, you can access an object by using its relative distinguished name instead of the object's fully distinguished name. All the objects in that container can be referenced by their object name alone because their context in the tree is the same.

The context helps the user and administrator access the objects in the tree more easily. See "User and Bindery Contexts" later in this chapter for more information.

The relative distinguished name must be unique only in a single context. The same relative distinguished names can exist in the tree if the objects are located in different contexts. For example, if World Wide Widgets employs Todd Anderson in the Engineering department of the San Francisco office and Teresa Anderson in the Sales department of the Los Angeles office, your tree might contain a CN=TANDERSO in the context OU=ENG.OU=SFO.O=WWW, and another CN=TANDERSO in the context OU=SALES.OU=LA.O=WWW.

You can give users the same names as long as they are not in the same context, but we recommend keeping user names unique across your entire tree. E-mail systems, for example, require unique names.

Typeful Names versus Typeless Names

Putting the name types in the object's complete name is called using *typeful* names. The examples we've been using, including the following, are typeful names:

```
CN=TAnderso.OU=Eng.OU=SFO.O=WWW
```

Typeful names are usually used in documentation to clarify the object's fully distinguished or relative distinguished name. In NetWare 4.11, however, it is not necessary to include the object's name type when you are entering names. (Prior to NetWare 4.11, the Novell utilities required the use of typeful names if you used the Country container object in your tree.) Instead of typeful names, you can use typeless names. A *typeless name* is one that does not include the name type in each segment, as in the distinguished name

```
TAnderso.Eng.SFO.WWW
```

Like typeful names, typeless names are not case-sensitive. The example above is equivalent to

```
tanderso.eng.sfo.www
```

In our example, a relative distinguished name also exists in the ENG container, as follows:

```
TAnderso
```

Notice that the names in our examples are short. As part of our naming standard, we keep our container names as short as possible. We also limit the user name to eight characters. The shorter the distinguished name, the easier it is to use.

As you can see, typeless names are easier for both administrators and users to use. Typeless names work in all situations in NetWare 4.11. Obviously, they are the preferred way to type names (unless you're getting paid by the keystroke).

Using Leading and Trailing Periods in Names

As you've seen, a period (.) separates the name segments in distinguished names, relative distinguished names, and contexts. By using leading and trailing periods in a name sequence, you can identify any object in the tree. Periods are useful for referencing objects located in another portion of the tree.

A leading period in a distinguished name instructs the client to ignore the current context that is set and start at the [Root] object. Thus, an object name with a leading period is treated like a fully distinguished name starting at the [Root] object. For example, if the context is

```
Sales.LA.WWW
```

then

```
.TAnderso.Eng.SFO.WWW
```

is resolved to the object CN=TAnderso in the container OU=Eng.OU=SFO.O=WWW in the tree. You can use only one leading period in the name.

You can use trailing periods with relative distinguished names to select a new context when resolving the object names. Each trailing period moves the context up the tree one layer. For example, if your current context is

```
OU=Mfg.OU=LA.O=WWW
```

and you want to reference the user BJONES in the container OU=Sales.OU=LA..O=WWW, you can use either of the following two forms:

```
BJones.Sales.

CN=BJones.OU=Sales.
```

NetWare 4 resolves the distinguished name as follows:

```
CN=BJones.OU=Sales.OU=LA.O=WWW
```

User and Bindery Contexts

Two types of contexts are considered in NetWare 4:

- Object (user) context

- Bindery context

The object (user) context, as described earlier, is the user's current view of the tree. Two users within the same OU object have the same context, as illustrated in Figure 3.3. The users with the same context are TAnderso and CSmith.

The user context is initially set in the NET.CFG file, and this context can be modified. It is easier for users to identify an object in the tree if their context or location in the tree is set to the container of the searched resource. For example, if user Todd Anderson wants to search for all printers in a particular OU object with NetWare utilities, he can set his context to that OU and search there for the desired printer.

The user's context can be changed by using the CX (Change Context) command-line utility that comes with NetWare 4. See Chapter 11 for details.

An NDS server uses the bindery context to determine which objects are accessible on a server through Bindery Services. A bindery context specifies which OU, O, or L object a server should search for bindery-based objects.

Bindery objects are objects created in NetWare 3 or other objects not recognized by NDS as NDS objects. Bindery objects reside in NetWare 4 with a feature known as Bindery Services. Bindery Services are installed automatically when you install NetWare 4. To enable Bindery Services, you must set the *Bindery Context* for that server.

FIGURE 3.3

Users TAnderson and
CSmith have the same
context because they
reside in the same
Organizational Unit.

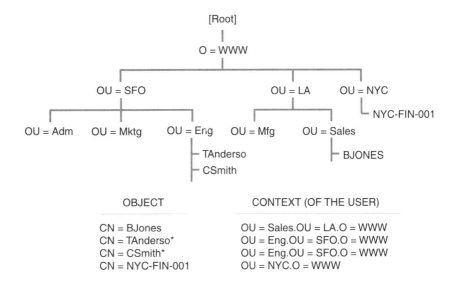

* TAnderso and CSmith have the same context
because they reside in the same OU.

When a bindery-based NLM (NetWare Loadable Module) application
or non-NLM application makes bindery calls to the server, the server sees
the container objects subordinate to the bindery context(s) as its bindery.
Only the NDS objects that existed in a NetWare 3 bindery are treated as
bindery objects. These objects are user, group, print queue, print server, and
profile. Bindery objects in the NDS database have plus signs in their names,
as in Bindery Type=Name+Bindery type=12.

The default bindery context is set to the server's parent OU, but you can
change the context to look to another OU. Versions up to and including Net-
Ware 4.02 allow you to set only a single context for your server. NetWare 4.1
and beyond allow you to set up to 16 contexts for a single server. This allows
a server to have, as its bindery, up to 16 containers, which gives you greater
flexibility in your tree design.

In Figure 3.4, a bindery context has been set for OU=ENG on Server SFO-
ENG-001. When an NLM or workstation application running on this server
makes a bindery call, the server will look in its bindery context for the appropriate bindery objects. In this example, the bindery context is set to

```
OU=ENG.OU=SFO.O=WWW
```

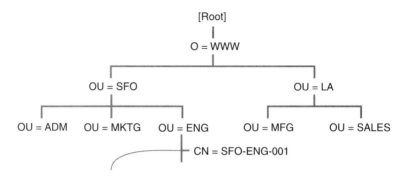

FIGURE 3.4
Server SFO-ENG-001 has
its Server Bindery Context
set to OU=ENG.OU=
SFO.O=WWW.

Server Bindery Context is set to: OU=ENG.OU=SFO.O=WWW.
The Context can be changed at any time to point to another OU.

The server can set any container for its Server Bindery Context. The server object does not need to exist in the context you specify.

Creating a Naming Standard

A CONSISTENT NAMING SCHEME provides guidelines to network administrators as they install file servers, create users or printers, modify existing objects, and move objects within the tree. A good naming scheme also allows users to quickly identify the resources available to them. It makes searches more efficient.

Even if your company's network is small, you should create a naming standard. The network will likely grow to include more users and resources. A consistent standard makes it easier for you and the other administrators in your company to install new resources. Even small network environments are plagued by the problem of duplicate internal addresses. Having a standard in place helps prevent this problem.

A naming standard must be global in nature. You want to be able to apply your naming standard consistently across the entire network so that all users and all departments, no matter where they are on the network, can readily and easily access resources. A global naming standard also helps administrators understand the names and uses of various objects.

The best time to create a naming standard is before you install NetWare 4 on a server. If you already have an existing standard, you may need to improve it to provide consistency across your entire network.

Using an Existing Naming Standard

If you are working in an established host environment, some naming standards are likely already in place. You can use these standards as the basis for your NetWare 4 naming standard. You don't need to undo the work you've already done and start from scratch. Your goal is to improve the consistency of resource information stored in NDS.

Consider how well your present naming standards fit into the NetWare 4 environment. For example, you may be able to transfer the names you have developed for your servers and printers to the NetWare 4 environment. Perhaps you have a naming convention for e-mail addresses you want to use, such as the first initial and last name of the user, as in TAnderso for Todd Anderson.

Producing a Naming Standard Document

To create your naming standard document, gather information from different organizations within the company. You likely need information from the people who handle the company's e-mail, network administration, and host (mainframe) environment.

Producing a naming standard document need not be a long process. Take the following steps to create your naming standard document as quickly and efficiently as possible:

- Decide on and list the object types you will use in your tree.

- Determine the properties you will use for each object.

- Provide an example of each object's naming standard.

The following sections discuss these steps in detail.

Listing the Object Types You Will Use

In order to set a proper naming standard, first determine which NDS object types you will use in your tree, such as:

- Servers

- Users

- Printers

- Print queues

- Groups

- Organizational Roles

- Profiles

- Directory Maps

- Organizational Units

Provide a definition of the object types to be implemented and supported in your Directory. Describe the required objects in detail and explain the reasons they are required.

Determining the Attributes to Be Used for Each Object

After you have created the list of objects you intend to use in the tree, decide which of the objects' attributes to use. Some attributes are required by NDS and must be entered when you create the object. When you create a user object, for example, you need to enter the Login Name and Last Name attributes.

In addition to the required NDS attributes, you may want to include other attributes if they are necessary for your site (such as a fax number or other information attributes for a user object). Specify those attributes in your naming standard, too.

Along with the other attributes you want to include with particular objects, explain why those attributes are necessary in your naming standard document. Currently, you cannot enforce the requirement for additional properties, but other administrators will be more likely to adhere to the standard if they understand your reasons for including a particular property.

Providing an Example of Each Object Used

To help administrators understand the purpose and use of each object and its properties, your naming standard document should include an example of every object used and how to name it. Here are examples of Organization and Organizational Unit objects:

Organization: World Wide Widgets

    O=WWW

Organizational Units: Atlanta, San Francisco, New York

    OU=ATL, OU=SFO, OU=NYC

General Guidelines for a Naming Standard

Following are some guidelines for developing your naming standard:

- **Keep object names simple.** The Organization object is almost always your company's name. Our example uses O=WWW for World Wide Widgets, Inc. Our Organizational Unit names for locations are short and descriptive, such as OU=SFO for the San Francisco location and OU=Sales for a sales office. The context for this name would be OU=Sales.OU=SFO.O=WWW.

The tree name can also be the same name as your organization (although this is not required). We gave our tree the name WWW_INC to distinguish between the tree name and the Organization name O=WWW.

- **Object names within the same context or container must be unique.** Duplicate names are allowed only if the objects are in different containers.

- **All network devices that communicate using the Service Advertising Protocol (SAP) must have unique object names in the entire tree.** Therefore, file and print server names must be unique on the entire network. The maximum length of these objects' names is 47 characters, but you should use far fewer. You cannot include spaces in server names. You may want to use a server name that designates a location, department, and server. For example, the server name ATL-Sales-001 indicates that the Sales department's server 1 is located in Atlanta. Use this naming convention for any device that uses SAP.

Use descriptive names with dashes (or underscores), such as ATL-SALES-001, for SAP devices to make them easier to recognize (for example, when you are troubleshooting packets on your network). A more general name such as SERVER1 does not give a very good description of where the server is located.

- **Avoid using spaces in object names.** (Spaces are illegal in all server names.) Use underscores instead of spaces. Spaces are often confused with the spaces used for delimiters in command-line parameters.

- **Decide how to standardize user names before you create user accounts.** User names can be up to 64 characters long, but we recommend limiting names to 8 characters. This way, you can use each user's name as his or her DOS home directory name as well. For example, Todd Anderson and his home directory could have the name TAnderso (the first character of the first name and the first seven characters of the last name) or AndersTo (the first six characters of the last name and the first two characters of first name).

- **Printer names can include the location, department, and printer number.** For example, an HP 4SI printer might be named ATL-SALES-HP4SI1 to indicate printer 1 in the Atlanta sales office.

- **Define print queue names by adding the letters PQ to the printer name.** For example, a print queue might be named ATL-Sales-HP4SIPQ or ATL-Sales-PQPH4SI. You may wish to change the order of the PQ designation if you prefer it in the front of the name.

An Example of a Basic Naming Standard

Following is an example of an NDS naming standard. This example includes only the naming standard for the objects in NDS, not for their attributes. A complete naming standard would specify what attribute values (telephone numbers, addresses, and so on) you will use for the objects.

File and Print Servers

XXXYYZ## (must be unique)

where:

XXX	Company or location (PRV, ORM, SJF, SUM, etc.)
YY	Department (IS, HR, TX, etc.)
Z	Server type (A=application server, C=communications server, D=database/SQL server, E=e-mail server, F=file server, M=network management server, P=print server, R=dial in/out server, S=SAA server, T=test server, X=fax server, etc.)
##	Server number (01, 02, 03…99)

Volume Names

*File server name*_SYS, APPS, USERS

Printers and Queues

Printer	*YY##P*
Queues	*YY##Q*
Queue Server	*YY##QS*

where:

YY	Department
##	Number of printer, queue, or queue server (01, 02, 03…99)
P	Printer
Q	Queue
QS	Queue server

User Names

Initial of first name and seven letters of last name

Organization

XXX (for company name)

Organizational Unit

XXXYYZ

where:

XXX	Location
YY	Department
Z	Division

Groups

*Function*_G

where *Function* is the activity that the group performs.

Organizational Roles

*Function*_OR

where *Function* is the administrative role that the Organizational Role performs.

Profiles

*Name*_P

where *Name* is the purpose of the Profile.

Directory Maps

*DIR*_DM

where *DIR* is the DOS directory name where the application has been installed.

Reserved and Invalid Characters

NDS reserves a few special characters for its own use. The following characters have specific uses or are not allowed in NDS object names unless they are preceded by an escape character:

SPECIAL CHARACTER	WHAT IT DOES
Period (.)	Separates the name segments of distinguished names.
Plus (+)	Ties names together for objects with multiple naming attributes that need to be put together. Bindery objects placed in the NDS database are examples of objects with the plus sign in the name, as in Bindery type CN=Name+Bindery Type 12.
Equal (=)	Ties name types and object names together.
Backslash (\)	Follows a reserved character if the reserved character is used as part of an object name. For example, to make *WWW Corp.* a valid name, you would need to enter *\WWW Corp.*
Forward slash (/)	Not allowed in Microsoft Windows naming rules. If you include a forward slash and try to use the Windows-based NWUser utility to map permanent drives or to capture a print queue, the operation will fail.

If you need to use the distinguished name and the name has spaces in it, enclose the name in quotation marks.

The best way to avoid naming problems is to make sure not to include any special characters as part of object names. Using special characters is cumbersome, because you must precede them with the backslash character. They can also make names confusing to users.

IPX Cable Address and Internal Network Number Naming Conventions

You may also need to consider the IPX cable address and internal network number for your NDS naming standard. The following sections offer some suggestions.

IPX Cable Address

The IPX cable address defines the physical cable segment that any file server will connect. Your cable segment may span a single location or many locations, depending on your network's infrastructure and size.

Here is an example of a naming convention for an IPX cable address:

AAASSSSN

where:

AAA	Designates a site location (such as SFO, LA, NYC, and so on)
SSSS	Designates a specific building, floor, wiring closet, and so on
N	Indicates a number of the segment (helpful if you have more than one cable segment in any location)

IPX Internal Network Number

The internal IPX number must be unique for each server in your network. The IPX number must also be different from the cable segment number. Take special precautions when you assign this value. A duplicate internal IPX number creates many conflicts with NDS and NetWare.

Here is an example of a naming convention for an IPX internal network number:

ARRSSSSN

where:

A	Designates an internal IPX number
RR	Designates a state, region, or country code (if you have servers in multiple regions or states)
SSSS	Designates a site location (special e-mail designators that are already in place can be used here; you can also use a building code designator if that makes more sense in your environment)
N	Designates the server number (if you have three servers in one location, you can use 1, 2, 3...; you can also use hexadecimal notation—0 through F hex—to allow up to sixteen servers per site or building)

With a naming standard in place, you are ready to begin designing your NDS tree. Remember that your naming standard will make administration of your tree easier and provide you with consistent naming across your entire organization.

Designing Your NetWare Directory Services Tree

4

QuickTips: Tree Design

- Will you have centralized or decentralized management? With centralized management, the entire tree structure is managed by a central IS group. With decentralized management, the individual network administrators are given rights to a portion of the tree and decide on the organization of the bottom layers.

- How will you structure the partitions? Usually, the most effective method is to partition locally. Split NDS into partitions so that they contain only the information needed by that set of users. You can make each remote location its own partition.

- Where are the physical devices located? In your tree, put network devices in container objects that meet the needs of the users who share the resources. For example, put printers that serve a single department in that department's OU object. If your file servers service many departments, place them in the highest applicable OU.

- What is the best design for taking advantage of login scripts? In order to use Container and Profile login scripts to configure the user's environment during login, your tree must include OU objects that allow the users and login scripts to be grouped together. Also, login scripts may depend on Group and Directory Map objects for drive mappings to applications. Put applications that all the network users will use on all file servers in the same place on the file system. This way, users can map the drives using Directory Map objects to identify those applications.

- Do you need to enable Bindery Services for your bindery-based client applications? If so, you must place all clients that require Bindery Services from a particular file server in the same container object as the file server's bindery context(s).

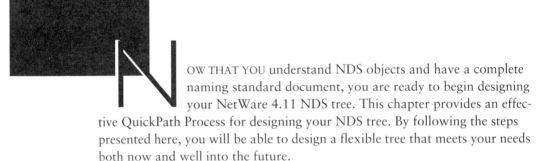

OW THAT YOU understand NDS objects and have a complete naming standard document, you are ready to begin designing your NetWare 4.11 NDS tree. This chapter provides an effective QuickPath Process for designing your NDS tree. By following the steps presented here, you will be able to design a flexible tree that meets your needs both now and well into the future.

NDS Tree Design: An Overview

OU SHOULD DESIGN the NDS tree before installing your first NetWare 4 file server. Although there is no "right" way to design an NDS tree for your company, some ways are markedly less efficient than others. Each company's network has different requirements. The approach we recommend gives you a good start on the NDS tree design and works well for companies of all sizes.

To produce the visual design of your tree, you can use either modeling software such as Preferred Systems's DS Standard or a software drawing package such as Visio.

Goals of Tree Design

A tree design has three goals:

- To structure network resources for ease of access

- To provide a blueprint for the implementation of NetWare 4.11

- To provide a flexible layout that can be modified to accommodate corporate changes

Steps for Tree Design

The tree design consists of these steps:

- Gather corporate documents

- Design the top level of the tree

- Design the bottom level of the tree

- Review your first draft

- Consider special design factors at the bottom of the tree

After you've gathered the corporate information, you are ready to plan the NDS tree. The tree design is logically split into two phases: the top of the tree design and the bottom of the tree design. The tree design takes the shape of an inverted tree with the [Root] object on top. The top of the tree design refers only to the first few layers of the tree (how many layers there are depends on the WAN infrastructure of your network). The bottom level refers to all OU layers below the top portion. The bottom of the tree is based on your LAN infrastructure and should be designed organizationally.

As shown in Figure 4.1, the top few layers of the tree usually reflect the WAN infrastructure of the network, whereas the bottom layers reflect the actual organization of the company from a departmental or divisional standpoint.

FIGURE 4.1

The top few layers of an NDS tree are representative of the physical WAN network.

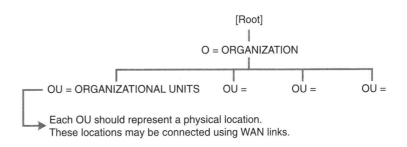

The bottom level of the tree will be affected by extenuating factors, such as the logical placement of partitions. After you've designed the bottom level of the tree according to your organization chart, you can apply the special factors one by one. This approach greatly simplifies the tree design process.

Trying to factor in all the possibilities and influences during the first stage of tree design is usually very frustrating. If you take this approach, your tree design will shift and change as you try to consider all the effects of Bindery Services, partitioning, and so on. Factoring in all the possibilities creates the (false) impression that a tree is unusually difficult (if not impossible) to design successfully. By using the tree design methods described in this chapter, you will discover that the NDS tree effort can be a simple process.

The actual number of layers in the tree is limited to 256 characters of a fully qualified name, which is 51 levels (using only two-character OU names). If your OU names are long, you can't have as many layers as you can if you devise shorter names.

Now that you have a general idea of the process, you can get started. The rest of this chapter describes the steps for designing an NDS tree in detail.

Gathering the Corporate Documents

THE FIRST STEP in actually designing an NDS tree is to gather the appropriate corporate documents. To create a suitable tree, you need the following documents:

- A wide area network (WAN) layout of your company

- A list of the major locations or campuses within your company

- Your company's general organization chart (listing items from the top down)

- A list of departments, divisions, and workgroups in your company

- A list of current servers, printers, and other resources

Designing the Top Level of the Tree

THE TOP LEVEL of an NDS tree comprises the [Root] object, which is created automatically and cannot be removed. Under the [Root] object comes either the Organization (O=) or the Country (C) object. The Country object is not necessary for use in private trees; it is used by public access providers (such as AT&T NetWare Connect Services). The following layers include the Organizational Unit (OU=) objects. Usually, only a few users and network resources are placed at the top levels in the tree. The ADMIN user is automatically created at the Organization layer, for example.

Functionally, the top level of the NDS tree is the most important because it serves as the foundation for the rest of the tree. As shown in Figure 4.2, the top three layers of the tree represent its top level. In this example, the top level contains a company name (WWW) and five OU objects that represent various geographic locations within the company. These locations are connected by the WAN infrastructure for WWW, Inc.

FIGURE 4.2

The top level of an NDS tree

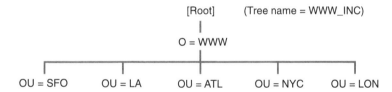

To design the top level, you choose names for the objects. How to do that is discussed in the following sections.

Naming the Tree or [Root] Object

The first thing for you to do is choose a name for the NDS tree. The name you choose usually represents the tree of the entire company. In our example in Figure 4.2, the tree name is WWW_INC for "World Wide Widgets, Inc." The NDS tree name is shown in a few NetWare 4.11 utilities, including SERVMAN, MONITOR, and others.

Keep in mind that the tree name must be a unique name on the entire network because the name is broadcast using the Service Advertising Protocol (SAP). Moreover, tree names cannot include spaces because SAP does not allow it.

The [Root] object is usually followed by the Organization (O=) object. The Country (C=) designator may be used to specify a particular country code based on the X.500 standard. However, as mentioned previously, the country code is not necessary for use in private corporate NDS trees. (See Chapter 2 for more information about the Country object.)

Naming the Organization Object

Every tree must have at least one Organization (O=) object. In most cases, the object gets its name from the company. Usually, at this layer in the tree, there is only one Organization object for your company, but if your company has more than one separate operating business you may want to use more than one organization designation.

Figure 4.3 shows an example of a tree design with two Organization objects. In this example, a conglomerate uses multiple Organization objects because each company under the parent company operates differently.

FIGURE 4.3

A tree structure with multiple Organization objects that represent entirely different companies under a single tree

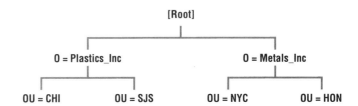

Remember, good tree design means giving meaningful names to each container object in the tree. Object names need to be easy to use and consistent with the naming standard already in place (see Chapter 3). NDS gives users the ability to have a single login from anywhere in the network, but confusing and inconsistent names can limit the usefulness of this feature.

Creating the Organizational Unit Locations

The next layer of the NDS tree—it comes directly under the Organization object—should include the physical locations or campuses of your company, placed as Organizational Unit (OU=) container objects. Typically, these location OUs are geographical sites within the company that are connected using WAN links. At each site, you could have multiple departments or divisions.

Using company documents that detail the physical layout of the WAN and how it connects your network, determine which locations should be OU objects in the NDS tree. It is extremely important to represent or match the WAN infrastructure to the top of the NDS tree design. In Figure 4.2, for example, we have Organizational Unit objects for our offices in San Francisco (OU=SFO), Los Angeles (OU=LA), Atlanta (OU=ATL), New York (OU=NYC), and London (OU=LON).

Using Regional OUs

In a company with multiple offices in different parts of the country, it is best to view the regional locations first and then group departments under each regional location. Most network administrators try to match the physical locations of their WAN at the layer under the Organization object in the tree.

For example, consider a large government agency with offices in many cities. The cities are connected via 56 Kbps links to regional offices. The same departments can be found in each city. For this tree design, you would not create an OU object for every location immediately below the [Root] and O= layers in your tree. Instead, you would insert a regional location OU and then group your location OUs under each appropriate regional OU. Figure 4.4 illustrates this example.

FIGURE 4.4

The top of the NDS tree based on the physical layout of a WAN

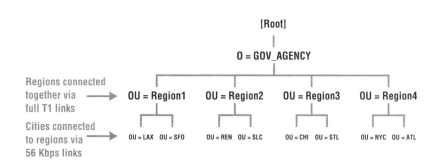

What Not to Include as Location OUs

It usually is not practical to include the floors of a building as location OU objects in a tree. Floors are usually not helpful for organizing a tree because they do not usually describe a location. However, if your company occupies several floors of a building and each floor is considered a unique or specific location, you might consider including the floors of a building as location OU objects in a tree.

Using the remote or field office sites as the first location OUs in a tree can be cumbersome. The design issue to consider with remote or field offices is the total number of sites that exist. Typically, you can gather small offices under a regional heading that distributes the offices appropriately. For example, in a company that is organized around one major headquarters and has a number of small sales offices, you would place the small offices in regional containers that are defined in the top of the NDS tree. Each office would then can be placed under the appropriate regional container.

Exceptions to the Geographical Approach

If your company does not have a WAN network infrastructure and is based completely on a LAN network, the NDS tree design should follow the design rules of the bottom of the tree. For example, suppose the company only has one site and is operating in a single building. In that case, use the company's departments, divisions, and workgroups as OU objects instead of the geographical sites.

If your company is connected using a campus network or metropolitan area network (MAN), your network is "geographical" and you should design the top of the tree accordingly. (This is true even if the links are very high-speed T3 links or greater.) At first, it might seem that the large WAN bandwidths nullify the geographical considerations, so NDS traffic and design considerations are not as great an issue. However, the stability and utilization of the links cannot be guaranteed and the NDS tree design should reflect the individuals sites.

Designing the Bottom Level of the Tree

THE BOTTOM LEVEL of the tree comprises the remaining hierarchy of OU and leaf objects. The bottom of the tree starts where the WAN network crosses over to the LAN network. Its design is based on the divisions, departments, and workgroups that contain the objects for users, servers, printers, queues, and other network resources.

The bottom of the NDS tree is where the issue of flexibility comes into play. A tree that has been designed with the company's organization at the bottom in mind is both flexible and easier for users and system managers to use. We recommend using your company's organization charts to design the bottom level of the NDS tree. Create OUs to represent the divisions, departments, workgroups, and teams at the various locations of your company.

By using your company's organization charts to design the bottom level, you can ensure that users have some familiarity with the tree layout. The example in Figure 4.5 highlights areas of a company's organization chart that you should include as OU objects in your tree.

Remember, for your first draft, follow your organization chart without trying to consider other factors. After you have sketched out the bottom of the tree, you can start adjusting it to meet users' additional requirements.

Reviewing Your Draft Design

AS SHOWN IN Figure 4.6, your NDS tree design should now consist of the top and bottoms layers of the tree.

The top of the tree should be stable and constant. Your first draft should show the skeleton or container objects and their placement in the tree.

Examine the draft of the NDS tree to ensure that there is a place for every user community in your current grouping of OU objects. Have you accidentally left out a group? Have you overlooked small departments or remote sites? If so, adjust your tree design to include these groups.

FIGURE 4.5

The portions of a
company's organization
chart that should be
included in the tree as
container objects

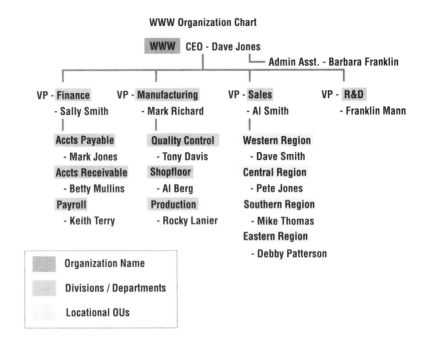

FIGURE 4.6

An NDS tree design with
top and bottom layers

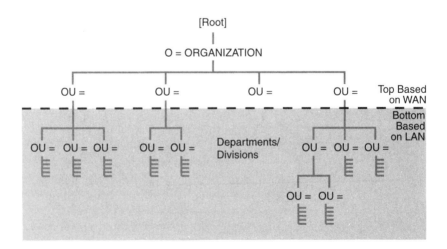

When you have completed your first draft of the NDS tree (on paper or with your design software), you're ready to apply special design factors to the bottom level of the tree. "Special design factors" is the name we've given to the "what-if" scenarios that you must consider in order to complete the tree design.

Applying Special Design Factors

THE SPECIAL DESIGN factors you need to consider apply to the bottom of the tree. They only impact the users and network resources that are in the bottom containers of the NDS tree. They do not alter the top of the tree design.

Five special design factors affect the bottom tree design:

- Centralized versus decentralized administration

- Network infrastructure and partitions

- Location of physical devices

- Login scripts

- Bindery Services

The following sections discuss these factors in detail.

Centralized versus Decentralized Administration

Your next step is to decide how the lower layers of your company's NDS tree will be managed and administered. There are essentially three options to consider:

- The NDS tree can be centrally managed, meaning only one IS (Information Services) group has the responsibility of managing the entire tree and all its changes.

■ The NDS tree can be managed by multiple and autonomous groups represented within the tree. For example, the tree can be managed by workgroup administrators at each department OU.

■ How the access rights of users and groups are administrated in the tree. Ideally, appropriate rights should be assigned as high in the tree as possible and should "flow down"—that is, be inherited—appropriately. For more information on rights, refer to Chapter 14.

Decentralized Management

A common approach to tree design is to break out the administrative functions in the bottom of the tree. In a tree managed in a decentralized fashion, each OU administrator decides independently how the tree is organized in the lower layers. The chief administrators create the tree down to the department OU objects and then relinquish control at that layer to individual LAN administrators. The OU administrator has the ability to create additional OUs below his or her own. At this point, the creators of the tree can only give directives as to how each OU object should be organized further down the tree.

For example, in your Los Angeles office (OU=LA), the administrator of the Sales department is responsible for the design of the layers beneath the OU=SALES object. (See Chapter 14 for more information about creating sub-administrators.) Figure 4.7 illustrates this example.

FIGURE 4.7

A tree's bottom design is set up by an OU administrator.

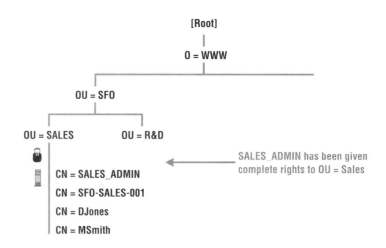

SALES_ADMIN has been given complete rights to OU = Sales

The number of layers you need for a decentralized management approach varies. But keep in mind that an NDS tree design must be flexible so that both users and administrators can find information easily.

Centralized Management

In the centralized management approach to the NDS tree structure, the central administration team has control of the tree from top to bottom. In this approach, we recommend letting the original creators continue to develop the tree design all the way to the bottom levels.

Rights are easier to administer when you use groups or other container objects. You can assign rights at a very high level in the tree to a few container objects, so that those rights are inherited and flow down to all the users involved. This technique allows for simple yet effective rights management. Keep the administration of rights in mind as you begin to create the bottom OUs. Chapter 14 has information about user rights and security.

Network Infrastructure and Partitions

You need to consider NDS partitions and the physical network infrastructure as you design the bottom level of your NDS tree. It is important to pay attention to infrastructure and partitions for a number of reasons. One of the most notable is that NetWare 4.11 must communicate with other servers in order to maintain synchronization of the NDS database. Based on the current design of NetWare 4.11, partitioning works best if it is localized and does not span a wide-area link.

However, NDS synchronization traffic is not the point here. The issue is that every server holding a replica in a partition must communicate with other such servers. If your link is slow or undependable, NDS will not synchronize until the links are back up. For this reason, we recommend that partitions do not straddle geographic sites.

You should split the NDS databases or partitions so that they contain only the information needed by a central set of users. Since the partitions of the tree should be based on the physical layout of the WAN, you can make each location its own partition.

Partitioning requires a container object to exist and be the [Root] (or topmost) object of the partition. To meet this requirement, you may need to create container objects and place them in the tree simply for partitioning purposes. For example, you might need to create a remote site container in order to partition its information and separate it from the rest of the sites.

As shown in the example in Figure 4.8, the topmost OU (it can also be an O or [Root]) is the root object of that partition. It is the highest OU in the partition and therefore is the name of that partition. As the highest OU in the partition, it is also known as the *partition root object* of the partition.

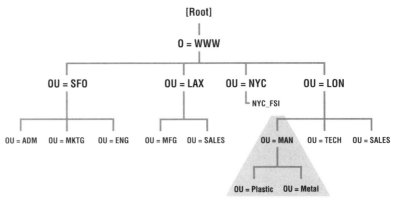

FIGURE 4.8

A partition's name is represented by the name of the uppermost OU object in the partition

If you have decided to manage the tree centrally, store all the master replicas for each partition at the hub sites or facilities where the best communication between partitions is available.

See Chapter 5 for more information about partitioning and replication rules and guidelines.

Location of Physical Devices on the Network

You should install network devices in the tree in container objects that meet the needs of the users who share the resources.

If the file servers and printers are departmental resources, place them in the department OU. On the other hand, if the file servers are superservers that service multiple departments, place them in the highest applicable OU.

Login Scripts

Use container and Profile login scripts whenever possible for configuring the user's environment during login.

Login scripts define the user's drive mappings, capture statements, variable settings, menus, and applications. To use login scripts, the appropriate OU objects must exist in the tree so the users and login scripts are grouped together according to their particular needs.

The same login script can be copied to many different container object scripts. With this strategy, however, the network administrator must be responsible for keeping all the copies up to date.

These login scripts also map the user's drive mappings to the appropriate servers for specific network applications such as databases. The login scripts depend on Group and Directory Map objects for these drive mappings. These groups and directory maps must be generic enough that all the users can find them during login.

Place the applications that all the network users need, such as word processors and spreadsheets, on all the servers in the same place on the file system. For example, you could create two Directory Map objects (WP and LOTUS) and use them in the login scripts for the servers on the network:

```
WP => SYS:APPS\WP

LOTUS => SYS:APPS\LOTUS
```

In this fashion, users can map the drives by using standard Directory Map objects to identify the key generic applications placed on all servers.

See Chapter 7 for the more information about login scripts.

Bindery Services

In order to respond to bindery calls made by the clients, NDS imitates the flat file structure of the NetWare 2 and NetWare 3 bindery. This feature, called Bindery Services, allows the clients to log in using NETX and run bindery-based client applications with NetWare 4.

When the Bindery Services feature is turned on at the server, the server sees the objects whose Directory Services base class is a bindery object, as well as users, groups, queues, printer servers, and profiles.

As you use Bindery Services, the most important issue to remember is the Server's bindery context. The bindery context of a server can point to as many as sixteen container objects in the NDS tree. You must place all bindery clients that require Bindery Services from a particular server in the same container object(s) as the server's bindery context. This consideration can affect the NDS tree design at the bottom level because it may require you to combine users and resources from multiple departments or workgroups into one OU object, when you would normally put them into several OUs.

See Chapter 3 for more information about the bindery context.

Before changing the design of your tree to accommodate Bindery Services, however, determine whether you actually need the bindery access. Identify the key applications used at your company and determine which ones require Bindery Services. By doing this, you can find out which servers need Bindery Services enabled.

After you have considered and applied the additional factors that might affect the bottom design for your company, you are ready to lay out the final draft design of the NDS tree (on paper or with a drawing application). Keep in mind that the tree design you have completed should not be "set in stone." Your design should be flexible enough that you can easily modify the tree structure when the organization of the company changes or its or network resources change.

NDS
Partitioning and
Replication

QuickTips: Partitions and Replicas

Use partitions to distribute the Directory 77

between servers. If your network has fifteen or more servers with replicas or it spans separate geographic sites, partitioning the Directory will increase the availability of the information and provide quicker access for users. However, if your network has less than ten to fifteen servers and is contained on one site, you probably do not need to partition the NDS tree.

Use replicas to provide fault tolerance, 79

quicker user access, and more efficient name resolution (finding information in the Directory). A replica is a copy of a partition. Any changes to a replica's objects or properties are updated to the other replicas of the same partition. These updates take place automatically at specific intervals. If a replica becomes unavailable, another replica of the same partition can be used for authentication.

Plan the placement of partitions carefully 85

by following these suggestions:

- Partitions should follow either a location OU (such as OU=REGION1 or OU=SFO) or an organization OU (such as OU=ENG at the lower levels of the tree).

- If a location or organization partition has more than ten servers that store replicas, consider partitioning that location container or organization container further.

- Plan your partitioning so that one partition does not span multiple physical locations.

Plan the placement of replicas to eliminate any single point of failure   90

by following these guidelines:

- Maintain three replicas of each partition. NetWare 4.02 and later versions automatically place up to three replicas on NetWare 4 servers, if available. You can create more replicas as necessary.

- Be sure to maintain three replicas of your [Root] partition (created by default on your first three NetWare 4 servers created in the [Root] partition).

- Replicate locally whenever possible.

- Create replicas as needed for Bindery Services.

ETWARE DIRECTORY SERVICES contains all the rules about NDS objects and their attributes. The rules that describe the NDS objects and their attributes constitute what is known as the NDS *schema*. The schema is distributed to all NetWare 4 servers in the network automatically.

When you create an object and add values to its attributes, this information is added to NDS and stored on the NetWare 4 servers in the form of data files.

In order to distribute the information in the Directory, the tree can be divided into smaller pieces. These pieces, or *subtrees*, are called *partitions* and can be stored on various NetWare 4 servers throughout your network. The partitioning process provides scalability to NDS. You can create as many partitions as you need to support the growth of your network.

Centralizing versus Distributing the Directory

HE INFORMATION IN your NDS tree may either be distributed among multiple servers or centralized, with all the information residing on one or two network servers. The size of your network usually determines which approach you take, the centralized approach or the distributed approach.

The Centralized Approach

In small network environments, centralizing the Directory (by not partitioning) makes it easier to manage NDS. The response time for the users is adequate as long as the number of users and devices in the partition remains small.

In this context, the term small means a network with roughly one to ten servers or up to 1500 objects, all located in the same location and not connected by WAN links.

If your network is small or contained to one site with only a couple of servers, you probably do not need to partition NDS. Instead, you can leave the tree as a single database that is replicated on one or two servers. If you choose not to create partitions and you have at least two NetWare 4 servers, you should maintain a replica (a copy) of your [Root] partition on each server.

The Distributed Approach

If your network is large or has several sites with many servers, the Directory should be distributed. By distributing the database, you increase the availability of the information and provide quicker access for users.

To distribute the Directory, you partition the NDS tree and locate the partitions in appropriate places, as discussed later in this chapter. Again, the partition is just a logical segment of the hierarchical Directory. Partitions are transparent to the user. From a workstation, the NDS tree appears as a single logical entity. When a partition is created or deleted, the user does not notice any differences.

Understanding NDS Partitions

ARTITIONING IS THE mechanism by which the logical NDS database is divided into subtrees, which are stored on different NetWare 4 servers in your network. Although an individual server may not physically contain the complete NDS database, your network users can still access all the NDS information. When you create a partition, special links are established to make the data available to all the servers.

Partitioning the database and storing the partitions on more than one server distributes the synchronization workload between NetWare 4 servers. NetWare's partitioning utilities allow you to choose where in the network you want to store the different parts of NDS.

The following sections describe how partitions are handled by NetWare 4. See "Planning Your Partitions and Replicas" later in this chapter for guidelines on setting up partitions for your NDS tree. See Chapter 13 for more information about NetWare's partitioning utilities.

The [Root] Partition

When you install your first NetWare 4 server, the [Root] partition is automatically created and placed on that server. You cannot delete this partition using NetWare utilities. An example of the [Root] partition is shown in Figure 5.1.

FIGURE 5.1

A [Root] partition for the tree WWW_Inc

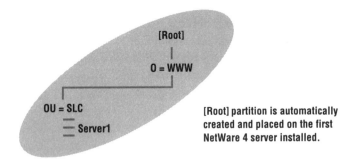

[Root] partition is automatically created and placed on the first NetWare 4 server installed.

During installation, four partitions are automatically stored on every server in the network: the System, Schema, External Reference, and Bindery partitions. These partitions store information that is local to that NetWare 4 server. All four are used internally by NDS.

The Partition Root Object

A partition can have only one container object as its root-most object. When you create additional partitions subordinate to the [Root] partition, you select a container object in the tree as the root of the new partition.

We refer to the root-most container object in the partition as the *partition root object*. The partition root object names the partition. For example, if the container OU=ENG were to be created as a partition, its partition name would be Partition Eng.

Do not confuse a partition root object with the [Root] object of the NDS tree. The [Root] object of the tree is a special container object that signifies the top of your entire NDS tree. The partition root object is the topmost container object in a particular partition.

Partition Attributes

When a partition is created, several additional attribute values are added to the container object that is the partition root object. These attributes' values are used to synchronize the data associated with the partition ("Synchronization of Replicas," later in this chapter, offers more information about NDS synchronization). The two most important of these attributes are the Replica Pointer and Synchronized Up To attributes.

The Replica Pointer attribute provides a list and the location of all the partition's copies. This list is commonly called the *replica list*, or *replica ring*, of a partition. It is used to find the other copies of the partition when NDS needs to update the information.

The Synchronized Up To attribute is a list of time-stamps, at least one for each replica in the replica list. It is used by each server to determine its state in regard to all other replicas of the partition. This attribute is commonly called a *vector of time-stamps*.

Another important attribute of the partition root object is the Inherited ACL (Access Control List). This attribute—a summary of all ACLs, from the [Root] object down to the object's context in the tree—helps determine access rights. (See Chapter 14 for more information about NetWare 4's ACLs.) The inherited ACL information is communicated through the partition root object.

Understanding NDS Replicas

THE NDS PARTITIONS can and should be replicated. By replicating them, copies of the partitions can be placed on different network servers. An identical copy of a partition physically stored on the server is referred to as a *replica*. A network server can store multiple replicas as long as the replicas are from different partitions in the tree. There can be multiple replicas for each partition.

You should try to maintain at least three replicas, which will be installed automatically during installation. You can create more replicas as your needs dictate, although we don't recommend using more than three replicas.

If your network has only one server, you probably have only a single copy of the [Root] partition, because no other partitions are necessary. Your redundancy is to create a copy of NDS using SMS-based backup software (SMS stands for Storage Management System). Make sure your backup software will back up NDS. You can also use products such as Preferred Systems' DS Standard to maintain a simple backup of NDS.

Any changes to information about the objects in the NDS tree or replicas are synchronized to the other replicas. Replica updates take place automatically at specific intervals. Some updates, such as changing a user's password, are immediate (within 10 seconds). Other updates, such as login updates, are synchronized every 30 minutes.

Functions of Replicas

Replicas perform three primary functions:

- **Fault tolerance:** If an NDS replica becomes unavailable, another replica can be used by NDS to authenticate users logging in to the network. Users can access the network, even when a server, router, or WAN link goes out of service, as long as a server communicating with those users contains a replica for those users. Your goal in replication is to have no single point of failure for NDS on your network. Fault tolerance is a major benefit and advantage of NDS.

- **Speed of access:** By placing replicas with frequently accessed NDS data closer to the group of users who use it most often, you decrease the time needed for authentication, modifications, and searches. This method increases the probability that the information will be retrieved from the nearest available server.

- **Name resolution:** Finding the requested object information in the Directory is referred to as *name resolution*, or *tree walking*. If the requested object information is not found in the portion of the Directory to which the user is attached, NDS performs the name resolution process to locate the information. Every partition stores references (pointers) to servers that contain the superior partition, as well as to any subordinate partitions. If necessary, NDS follows these pointers to find the data requested.

Replica Types

Before you decide where to place replicas in your network, you should understand the different replica types. There are four types of replicas: master, read/write, read-only, and subordinate. The following sections describe these types. See "Placing the Replicas" at the end of this chapter for guidelines on which types to use and where to put them in your NDS tree.

Master Replica

The master replica of the partition is the first replica created when the partition is defined. There can be only one master replica for each partition. Other replicas are either the read/write or read-only type.

The [Root] partition, which is created during the installation of the first NetWare 4 server, is stored as the master replica for the [Root] object.

The master replica is important because it is used to perform partition operations. NetWare 4 checks the master partition to ensure that only one partition operation is being performed at a time. While a partition operation is being performed, the master replica "locks" the replicas in its list so that no other partitioning operations can be performed. This gives NDS database integrity. Like a read/write replica (discussed in the next section), a master replica accepts client updates.

Read/Write Replica

A read/write replica is usually the second replica created for a specific partition. Maintaining up to three replicas, including the master replica, is recommended for fault tolerance. You can create multiple read/write replicas for each partition. However, we recommend that you create additional replicas (beyond three) only when the need arises (see "Placing the Replicas" at the end of this chapter for more information).

The read/write replica type accepts client updates. Since these replicas can receive updates, they can be used for users' login and authentication requests.

The NDS Bindery Services feature requires that a read/write or master replica of the partition containing the bindery context be stored on the NetWare 4 server where the services are needed. The Bindery Services feature is discussed in detail in Chapter 7.

Read-Only Replica

A read-only replica does not accept client updates; it can only be updated from master or read/write replicas. You probably will not use read-only partitions because they are so limited. For example, users cannot log in to the network using a read-only replica. Since the server with the read-only replica cannot service these requests, it would need to pass the request to a server with a master or read/write replica.

Subordinate Reference Replica

A subordinate reference replica basically links the partitions in the tree. These replicas are created and managed completely by the system. You can see which subordinate reference replicas exist by using Novell's NWAdmin and DSRepair utilities, but these replicas are not visible from the DOS-based NetAdmin utility. The DSRepair utility provided with NetWare 4.11 does allow you to convert a subordinate reference replica to a master or read/write replica.

The only situation in which you would convert a subordinate reference replica to a master or read/write replica is if all the replicas for a partition were destroyed and you had no other replica. The conversion only restores a link within your tree between higher partitions and downstream partitions. It does not restore a replica's objects, because the subordinate reference replica does not contain them. You would still need to restore your partition's objects from your NDS tape backup.

The subordinate reference replica links a parent partition with its child partition. A *child* partition is one that is subordinate in the tree to another partition (the *parent*). A subordinate reference replica is created whenever a parent partition exists on a server, but the child partition is not on that server. Figure 5.2 shows how this process is handled automatically by NDS.

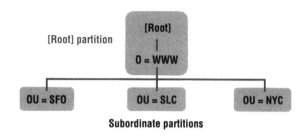

A subordinate reference replica does not contain all of the NDS objects that are normally stored in a partition. Instead, this replica contains only a copy of the child partition's root-most object (including all of its attributes). A subordinate reference replica contains these attributes: Replica Pointer and Synchronized Up To (they are described earlier in the chapter, in the section called "Partition Attributes").

Since the subordinate reference replicas contain a list of all the replicas and their locations (the Replica Pointer attribute), NDS can quickly locate information that is stored in those replicas. Name resolution is handled quickly and efficiently by means of subordinate references and is impossible without them.

Replication for Bindery Services

NetWare 4.11's Bindery Services feature enables the NetWare 3 bindery utilities and applications to run under NDS without modifications. Using Bindery Services, NetWare 4.11 responds to the bindery calls as if it were a NetWare 3 bindery. The objects in the replica that are currently in a NetWare 3 bindery (User, Group, Print Queue, Print Server, and Profile, plus any object whose base class is a bindery object) are the only objects recognized by Bindery Services.

To operate properly, the NetWare 4.11 server must have a master or read/write replica of a partition and the proper server bindery context set for Bindery Services. Figure 5.3 shows an NDS tree with a server using Bindery Services.

FIGURE 5.3

Any server that uses Bindery Services requires a read/write or master replica.

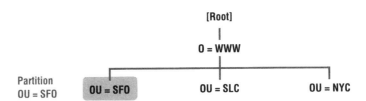

A server in the tree has Bindery Services enabled. It must have a read/write replica of a partition. In this example, we specify that OU = SFO be our bindery context. You can specify up to 16 bindery contexts in NetWare 4.11.

Synchronization of Replicas

The responsibility of NDS is to keep all the information in the database synchronized. However, the NDS database can be partitioned and replicated, so we describe NDS as "loosely consistent" because not all replicas of a partition are synchronized simultaneously. When changes are made on the system, a variable amount of time passes before these changes are recorded on all replicas. During that time, the database is considered to be in an inconsistent state, yet moving toward consistency.

Synchronization of the data across replicas is performed by sending only the delta (changed) information of the object. The only time that an entire object is synchronized with all of its attributes is upon initial creation and after some partition operations. Other times, only the changes made to that object are sent to the replicas of that partition. This minimizes the amount of data traveling across the network.

See Chapter 15, which covers troubleshooting, for more information about NDS synchronization.

Partition and Replica Operations

P ARTITION OPERATIONS USUALLY include any function that affects the partition hierarchy, such as the following:

- Creating a partition (also called *splitting*)
- Deleting a partition
- Changing a replica's type
- Rebuilding a replica
- Moving a partition
- Moving a subtree

Partition operations can potentially involve a large number of objects, so they should be performed when the network is less active. For example, joining partitions is fairly band-width-intensive and may interfere with users' network response time. On the other hand, splitting a partition is not as bandwidth-intensive and can probably be performed anytime. If you have more than ten replicas of a partition, these operations should be performed after hours.

Partition operations require that the master replica be available, because the master replica is where the operations start. All the other replicas of the same partition must be up in order to complete any partition operation.

The following sections describe partition and replica operations and their effects. See Chapter 13 for information about NetWare's utilities for creating and managing partitions and replicas.

New Servers and Default Partitions

By default, if a NetWare 4.11 server is installed into a new container object that is created during the installation process, a new partition is not created (just the opposite occurs in version 4.02: a new partition *is* created for the new container object). The NetWare 4.11 installation program does not do partitioning for you.

If you are installing a new NetWare 4.11 server, rather than upgrading from NetWare 3, and the current number of replicas of the partition is less than three, the installation program places an additional replica on the newly installed server. If you need to maintain more than the recommended three replicas, you can use the NWAdmin or DOS PARTMGR utility to add more replicas.

If you are upgrading the server from NetWare 3 (and therefore the server has bindery files), a replica is added to the server, regardless of the current replica count.

Figure 5.4 illustrates how a new server is installed into a newly created OU object using NetWare's 4.11 installation utility. The OU is not partitioned. It remains part of its parent until you partition the OU using the NetWare utilities. In this example, if you enabled Bindery Services during installation, the server would automatically receive a read/write replica of OU=NYC.

FIGURE 5.4

A partition is not automatically created when you install a new server into a new OU with the NetWare 4.11 Install utility.

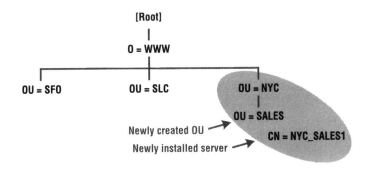

By using the NWAdmin or Partmgr utility, you can create a new partition for a new container, even if you have not yet installed a server into that partition. For example, you might create partitions before installing servers when you are setting up an entire NDS tree, including partitioning, and then ship the servers to their actual locations. In this case, the master replica of the new partition is placed on a server that contains the parent partition. When you install a server in the new partition, a read/write replica of the new partition is placed on that server. Figure 5.5 shows where the replicas are placed.

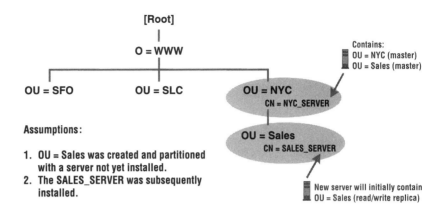

FIGURE 5.5

Creating a new partition
for a newly created OU
with a server

Creating Partitions

Creating a new subordinate partition from a parent partition is commonly
called *splitting* a partition. This operation is relatively fast and does not generate a lot of network traffic, because all the object information (values) stays
on the same servers. The process is similar to drawing a boundary between a
database, with all the data remaining on the same server. The new partition
resides on all servers that store the original partition.

When the subordinate partition is created, all the objects in the tree under
the partition root object are included in the new partition. However, if
another partition has already been defined lower in the tree, that partition is
not affected; the existing partition still contains the objects below its partition
root object. The subordinate partitions are not included in the new partition.
Figure 5.6 shows an example of a tree with the names of the partitions
highlighted.

Partitions cannot overlap. As a consequence, NDS objects reside in only
one partition.

Merging, or Joining, Partitions

When you merge partitions, you combine subordinate partitions with the
parent partition. This is commonly referred to as a *join* operation.

FIGURE 5.6

A partition is named by the highest container object in the partition. Its name is known as the partition root object.

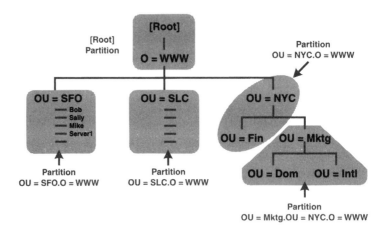

The length of time a merge operation takes and the impact it has on network traffic depends on where the information is stored. If all the servers that have replicas of the subordinate partition also have replicas of the parent partition, the merge process goes quickly because no data has to move across the network.

However, if some servers have only a replica of the subordinate partition and other servers have only replicas of the parent partition, the merge process takes more time. Before the merge can take place, NDS must add the replicas to all the servers that do not have information about both partitions.

Adding Replicas

You can add a new replica quickly if the size is small (less than a thousand objects), because a new replica comes from an existing partition. When you add a replica to a server, NDS sends all the data in the partition to the replica on the other server.

The amount of network traffic generated when you add a replica depends on the number and size of objects in the partition. Obviously, this operation takes much longer if the partition has several thousand objects and multiple replicas.

Removing Replicas

When you remove a replica, you delete a copy of the partition information from a specific server. Because you are simply removing the data from the server, the operation appears to take place quickly from a utility standpoint. However, every object in that partition will automatically be set up as an external reference (pointer) with backlinks on the real object in another replica until the NDS process can inform every server that holds the replica.

Although the replica itself can be deleted quickly, setting up each object in the replica as an external reference takes time. Therefore, the more objects in the replica, the more time required to delete it.

If you are removing a server from your NDS tree, the NetWare 4.11 utilities prompt you to redesignate the replicas that reside on that server. Because of the backlinks, simply deleting the server object (by using NWAdmin) rather than deleting the replicas on that server creates less network traffic. Deleting the server object removes the server entry from the replica list and does not create backlinks. Removing replicas requires NDS to establish backlinks for each object in the partition.

Be careful not to delete a server object that contains the only copy of a partition.

Managing Partition and Replica Operations

If possible, we highly recommend that you centralize partition operations management. By doing so, only one person or a small group of people are responsible for all the partitioning and replication operations for your company.

We also recommend using only one client on the network for partition operations. Replica management should be done from only one client workstation at a time. This way, you can eliminate the possibility of two clients making different changes to the same partitions.

You should check the status of the replicas of the partitions before you perform any partition operation. Make sure that the status of the synchronization is error-free before starting a new operation.

The DSRepair utility for NetWare 4.11 shows the replica status on a given server. See Chapter 15 for more information.

Partitioning operations are not usually instantaneous. As explained earlier, NDS is a distributed, replicated database that is loosely consistent, which means that the information in the database is more or less consistent depending on the time factor. To achieve consistency after a major change, therefore, the replication and synchronization of information throughout the database requires a variable amount of time. The time varies depending on the amount of information or objects, the number of servers, the number of replicas, the speed of the WAN links, and so on.

Each time that you perform partitioning operations in the NDS tree (such as add, delete, split, or join operations), wait a sufficient amount of time to let conditions in the tree settle down before you take further action. You can verify that an operation is complete with the NetWare utilities (see Chapter 13 and Chapter 15 for details).

Planning Your Partitions and Replicas

ONCE YOU HAVE a basic understanding of partitions and replicas and the operations in which they are involved, you are ready to determine where you want to place the partitions for your NDS tree.

For medium to large installations of NetWare 4, a replication matrix can help you design your partitions and replicas. Figure 5.7 shows an example of a matrix for this purpose.

Designing the Partitions

In general, you should define your partitions by following the physical layout of your network infrastructure. Plan the partitioning so that one partition does not span multiple physical locations over a WAN link. Since a

FIGURE 5.7

A replication matrix can assist you in the creation and placement of replicas.

M - Master replica R/W - Read/write replica			Partitions					
Site Name	Address	Server Name	Abilene	Baird	Colorado City	Snyder1	Snyder2	
Abilene	114 4th St.	ABL-001	M	R/W				
Baird	205 Jonson Ave.	BRD-001						
Colorado City	312 Industry Rd.	COC-002	R/W	M				
Snyder	4822 Longson Ave.	SNY-001				M	R/W	
Snyder	33 2nd St.	SNY-002				R/W	M	

partition is defined by a container object, a partition should contain servers that are physically close together on the network.

The first layer of partitions (after the root object partition) are typically defined according to the physical locations of the company and the network infrastructure. Subsequent layers are based on the company's divisions, departments, or workgroup OU objects.

For a company with several sites scattered around the country, for example, you would create partitions at the location OUs to localize the NDS information. If the local sites have several divisions or groups, you might need to split the tree into smaller pieces by partitioning further if the partitions are too large. On the other hand, for a company based at a single site with a small number of users, you would probably not need to partition the NDS tree at all.

If you don't partition your NDS tree, you will have the default [Root] partition. For redundancy purposes, you should create another read/write copy of the [Root] partition and place it on a second NetWare 4 server. If you do not have a second NetWare 4 server, you should rely on tape backup for NDS as well as your file system.

A good design for partitions is a pyramid shape with a few partitions at the top level of the tree and more partitions as you move toward the bottom. The [Root] partition, which is created automatically during installation, is at the top. A pyramid design creates fewer subordinate reference replicas than a tree that has more partitions at the top than at the bottom. ("Placing the Replicas" at the end of this chapter discusses the effects of subordinate reference replicas on replica replacement.) An example of partition placement is shown in Figure 5.8.

FIGURE 5.8

Partitioning should look like a pyramid, with a few partitions at the top and more at the bottom of your tree.

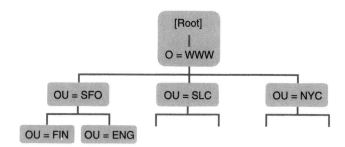

The pyramid design can be accomplished if you always create the partitions relatively close to the leaf objects (particularly the users). Placing the partitions close to the leaf objects encourages you to create small partitions, because you don't place many levels of container objects in one partition. With the pyramid design, replication and synchronization times are dramatically decreased because the replicas are smaller and fewer servers need to hold the replicas. (Remember that during the synchronization process, each replica is updated with all the partition's changes.)

We are not suggesting that every OU object be its own partition as a rule. Each location OU should be its own partition. Further partitioning beneath this OU depends on the number of servers, objects, performance requirements, and so on. We are also not suggesting that you add additional OUs to balance the tree on both sides. Simply remember to have more containers at the bottom of your tree than the top.

The size of the partitions and the number of replicas can significantly affect the synchronization and responsiveness of the system. You should avoid the following extremes:

- Partitions that are too large (greater than 3000 objects), with too many servers (more than ten) holding replicas, because they take too long to synchronize and managing all replicas becomes more complex.

- Partitions that are too small (less than 100 objects). If a partition contains only a few objects (just users and a server, for example), the benefits of the partition may not be worth the time you must invest in managing it.

It has been stated that there is a limit on the number of objects in a single container object. Some say 100 objects, others say 500, and still others say 1000 or 1500. The truth is that there is no limitation within the data files of NDS other than disk-space limitations. Displaying the objects within a container from the NetWare utilities screen will be delayed if the number of objects is extraordinarily large.

Placing the Replicas

Introducing replication into a distributed system presents a new level of complexity. Placing replicas correctly on the network servers is important to the efficient operation of the Directory.

First, you must decide whether changes or updates to the Directory should be directed to any copy or only to the original copy that is stored on the network server. You decide which copies will accept updates by choosing which type of replica to place in service. As explained earlier, the four types of replicas are master, read/write, read-only, and subordinate reference. Master and read/write replicas accept updates; read-only replicas do not. Subordinate reference replicas are created automatically by NDS.

Guidelines for Replica Placement

Designing the placement of the NDS replicas involves distributing or allocating replicas to specific network servers. The determining factors for the proper distribution are fault tolerance and speed of access. The following general guidelines will help you decide where to put your replicas:

- Be sure to maintain the [Root] replicas. The [Root] partition is created by default when the first NetWare 4 file server is installed. If you have not yet partitioned, the installation utility places two other replicas of the [Root] partition on the next two servers you install. Do not go overboard in replicating this partition; two or three replicas are sufficient at your key hub sites.

- Always have both a master and one to two read/write replicas for every partition. By having two to three replicas, you eliminate any single point of failure in your network—any one server can fail without affecting NDS availability. Multiple copies of the same partition are your best backup of data stored in NDS. Ideally, there are at least two replicas of each partition. Place at least one read/write replica of each partition in the same physical location as the master replica for the partition (if possible) to localize synchronization traffic.

■ Place a replica that contains the users' information on a server that is local to the users. Ideally, the server containing the replica is the same server that stores the users' home directories. This design gives users rapid access to the objects they use most often. For example, a user's login script maps drives to volumes, sets captures to print queues, and sets the user's working configuration. NDS accomplishes these tasks regardless of where the resources are placed on the network, but it does require more time to resolve requests from a remote server.

■ Place the master replica of the partition in the same location or site as the administrators of the partition. If your company wants to centrally manage the NDS partitions and replicas, place all the master replicas for each of the partitions at your central facility.

■ Avoid having too many replicas on one file server. Use your high-end file servers to hold the replicas. Most servers can adequately hold five to ten partitions in addition to their regular responsibilities.

■ The use of dedicated replica storage servers is acceptable in branch office situations where you need to store an additional replica of the branch's partition. Make sure that these dedicated servers use Pentium-class hardware.

■ Determine which NetWare 4 servers need Bindery Services. Give those servers at least a read/write replica of the partition. Remember, in NetWare 4.11, a bindery context can be set to up to sixteen containers.

Placing replicas on too many servers that require Bindery Services can affect replica synchronization performance. If you get beyond seven to ten servers with read/write replicas of the same partition, consider creating another partition to minimize this issue.

The Effects of Subordinate Reference Replicas

Although the subordinate reference consists of only the partition root object, the server name is included in the replica list of the partition. Too many subordinate reference replicas can cause problems, but not from an NDS traffic standpoint. Rather, the problem arises because a NetWare 4.11 server holds too many subordinate references (a single point of failure).

Subordinate references are a necessary and an automatic part of NDS. Their design was intentional. The purpose of this section is to explain methods for managing and distributing them for greater efficiency in your tree design.

During partitioning operations, all the servers in the replica list must be available. A partition operation (create, delete, merge, and so on) affects the subordinate reference replica because the partition root object changes. If you cannot contact the servers that hold subordinate reference replicas, you cannot complete the partitioning operations. For example, if you wanted to merge partitions and the link was not available, you would not be able to complete the merge until the subordinate reference replicas across the link became available. In the meantime, the NDS tree would not be synchronized for that particular partition.

Consider the example shown in Figure 5.9. In this figure, the tree has a [Root] partition and 100 geographic sites, each with its own partition. The [Root] partition is replicated on one other server in addition to the server holding the master replica. Each server that contains the [Root] partition also has 100 subordinate reference replicas for the partitions below.

FIGURE 5.9

A tree with two [Root] replicas and 100 partitions below places 100 subordinate reference replicas on each of the [Root] partition servers for a total of 200 subordinate references.

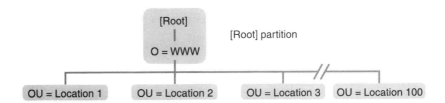

Each server containing a replica of the [Root] partition will also have 100 subordinate references; one for each subordinate partition (100 in our example).

The most effective way to reduce the number of subordinate reference replicas is to reduce the number of servers that contain a copy of the parent partition but not the child partition. Having fewer subordinate reference replicas decreases the number of replicas NetWare needs to update when you make partition changes, thus reducing the chance that synchronization will not occur because file servers or communication links are not available.

If your tree is partitioned below the [Root] partition, the server that contains the [Root] partition also has subordinate references to the partitions below (unless that server has a replica of the subordinate partitions). Each additional copy of the [Root] partition also contains subordinate references to all subordinate partitions. By reducing the number of servers that hold a copy of the [Root] partition, you can reduce the number of subordinate reference replicas on your network. Three copies of the [Root] partition are usually adequate.

Placing a read/write replica on a server in order to eliminate a subordinate reference is not recommended. You will actually add more traffic to your network this way. Remember that the subordinate reference contains only a copy of the subordinate partition's root-most object. Other types of replicas contain all the objects in the partition.

The only design option available is to distribute the number of subordinate reference replicas among more servers, thus reducing the chance that a server that contains subordinate reference replicas will not be in service during partitioning operations. This process would be handled by adding another group of regional OUs to distribute the load of subordinate reference replicas, as shown in Figure 5.10.

F I G U R E 5.10

To distribute the load of subordinate references, add another layer of OUs that are made into partitions.

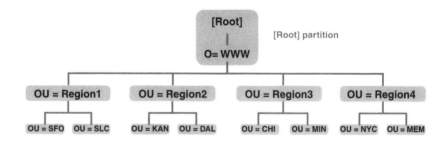

Creating regional OU objects can distribute subordinate reference across your NDS tree. Each regional OU will share the responsibility of holding the subordinate references. You eliminate one server having to hold all the subordinate references.

Partitioning is a logical distribution of the NDS database. Replication is the physical placement of partitions. Keep in mind that partitioning allows you to scale the network according to your needs. This process can be as simple as doing nothing (using the defaults) or designing a partitioning/replication matrix to define many locations for your partitions.

NDS Time
Synchronization

QuickTips: Time Servers

if the number of servers at your company is fewer than thirty or the file servers are all in one location and are not separated by a WAN. The default configuration designates one Single Reference time server and configures the rest of your servers as Secondary time servers. You should have only one Single Reference time server on the network to provide the network time to the other servers.

if your company

- Has more than thirty file servers

- Is separated by a WAN

A time provider group requires one Reference time server and at least two other Primary time servers. To set up a time provider group, you need to modify the time server type parameter for the servers chosen as the time provider servers in the group.

to suit the size of the site:

- At small, remote locations, servers can remain as Secondary time servers and get their network time from either a Single Reference time server or a time provider group, which could be across the WAN link. With this method, each Secondary server requests and receives the network time from a Primary time provider, thus minimizing time synchronization traffic on the wide-area link.

- At large, remote locations, you may need to make at least one server a Primary time server. This local server can participate as a member in the time provider group, thus eliminating the need to pass time requests from the remote Secondary servers across the WAN. Instead, the remote servers can go to their local Primary time server for network time.

Choose a method for time synchronization   109

to suit your network:

- Use the Service Advertising Protocol (SAP) to communicate between the time servers. SAP is the default configuration at installation.

- Consider using the configured lists method to reduce SAP communication broadcasts and reduce network traffic after your network is in place.

Use caution when adjusting SET parameters   115

for NDS time synchronization. The default settings work very well for NetWare 4 time synchronization. For example, the daylight saving time SET parameters are automatically added to your AUTOEXEC.NCF file. If you change the load order of these time parameters in AUTOEXEC.NCF, DS.NLM may not load properly because that NLM must first get the time as it is loading.

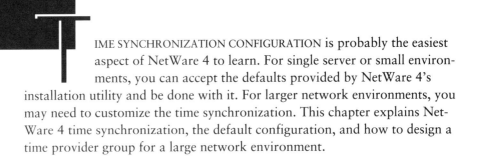

IME SYNCHRONIZATION CONFIGURATION is probably the easiest aspect of NetWare 4 to learn. For single server or small environments, you can accept the defaults provided by NetWare 4's installation utility and be done with it. For larger network environments, you may need to customize the time synchronization. This chapter explains NetWare 4 time synchronization, the default configuration, and how to design a time provider group for a large network environment.

What Is NetWare 4 Time Synchronization?

IME SYNCHRONIZATION, A NEW feature in NetWare 4, maintains the same time on all NetWare 4 servers in the tree. Time synchronization actually keeps each server's time set to UTC (Universal Coordinated Time), the world time standard coordinated to the zero meridian.

UTC was previously called Greenwich Mean Time (GMT). The abbreviation UTC is from the French translation.

UTC for each server is calculated from the local server time by applying the time zone and daylight saving time settings. Time synchronization ensures that all servers in the NDS tree have the same UTC time for time-stamping NDS events in the network.

The main purpose of time synchronization is to provide a common UTC time across all NetWare 4 servers. You can ensure that the time of day is accurate by attaching your main NetWare 4 time providers to an external time source service, such as a radio clock, an atomic clock, or the Internet time.

You can get the UTC time from many outside sources, including the Internet. You can also use a UNIX host that has been connected to an external time source.

If you do not use external sources, NDS time synchronization can still provide an accurate and predictable time to all NDS servers if you manually set the time on each server. PCs manufactured in the past few years have very accurate and stable clocks.

Why You Need Time Synchronization

T HE NDS DATABASE is a distributed and replicated database, so individual pieces of the NDS database are kept in different locations on various servers. To ensure that all the changes are applied in their proper order, NDS marks each event in the database with a time-stamp.

An event is any change to any object or property in the NDS database. Creating a user object and changing a user's password are examples of events.

A *time-stamp* is a unique value that records the time (UTC) and identifies the event. Time-stamps resolve collisions (multiple changes to the same object or property on different servers) by updating the events properly to all copies of the database. They are also used to mark objects or properties for deletion from the database when deletions are made through the NWAdmin and Partition Manager utilities.

Another benefit of keeping a consistent time on each network server is that NetWare records date and time information about each file when it is created, modified, archived, and deleted. Backup systems, document managers, and other file-based programs often rely on the accuracy of that information.

How Time Synchronization Works

TIME SYNCHRONIZATION USES a NetWare Loadable Module (NLM) called TIMESYNC.NLM that automatically loads whenever a NetWare 4 server is booted. TIMESYNC.NLM communicates with other TIMESYNC NLMs on other network servers and receives their time information. The *Secondary servers* (time servers that obtain their time from another server, as explained later in this chapter) adjust their internal clocks by speeding up or slowing down their tick rates.

Do not manually unload the TIMESYNC.NLM module. Time synchronization is only active when the NLM is running on each server.

Each NetWare 4 server on the network is responsible for its own synchronization and status. The server determines whether its internal clock is within a synchronization radius of the network time. The s*ynchronization radius* specifies a time value, with the default being 2000 milliseconds (2 seconds). You can adjust this value through the SERVMAN utility. (You may need to adjust the synchronization radius of your time servers if they are connected by satellite links that cause a significant delay in the transmission of packets.)

If the server determines that its time is within its radius, it raises a time synchronization flag to indicate that synchronization has been achieved. To see the value of the time synchronization and the status of the time server, type the following at the server console:

    TIME

As shown in Figure 6.1, you will see information about the time zone and daylight saving time (DST) settings, and the status of time synchronization. You also see current time values for both local time and UTC.

```
CSI1:TIME
  Time zone string: "MST7MDT"
  DST status:  OFF
  DST start:    Sunday, April 2, 1995    2:00:00 am MST
  DST end:      Sunday, October 29, 1995  2:00:00 am MDT
  Time synchronization is active.
  Time is synchronized to the network.
Wednesday, November 30, 1994   12:34:43 am UTC
Tuesday, November 29, 1994    5:34:43 pm MST
CSI1:
```

Types of Time Servers

HERE ARE TWO categories of time servers: time providers and time consumers. *Time provider* servers provide the time and fall into the following server categories: Primary, Reference, or Single Reference. *Time-consumer* servers request the time from a provider. They are called Secondary servers.

Internally, the four types of time servers are similar. All are both time providers and time consumers. They have the same fundamental responsibilities:

- Providing time to a time provider, time consumer, or workstation that requests it.

- Deciding whether it is synchronized to the network time and raising a time synchronization flag when it is synchronized.

- Adjusting the clock rate to correct discrepancies and maintain time synchronization with other servers.

Secondary Time Servers

Secondary time servers are time consumers. They get the time from a time provider (a Primary, Reference, or Single Reference server). They always try to stay synchronized to the time provider that sends them the time.

The majority of the time servers on a network (90 percent or more) are Secondary time servers. After you install NetWare 4.11 on the first server, the Secondary time server type is the default installation option when you install subsequent servers in the network.

During installation of your second and subsequent servers, always accept the default Secondary server type. If you need to, you can change the time server type, as explained later in this chapter.

Secondary time servers perform the following functions:

- Request network time from a time provider.

- Adjust their internal clocks to correct 100 percent of the time discrepancy during the polling interval.

- Provide time to clients or workstations.

Secondary servers do not vote with time providers to determine network time.

Secondary time servers raise their time synchronization flags when their time is within their configured synchronization radius.

A Secondary server can also act as a time provider to other servers in special cases. This configuration requires the Secondary server to retrieve the time from a Primary server first. The Secondary server can then distribute time to other Secondary servers. To get this configuration, you have to use the Configured List option in NetWare's ServMan utility, as explained later in this chapter.

Primary Time Servers

A Primary time server is a time provider and votes with other time providers to determine the network time. As you design your time synchronization configuration, keep in mind that each time provider must be able to reach all the other time providers.

A Primary time server performs the following functions:

- Polls all other time providers and votes to help determine network time. Each Primary server has a voting weight of 1.

- Adjusts its internal clock to correct 50 percent of its time discrepancy before the next polling interval.

- Provides network time to requesting time consumers.

- Provides network time to the clients or workstations.

A Primary time server must confirm with at least one other time provider that its internal clock is correct before raising its time synchronization flag.

Never reset a Primary or Reference server's clock to a time that is behind its current time. This leads to problems with time synchronization and causes the server to issue Synthetic Time for the NDS partitions on the server.

Reference Time Servers

A Reference time server is a time provider that adds to the functionality of a Primary time server. Like a Primary time server, the Reference time server votes with other time providers to determine the network time. However, the Reference server's vote has a much greater weight than that of the Primary server. This guarantees that the Reference server has the absolute vote in determining the time as long as it is online, with the result being that the network time converges to the Reference server.

The Reference time server performs the following functions:

- Polls all other time providers and votes to help determine network time. The Reference time server has a voting weight of 16.

- Does *not* adjust its internal clock.

- Provides time to requesting time consumers.

- Provides time to clients and workstations.

Like a Primary time server, a Reference time server must confirm with at least one other time provider that its internal clock is correct before it raises its time synchronization flag.

Because the Reference time server has sixteen votes during the voting process and does not adjust its internal clock, all other time servers converge to its time. Thus, your Reference server is a single point for placing an accurate external time source. Although the server's own clock can be used, ideally the Reference server is connected to an external clock source so that highly accurate time readings can be obtained at automated intervals. You can get products that connect PCs to external time sources. A list of most of the third-party external time sources is available on Novell's NetWire and Novell's Web server.

Generally, you place only one Reference time server on your network, but if your network consists of large, worldwide installations that span several continents, you might consider using more than one time provider group. If this is the case, multiple Reference servers will be on the network. However, the two Reference time servers will not synchronize with each other. So, you must create separate time provider groups for your network. To do this, isolate each group by filtering the time synchronization SAP type (0x026B) or create a configured list for each time server.

In order to properly establish two time providers, you need to make sure that the time is exactly the same in each time provider group. You can do this by connecting each Reference server to the same external time source. This way, the clocks for each time provider group will be exactly the same time on each side.

Single Reference Time Servers

The Single Reference time server is a stand-alone time provider. It is the default setting when you install your first NetWare 4 server. Any other NetWare 4 servers default to the Secondary time server type.

A Single Reference time server can raise its synchronization flag without confirming its time with any other time providers. Therefore, you should not use a Single Reference time server on the network with any other time provider (other Primary, Reference, or Single Reference time servers). The Single Reference server does not check with other time providers. The Single Reference time server always has the proper synchronized network time, but the other time providers might not.

A Single Reference time server performs the following functions:

- Stands alone as the only time provider on the network.

- Can raise its own synchronization flag without confirming the time with other servers.

- Provides time to requesting time consumers.

- Provides time to the clients and workstations.

Secondary time servers synchronize to the Single Reference server's time. You can use the Single Reference server's own clock or you can connect your Single Reference time server to an external time source, such as a radio clock or atomic clock.

If you choose not to use an external source for your Single Reference server, you must make sure that the server is keeping accurate time on your network. Check the Single Reference server's time periodically against a reliable source.

Configuring Time Synchronization

NOW THAT YOU understand the differences between the time servers, you are ready to configure time synchronization for your network. Because the default time configuration uses SAP broadcasts to obtain the correct time, you must consider the location of your time providers and time consumers.

The configuration of time synchronization has a little to do with the logical layout of your NDS tree and more to do with your physical network infrastructure and WAN connectivity. Basically, there are only two efficient time server configurations:

- Single Reference (the default)

- Time provider group

Read the following sections to determine which of these configuration options best meets the needs of your network.

Option One: Using a Single Reference Time Server

Using a Single Reference time server is the simplest configuration if your site is a small one. This configuration requires you to do nothing during installation; it is set up automatically by the NetWare 4.11 installation program. Single Reference is the default for the first server you install. When you accept this default, every subsequent NetWare 4 server is installed automatically as a Secondary time server.

The Single Reference time server configuration is suitable to networks with fewer than thirty file servers located in one site or campus. Your first NetWare 4 server—the network's Single Reference time server—should be centrally located in order to serve its time synchronization purpose.

Figure 6.2 shows an example of a Single Reference time server configuration.

FIGURE 6.2

A Single Reference time server configuration with only one server providing time to the entire network. This configuration is suitable for a network that has fewer than thirty file servers and is situated in one geographical site.

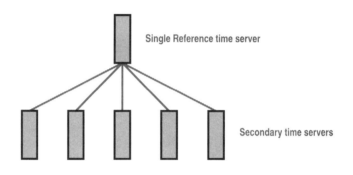

Single Reference time server

Secondary time servers

• **One Single Reference time provider**
• **Remaining servers are Secondary**
• **Less than thirty NetWare 4 servers**

The disadvantage of this type of configuration is that all the network servers could lose UTC time synchronization if the Single Reference time server goes down for an extended period of time. However, if you have a small network (with five or so NetWare 4 servers), this is not a big problem, because you can always designate another server as your Single Reference time server.

Option Two: Using a Time Provider Group

The second option, using a time provider group, requires one Reference time server and at least two other Primary time servers. All the time servers vote and converge to the network time. Together, they form the time provider group and provide the correct time to the rest of the time servers or time consumers, which are Secondary servers.

The time provider group configuration is appropriate for networks with more than thirty NetWare 4 servers or networks that are situated in several locations in a wide-area configuration.

To set up this configuration, you must modify the time server type parameter for the file servers you have chosen for the time provider group. Make one a Reference server and the others Primary time servers.

Designate a centralized server as your Reference server. Distribute the Primary servers across your wide-area links. If your network is a large WAN, place a few extra Primary servers in strategic hub locations.

We recommend including at least two and no more than seven Primary servers in a time provider group. You need at least two Primary servers to provide redundancy. But having too many Primary servers adds traffic to your network when they all need to synchronize. The rest of the installed file servers are Secondary servers (the default at installation).

Ideally, you should connect the Reference Server to an external clock source. Accurate time is especially critical in a time provider group because you need to avoid drift of the Reference Server's clock.

Figure 6.3 shows an example of a time provider group connected to an external time source. The time provider group contains one Reference time server and two Primary time servers, thereby providing redundancy.

Communicating Time Synchronization

TO RECEIVE THE network time, time consumers (Secondary servers) need to communicate with time providers on the network. Time providers need to find other time providers in order to vote and negotiate the network time.

Time servers communicate using one of two methods: SAP (the default) or configured lists. The following sections describe these methods.

You can use SET TIMESYNC commands at the file server's console to set the time synchronization method to SAP or configured lists. See "Time Synchronization Commands" a couple of pages hence.

FIGURE 6.3

A time provider group connected to an external time source for accurate time. This time provider group consists of one Reference and two Primary time servers. You have redundancy with the three servers.

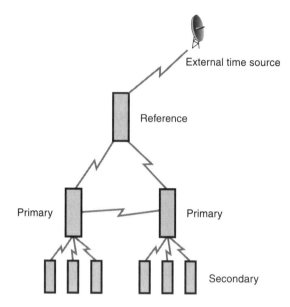

External time source

Reference

Primary

Primary

Secondary

• Requires one Reference and 2-7 Primary time providers
• Can be used with multiple campuses or across a WAN
• Used in environments with more than thirty NetWare 4 servers

Time Synchronization Using SAP

The SAP method is simple and self-configuring. You do not need to provide custom configurations to the existing time server or to new servers as they are added to the network. Time providers (Primary, Reference, and Single Reference servers) advertise their presence on the network using SAP. Time consumers only use SAP type 4 for address location.

Consider these issues when you use the SAP method of time synchronization:

- It can cause additional SAP information to be propagated around your network. This can be a cause for concern if many devices use SAP on your network.

- Since SAP is self-configuring, a time server that is configured incorrectly could disrupt your time synchronization.

Time Synchronization Using Configured Lists

In the configured list method of time synchronization, you perform custom configurations to enable the time providers to communicate with each other. You also determine which time providers service which time consumers.

Configured lists give you complete control of the time synchronization hierarchy. They also reduce SAP traffic on your network, because each time server only communicates with a time server found in its configuration list.

To use the configured list method, run NetWare 4's SERVMAN utility and choose the Configured List option. Then specify, by name, the server(s) you want to contact. As shown in Figure 6.4, the Configured List feature is very easy to use. If you specify more than one server, separate server names with semicolons.

FIGURE 6.4

Using SERVMAN to create a list of time servers to exchange time. In this example, the server is specifying a Primary server and a backup server to exchange its time.

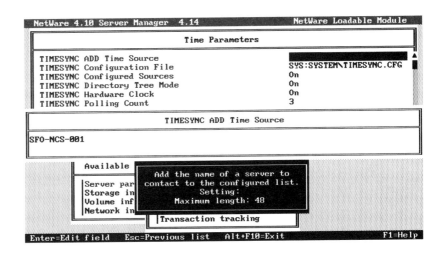

Choose either the Single Reference option (the default) or use a time provider group to provide time to your network. If you must use two time provider groups, make sure that both groups go to the same external source for the time. Because the two Reference servers never synchronize, you need a consistent external time to avoid time drift in the network.

Once configured, time synchronization is stable and dependable. It is one of those functions that almost never needs changing unless your network changes its size or location or you remove a server that was a time provider from operation.

Time Synchronization Commands

ONCE TIME SYNCHRONIZATION is functioning, your only job is to occasionally monitor time on your network.

Before a repair operation or network change, you should check the status of time synchronization. As mentioned earlier in the chapter, you can enter the TIME command at the file server console to see the status of time synchronization. You can also run DSREPAIR and select the Time Synchronization option from the menu. Both procedures return the status of time synchronization for all the servers that are known by the server where it is executed.

Debug Commands

In conjunction with the TIME command, you can use the following DEBUG command at the server console:

```
SET TIMESYNC DEBUG = 7
```

This command turns on the Debug utility, which shows you the status of time synchronization on that server.

To turn off the utility, type

```
SET TIMESYNC DEBUG = 1
```

Daylight Savings Time Commands

The following commands are used to set daylight saving time. They can be typed at the server console or placed in the server's AUTOEXEC.NCF file.

The daylight savings time SET parameters are automatically added to your AUTOEXEC.NCF file. Never change the load order of these time parameters in the AUTOEXEC.NCF file. Changing the order could cause problems when DS.NLM begins to load, because that NLM gets the time as it is loading.

The following command sets the UTC offset for your time zone:

```
SET Daylight Savings Time Offset =
```

The offset is set automatically during installation according to your time zone, but you can change it if a server is physically moved to a new time zone.

These commands set the status:

```
SET Daylight Savings Time Status = YES

SET Daylight Savings Time Status = NO
```

The default is NO, so that the daylight saving time status is not displayed on the server.

The following commands sets the date and time when you want daylight saving time to go into effect on that server:

```
SET Start of Daylight Savings Time =
```

By default, this is set to the time zone specified during installation and looks similar to

Sunday, April 2, 1995 2:00:00 am MST

This command sets the date and time when you want daylight saving time to no longer be in effect on that server:

```
SET End of Daylight Savings Time =
```

By default, this is set to the time zone specified during installation and looks similar to

Sunday, October 29, 1995 2:00:00 am MDT

Time Synchronization Configuration Commands

The following commands are some of the SET commands available for adjusting time synchronization on your server.

You should rarely need to adjust time synchronization. Most of the default settings work extremely well. Adjusting these time commands may cause problems with NDS and should only be attempted if you have an advanced understanding of the time parameters and understand the consequences. If you do not understand the issues and still want to change a parameter, you may wish to contact Novell Technical Support for assistance. Also refer to the Novell manuals for descriptions and documentation of these commands.

To set the time synchronization method to SAP, use the command

```
SET TIMESYNC Service Advertising =
```

To set the time synchronization method to configured lists, use the command

```
SET TIMESYNC Configured Sources =
```

Time synchronization can be straightforward and easy to use. If your network has less than thirty servers, you do not need to configure time synchronization. Your first server will be a Single Reference time server, and all subsequent NetWare 4 servers will be Secondary servers. If you have more than thirty servers, you should create a time provider group that consists of a Reference server and at least two Primary servers.

You have two options for configuring time: the SAP method (the default) or the configured list method. Use the configured list method if you need to reduce SAP traffic on your network or you are using a Secondary server to provide time to other Secondary servers.

Accessing
NetWare
Directory
Services

QuickTips: NDS Access

Use NetWare 4.11's additive licensing   **122**
feature to add connections

to an existing network. To expand your network, you can buy a license for closer to the number of users you want to add, instead of investing in a version of NetWare 4 for a greater number of users. Note that in NetWare 4, licensed connections are used only when a user has mapped drives or captured printers to a NetWare 4 server. Licensed connections are not required for clients who are just accessing NDS.

In mixed NetWare 3 and NetWare 4   **122**
environments, take advantage of
NetWare 4's single login feature

by using an identical user ID and password for each user who needs access to both versions of servers. Users must log in to a NetWare 4 server first, then ATTACH to additional NetWare 3 servers. The NetWare 3 connections will be bindery-based. With single login, you only need to manage a single account per user in a pure NetWare 4 environment. If you are running in a mixed NetWare 3 and 4 environment, you will still need to maintain user accounts on your NetWare 3 servers.

If you use the # command in your   **124**
login scripts

to execute a .EXE, .COM, or .BAT file, be sure to do all your MAP assignments first. If you try without first mapping a drive to the program, it will not execute.

Avoid using user login scripts in large   **130**
organizations

with more than 20 people. Instead, set up the user environment with container login scripts, which execute first (for the users who are part of the container and any other users who are aliased to the container). When necessary, provide additional environment settings for a set of users by using Profile scripts. Use individual user login scripts only for those users who can maintain their own user scripts or who require special settings.

Create login scripts for mobile users 130

to log in from various locations. Mobile users can set a site location in their CONFIG.SYS file to designate their home site name. The CONFIG.SYS file can also contain a location variable to provide more specific drive mappings based on location. Those mobile users who do not carry their own computer will log in from an available machine at their site. NDS must know their distinguished name before they can log in. Use one of these methods to accomplish this:

- The user first enters the context at the machine by using the Change Context (CX) command. (The user must know his or her context in the tree.)

- Set the context through the use of Alias objects. Create an Alias object below the Organization object for each mobile user. It should point to the user's primary object in the container where the user resides. (This method will work for up to 20 mobile users.)

Run bindery-based applications 138

using NetWare 4's Bindery Services feature. NDS can run bindery-based applications as long as your NetWare 4 server has a bindery context set. This context tells the NetWare 4 server the location or context of the bindery-based users. In NetWare 4.1 and later, you can set up to 16 bindery contexts per server. This means that you are not as limited in your NDS tree placement of users who need to access a bindery-based application on a particular server. Use the SET BINDERY CONTEXT=*<server location>* command at the NetWare 4 server prompt or in your STARTUP.NCF file, or use the SERVMAN utility to set up bindery contexts.

Access NDS from other types of clients 140

using normal login procedures. The different clients log in as follows:

- OS/2 clients log in as NDS users. They will execute either their personal login script or an OS/2 default login script. They will not execute a container login script.

- Macintosh clients can log in as NDS users. However, there are no NDS utilities currently available that run on the Macintosh. The user's activity will be bindery-based after NDS login.

- UNIX clients (running the UnixWare client software) log in as bindery-based clients and will not execute a login script of any kind.

ETWARE 4.11 PROVIDES users access to the network and its resources. The clients may be of the following types:

- VLM client

- NETX.COM bindery-based client

- OS/2 client

- Macintosh client

- UNIX client

Before users can access the network, they must go through the login and authentication processes. Although a particular server authenticates user login, other NDS servers in the network may participate in the login process. If one server cannot respond to the request, that server will contact another server that can process the request. As necessary, connections are authenticated across multiple servers until the login process is completed. This is known as *background authentication*.

This chapter explains the login process and how users can access and use NDS and its file system. It also provides examples of how to create various login scripts for both local and mobile users. The last section of this chapter covers Bindery Services and how the Bindery Services feature can help you with your design of a NetWare 4.11 network.

The current VLMs allow clients to connect to only one NDS tree at a time. If users need additional connections to other trees, those connections will be made through Bindery Services. If you map a drive to a server in another tree, the user will need to enter a user name and password, because background authentication currently does not span multiple trees. This process will allow you to access the server data but not NDS data on the second tree.

Types of Connections to NetWare 4 Servers

ONNECTIONS TO A NetWare 4 server can be one of three types:

- **Connected (not logged in):** Indicates a user who is currently not logged in but still is attached with the NETX.COM shell or VLM client loaded at the workstation. No licensed connection is being used at this point.

- **Authenticated:** Indicates that a user is accessing NDS, but has not accessed any physical resources such as files or printers. This status will be displayed in the MONITOR.NLM utility with an asterisk (*) next to the user name. These types of connections are not applied toward your total available license count.

- **Licensed:** Indicates a user that has logged in to the network and has mapped a drive or captured to a printer resource on that server. This type of connection is applied toward your total available license count.

Clients who are accessing NDS do not require a licensed connection. For example, if a user is browsing the NDS tree before logging in to the server, that user has not used a connection. (The [Public] trustee is granted Browse rights at [Root] so that users can see the objects in the tree and not be logged in to the network.) Pass-through operations, such as when a user attempts to log in to a server and NDS passes the request to another server, also do not use a licensed connection. Only when the user has mapped drives or captured printers to a NetWare 4 server is a license connection used.

Administrators who want to browse the NDS tree and not use a licensed connection can load the NWAdmin or NetAdmin utility at their workstations and run it locally. If they log in to a NetWare 4 server and run the applications from the server, they will be using a licensed connection.

Bindery-based logins are counted toward your total licensed connections. For example, a licensed connection is used when a NETX client logs in and accesses a file on a NetWare 4 server or a printer logs in to a NetWare 4 print server.

Expanding Your Network with Additive Licensing

A feature available in NetWare 4.1 and higher is additive licensing, which allows you to scale your licensed connections additively as your network grows. For example, you may currently have a 250-user version of NetWare 4.11, and now your company has decided to hire 40 more people. Rather than buying a 500- or 1000-user version of NetWare 4, you can purchase a 50-user license, which can be added to your 250-user license for a total of 300 connections. You can continue to add licenses as your network grows.

There is no limit to the number of connections through additive licensing using any combination of NetWare licenses. However, your server hardware may be limited in the number of connections it can handle. As your connections increase, the speed and memory of the machine you are using as a server must also increase.

Logging In Once and Only Once

ONE OF THE great benefits of using NetWare 4 is its single login feature. Single login means that a user logs in to the network only once. Additional connections and drive mappings to other NetWare 4 and NetWare 3 servers in your tree are handled automatically in the background through NetWare 4.11's authentication process.

With single login, you only need to manage a single account per user in a pure NetWare 4 environment. If you are running in a mixed NetWare 3 and 4 environment, you will still need to also maintain user accounts on your NetWare 3 servers.

The user's user ID and password must be identical for both NetWare 3 and NetWare 4 servers if you want to use the single login feature of NetWare 4.11. Users must also log in to a NetWare 4 server first, and then attach to additional NetWare 3 servers. The NetWare 3 connections will be bindery-based.

ATTACH.EXE is no longer used as a command-line executable command in NetWare 4. Instead, attachments to another server are handled through the MAP command. However, NetWare 4 still allows you to use the ATTACH command in your login scripts for compatibility with prior versions of Net-Ware. You can create login scripts that involve NetWare 3 and NetWare 4 servers, as discussed in this chapter.

Creating Login Scripts

L OGIN SCRIPTS AUTOMATICALLY set up your users' workstation environment at the time of login. As in prior versions of NetWare, you can use login scripts to map drives, set environment variables, execute programs or menus, and display messages. However, NetWare 4 provides more options for login scripts than NetWare 3. In NetWare 4, you can execute up to three out of four available types of login scripts.

Our focus in this chapter is to provide examples of how scripts can be used effectively in your environment. For a list of all the NDS script variables and commands, see Appendix B.

The Order of Login Script Execution

Before you decide which type of login script to use, you need to know the order of login script execution. Note that any NetWare login script should be executed before Windows is launched.

The NetWare 4 Login program executes login scripts in the following order and with the following conditions:

1. **Container login script:** When a user first logs in to the network, the script of the container in which the user resides will execute, if a container script is defined. Login scripts for containers above the one in which the user resides will not be executed. For example, Figure 7.1 shows user JSorenso under OU=Sales. If OU=Sales does not have a container login script, a script higher in the tree at OU=Parts would not execute for user JSorenso.

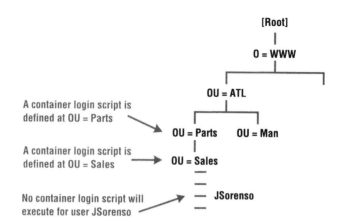

FIGURE 7.1

A container login script
executes only for users
that are directly beneath
its Organization or
Organizational Unit.

2. **Profile script:** If a user has a Profile script assigned, that script will be executed next. Its purpose is to set additional environment variables that were not assigned to everyone in the container.

3. **User login script:** This script is the third script to execute, if available. It is only run by the user who owns the script and is used for specific script assignments. If there is a container login script and also a user login script, the container script will execute, then the user script.

4. **Default login script:** The Login utility contains the default login script. This script includes minimal drive mappings and is intended for users who are not executing their own user script. If you do not create user login scripts and you do not want the default script to execute, you must specify the NO_DEFAULT command in the container login script or in a Profile script, or add an EXIT command at the end of the script.

Figure 7.2 shows where in a NDS tree login scripts are located.

Note that you if use the # command in your login scripts to execute a .EXE, .COM, or .BAT file, you should make all your MAP assignments first. If you try to execute a program using the # command without mapping a drive to the program, it will not execute.

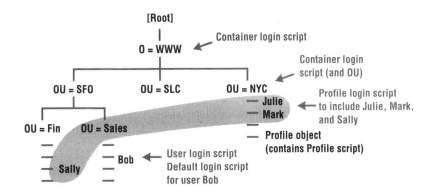

The Container Login Script

The first login script, if available, to execute in NetWare 4 is the container login script, also referred to as the O, OU, or system login script. The container login script for NetWare 4 executes for only the users who are part of the container and any other users who are aliased to the container. The primary object is contained in the OU object. Users in other containers usually will have their own container login script.

The purpose of the container login script is to set up an environment specific to an O (Organization) or OU (Organizational Unit) object. You can define available variables, drive mappings, and CAPTURE statements. You may also want to create menus or call applications from within login scripts.

Figure 7.3 shows an example of a container login script. This container script maps drives to a NetWare 4 server and also attaches and maps drives to a NetWare 3 server.

The Profile Login Script

The Profile login script is a special-purpose script that can provide more flexibility when establishing a working environment for a group of users. Any number of users can be assigned to execute the Profile script, and they can reside in any container in your NDS tree.

FIGURE 7.3

A container login script
that maps drives to
NetWare 4 and
NetWare 3 servers

```
;****************************************************
; Container Login Script
; Creation Date: 11/4/94
; Created by:
; Revisions:
;****************************************************
COMSPEC=C:\DOS\COMMAND.COM
REM Do not execute default script
NO_DEFAULT
WRITE "Good %GREETING_TIME, %LOGIN_NAME."
MAP DISPLAY OFF
IF
COMSPEC=C:\DOS\COMMAND.COM
REM Do not execute default script
NO_DEFAULT
WRITE "Good %GREETING_TIME, %LOGIN_NAME."
MAP DISPLAY OFF
IF <NW_DEBUG> <> "" THEN MAP DISPLAY ON
CONTEXT .%LOGIN_CONTEXT
MAP ROOT P:="%HOME DIRECTORY"
IF "%ERROR_LEVEL" <> "0" THEN
    WRITE "NO HOME DIRECTORY AVAILABLE, NOT MAPPED"
END
IF LOGIN_CONTEXT <> REQUESTER_CONTEXT THEN
    CONTEXT .%REQUESTER_CONTEXT
END
MAP ROOT INS S1:=%FILE_SERVER/SYS:PUBLIC
IF "ERROR_LEVEL <> "0" THEN
    MAP ROOT INS S1:="PUBLIC_BACK"
    IF "%ERROR_LEVEL" <> "0" THEN
        CONTEXT .%LOGIN_CONTEXT
        MAP ROOT INS S1:="PUBLIC"
    END
END
MAP ROOT N:=NETWARE3\SYS:APPS\TOOLS
```

As discussed in Chapter 2, a Profile script can be used in three different
ways: as a company-wide login script, a locational login script, or a special-
purpose login script. An example of the scope of the Profile script is shown in
Figure 7.4.

FIGURE 7.4

A Profile script can encompass your entire tree, a group of containers, or users in a single container.

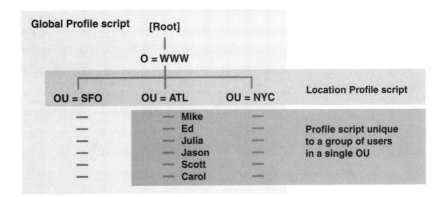

The Profile Script as a Company-wide Login Script

A company-wide Profile script works best if your NDS tree is small (20 container objects or less) and you want to include many people in the Profile script across your entire tree. For example, you could use a company-wide Profile script for creating a group of administrators who need special access to resources in the tree. When administrators log in to the network, they receive the additional drive mappings to perform their job functions.

For example, rather than leave the NWAdmin utility in the PUBLIC subdirectory, you could move it along with other utilities to a special directory called \APPSMGR. You could then map a drive in a Profile script to access the APPSMGR subdirectory, thus providing mapping to NWAdmin only to the administrators.

The Profile Script for Particular Locations

The Profile script can also be used as a locational script, which means that you can have the script execute for people residing in a particular division, building, or other location.

For example, if you wanted to designate that a floor of users capture to a particular printer, you could create a Profile script that assigns all users of a particular division rights to access a printer. Another example would be to have a particular group of users attach to a specified server to run their applications. Figure 7.5 shows how a Profile script can be used to capture a specific printer for the secretarial pool of a company.

FIGURE 7.5

Using a Profile script to capture a printer in a particular division

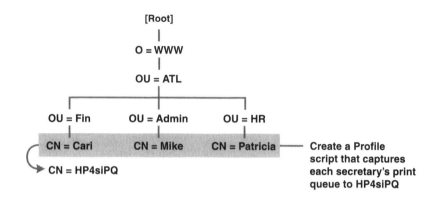

Create a Profile script that captures each secretary's print queue to HP4siPQ

The Profile as a Special-Purpose Script

Another use of the Profile script is to assign drive mappings and access for people within a single container. This allows you to assign a group of people within a container object a specific set of drive mappings. In this role, the Profile script is much like a Group object, but its sole purpose is script execution.

An example of a special-purpose Profile script is shown in Figure 7.6. This script defines specific drive mappings for a particular set of users in the tree.

FIGURE 7.6

A special-purpose Profile script with drive mappings for a set of users

```
MAP DISPLAY OFF
MAP ERRORS OFF
MAP INS S16:=VOL1\APPSMGR
MAP INS S16:=VOL1\ACCOUNTS\DATA
MAP INS S16:=VOL2\USER\RECORD
```

The User Login Script

The user login script allows you to customize a user's environment for his or her unique circumstances. If you cannot place drive mappings in the container or Profile login script, put these mappings in a user login script. However, keep in mind that allowing your users to have their own personal scripts can add extra maintenance tasks for network administrators.

An example of a user login script is shown in Figure 7.7. This script maps a drive to a data directory and to a common directory. This script also captures a specific print queue.

```
MAP DISPLAY OFF
MAP ERROR OFF
MAP *7:=VOL1:\JEFF\TASKS\DATA
MAP *8:=VOL2:\COMMON
SET USR="JFHUGHES"
SET WP="/U-JFH/B-5"
CAPTURE /SERVER=NCS /Q=HP-4SI /L2 /NB
```

The Default Login Script

The default login script is provided to give you some basic functionality. When a user logs in to the server for the first time, the default script is executed because there is no other script currently available. Also, if a user who does not have a user login script logs in to a server, the default script will execute. Figure 7.8 shows an example of a default login script.

```
WRITE "Good %GREETING_TIME, %LOGIN_NAME."
MAP DISPLAY OFF
MAP ERRORS OFF
MAP *1:=%FILE_SERVER\SYS:
MAP *1:=%FILE_SERVER\SYS:%LOGIN_NAME
IF "%1" = "SUPERVISOR" || "%1" = "ADMIN" THEN MAP
*1:=%FILE_SERVER\SYS:SYSTEM
MAP INS S1:=%FILE_SERVER\SYS:PUBLIC
MAP INS
S2:=%FILE_SERVER\SYS:PUBLIC\%MACHINE\%OS\%OS_VERSION
MAP DISPLAY ON
MAP
```

Deciding Which Type of Scripts to Use

Because user login scripts are difficult to maintain in a large organization, most companies with more than 20 people should avoid the use of user login scripts. Instead, create the user environment by using container login scripts. This approach will save you a great deal of time, because the general script can be applied to many, if not all, your users.

If you have several users who need the same environment outside the normal container login scripts, use a Profile script to provide them with additional environment settings.

Allow user login scripts only for particular users:

- Those who are knowledgeable enough to be able to maintain their own user scripts

- Those who cannot have their settings included in a container or Profile login script because they require a different environment than other users

Keep in mind that up to three login scripts can execute for each user. If a particular drive letter is mapped in the container login script, and the Profile script maps the same letter to another location, the latter drive mappings will override any previous mappings.

Defining Login Scripts for Mobile Users

FOR PURPOSES OF our discussion, a *mobile* user is someone who has a home server, but also travels away from his or her workstation to any local or remote location and accesses the network (via a stationary or portable computer).

We assume that you maintain consistency in your file system across all your network servers. This means that all applications reside in the same locations on your file systems, so that your login scripts will map to the proper locations.

Most mobile users have the same needs when they travel as they do while in their permanent location. They want to access applications such as word processors or spreadsheets on servers locally, but retrieve their data from their home or current server. They also want the ability to print anywhere. And of course, they want this whole operation to be as simple and painless as possible.

The mobile user presents some unique situations in a NetWare 4.11 environment. As users move about from one location to another, they are logging in to the network from a different location in the NDS tree. NDS is more manageable if a user context is set for every NDS user logging in to the network. NDS must know the user's distinguished name to find a NetWare 4 server that can authenticate the user ID and password. While a mobile user's physical location may change from time to time, that user's context will remain static as long as the user remains part of a particular container.

Keep in mind that your approach to designing a NetWare 4.11 network should be to first design for the masses and then design for the mobile user. Not because the mobile user is any less important, but because your approach is to first design generally, then specifically.

When you are creating login scripts for mobile users, you need to consider where they will be logging in to the network:

- **Mobile user/mobile computer:** This type of user travels to different locations with a notebook or laptop machine. When the user arrives on site, he or she connects to the network using the portable computer. The user's name context is stored in the NET.CFG file on the portable machine.

- **Mobile user/stationary computer:** This user travels to different locations but does not carry a portable machine. Instead, the user employs any available computer in the office he or she is visiting and logs in to the network. The issue in this case is how to determine the user's name context for login purposes.

Both of these cases are discussed in the following sections.

Keep in mind that during login for any users accessing NDS, LOGIN.EXE first checks the current context of the computer. Is the user's name context set in the user's NET.CFG? Try connecting based on current context setting? If the context is valid, the user name is appended to the context, and the Login utility then attempts to log in. If this step fails, the user name with the server's context is tried. Following a successful login, drives are mapped based on the login script(s) present for that user. If the context is invalid, the user will see an Invalid Context message.

Creating Scripts for Mobile Users with Mobile Computers

The first step for any user (mobile or nonmobile) connecting to the network is for the Login utility to know the user's name context in the NDS tree. Normally, this name context is set in a user's NET.CFG file and is read by the Login utility during execution.

As shown in the example in Figure 7.9, a name context is set for user Joe in his NET.CFG file stored on his PC. At the time of login, Joe only needs to type his user name: Joe.

FIGURE 7.9

A name context for user Joe has been set to a server that can authenticate his user ID and password.

```
Netware DOS Requester
    Auto Reconnect = on
    Cache Buffers = 10
    File Handles = 60
    First Network Drive = f
    Handle Net Errors = on
    signature level = 0
;   Local Printers = 0
;   Large Internet Packets = on
    Name Context = "OU=SALES.OU=SFO.O=WWW"
;   Pb Buffers = 3
    Preferred Server = SFO-SALES-002
;   Preferred Tree = WWW_INC
    Print Buffer Size = 256
    Show Dots = on

Link Support
    Max Stacks 8
    Buffers 8 1536
    Mempool 0

Link Driver NE2000
        INT 3
        PORT 300
Strike a key when ready . . .
```

NDS reads Joe's name context in his NET.CFG file and is able to complete the login process with the entry of the correct password.

Figure 7.10 shows a login script for mobile users with their own mobile machines. This script will allow the user to easily log in to the network from three cities: Atlanta, Chicago, and San Francisco.

```
REM Mobile login script
REM Do not execute default script
NO_DEFAULT
Write "Good %GREETING_TIME, %LOGIN_NAME"
REM Map NetWare drives according to the site variable
REM Map root drive to Public and another drive to home
REM directory.
MAP ROOT INSERT S1:=SYS:\PUBLIC
MAP ROOT M:="HOME_DIRECTORY"
IF <NW_SITE> == "ATL" THEN BEGIN
    MAP ROOT R:= ATL-SALES-001\SYS:APPS\MAIL1
    MAP ROOT V:= ATL-SALES-001\SYS:WORK\WP
    MAP ROOT W:= ATL-SALES-001\VOL1:\APPS\QUATTRO
    END
IF <NW_SITE> == "CHI" THEN BEGIN
    MAP ROOT R:= CHI-SALES-002\SYS:APPS\MAIL1
    MAP ROOT V:= CHI-SALES-002\SYS:WORK\WP
    MAP ROOT W:= CHI-SALES-002\SYS:APPS\QUATTRO
    END
IF <NW_SITE> == "SFO" THEN BEGIN
    MAP ROOT R:= SFO-SALES-003\SYS:APPS\MAIL1
    MAP ROOT V:= SFO-SALES-003\SYS:WORK\WP
    MAP ROOT W:= SFO-SALES-003\SYS:APPS\QUATTRO
    END
EXIT
```

If you have the same file structure on all servers in your network, you can also use the preferred tree = statement in your NET.CFG, as in MAP ROOT R:=%FILE_SERVER\SYS:APPS\MAIL1.

The user sets a site location in his or her CONFIG.SYS file to designate the user's home site name. The CONFIG.SYS file will also contain a location variable that says:

```
SET NW_SITE=<site location>
```

The site locations for our example are Atlanta (ATL), Chicago (CHI), and San Francisco (SFO). For example, use:

```
SET NW_SITE=SFO
```

to represent San Francisco. Testing against the site variable in your script allows you to map drives to local resources. For example, you can use the following command in a login script:

```
IF NW_SITE="ATL"
THEN MAP [local resource]
```

Creating Scripts for Mobile Users without a Mobile Machine

The mobile user who uses any machine available will not have his context stored on the machine he or she is using temporarily. Since NDS must know the user's name to log in, what can be done in this situation? There are ways around this problem.

Mobile User Changes Context

One way a mobile user can log in is to first manually enter the context at the machine he or she is using. This solution requires your mobile users to understand and know their context in the NDS tree.

The Change Context (CX) command sets the appropriate context. For example, user Joe, mentioned in the previous section, would type:

```
CX SALES.ATL.WWW
```

at the C:\ prompt. Then Joe would enter:

```
Login Joe
```

and then type his password.

Joe could also type:

```
LOGIN JOE.SALES.SFO.WWW
```

and skip the step using the CX command. This method does not change the PC's context. Instead, it logs Joe in with the correct context.

Figure 7.11 shows an example of user Joe's context in the tree and how Joe could set his context. Figure 7.12 shows the Help screen that explains the use of the CX command to set the user's context.

There are also some third-party utilities available that help search the tree for a particular user and then set the user context. The issue to consider is time. Can users use the CX command and change their context in the same amount of time or less than it takes a utility to find their name in the tree? You must weigh these considerations in your support for your mobile users.

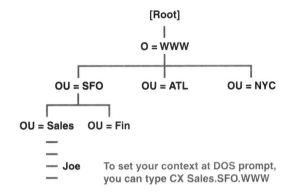

FIGURE 7.11

User Joe's context in the NDS tree

To set your context at DOS prompt, you can type CX Sales.SFO.WWW

FIGURE 7.12

The Help screen explaining how to enter your context with CX

```
CX                           General Usage Help                        4.20

Purpose: View and set current context.
Syntax:  CX [new context | /VER] [/R] [/[T | CONT] [/A]] [/C] [/?]

New context:
    A context can be entered either relative to your current context or
    as a distinguished name relative to the directory root.
    Use trailing periods (.) to change to a context relative to a higher
    level of your current context.
    To change to a context relative to the root of the directory put a period
    at the beginning of the new context or use the /Root flag.

To view your current context type CX
Current context is OU=Engineering.O=Novell

For example, to change context:                          Type:
    O=Novell                                             CX .
    OU=Testing.OU=Engineering.O=Novell                   CX OU=Testing
    OU=Marketing.O=Novell                                CX OU=Marketing.

C:\>
```

Using Aliases

Another approach for setting the context of mobile users is through the use of Aliases. You could create an Alias object below the Organization object for each mobile user. The Alias object will point to the user's primary object in the container where the user resides. (See Chapter 2 for more information about Alias objects.)

Note that when you use Aliases, NDS must search for the actual user object further down in the tree, so this method is not as fast as changing the context.

The Alias method will work if you have a small number of mobile users, say no more than 20.

Figure 7.13 shows how you can create Alias objects beneath the Organization object so that the users only need to remember a shortened context in the tree.

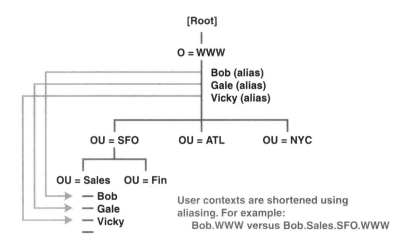

FIGURE 7.13

Create an Alias for each mobile user just below the O=WWW. This will shorten the context for each user to USER.WWW.

An Example of a Login Script for Mobile Users without a Mobile Machine

After the user has logged in to the network, the container login script maps the appropriate drives for local and remote access to server resources. A login script with site designators works best for any type of mobile user after that user is logged in to the network. Figure 7.14 shows a universal script used in every container. This script determines where the user resides in the tree and maps resources appropriately.

Like the script for mobile users with their own machines, the sample script will allow the user to log in to the network from Atlanta (ATL), Chicago (CHI), or San Francisco (SFO). The container login script determines the site location of the machine the user is using, and then maps the appropriate drives and the user's home directory. As with the script shown earlier in Figure 7.10, each computer will have a location variable set in its CONFIG.SYS file. This example maps the user's home directory and then maps other applications locally.

FIGURE 7.14

A login script for mobile users without a mobile machine

```
REM Mobile login script/nonmobile PC users
REM Do not execute default script
NO_DEFAULT
Write "Good %GREETING_TIME, %LOGIN_NAME"
REM Map NetWare drives according to the site variable
REM Map root drive to Public and another drive to home
REM directory.
MAP ROOT INSERT S1:=SYS:\PUBLIC
MAP ROOT M:="HOME_DIRECTORY"
IF <NW_SITE> == "ATL" THEN BEGIN
    MAP ROOT R:= ATL-SALES-001\SYS:APPS\MAIL1
    MAP ROOT V:= ATL-SALES-001\SYS:WORK\WP
    MAP ROOT W:= ATL-SALES-001\VOL1:\APPS\QUATTRO
    END
IF <NW_SITE> == "CHI" THEN BEGIN
    MAP ROOT R:= CHI-SALES-002\SYS:APPS\MAIL1
    MAP ROOT V:= CHI-SALES-002\SYS:WORK\WP
    MAP ROOT W:= CHI-SALES-002\SYS:APPS\QUATTRO
    END
IF <NW_SITE> == "SFO" THEN BEGIN
    MAP ROOT R:= SFO-SALES-003\SYS:APPS\MAIL1
    MAP ROOT V:= SFO-SALES-003\SYS:WORK\WP
    MAP ROOT W:= SFO-SALES-003\SYS:APPS\QUATTRO
    END
EXIT
```

Novell's NetWare Application Manager

NTRANETWARE PROVIDES another tool for managing a user's access to server applications: the NetWare Application Manager in Client 32 for DOS/Windows and Client 32 for Windows 95. The NetWare Application Manager gives an administrator the ability to easily manage applications on the network by defining applications as NDS objects. As an administrator, you now have the ability to define NDS application objects and assign security to those objects for any number of users that are part of the NDS tree.

The NetWare Application Manager consists of two components that are easy to install and configure. First, NAM provides a Dynamic Link Library (DLL) that snaps into Novell's NWADMIN utility and allows an administrator to define a user's access to NDS application objects. The second component is the NetWare Application Launcher (NAL), which allows users to see and access the NDS application objects that have been defined by the administrator.

For more information on using the Application Manager see Novell's Web site, at www.novell.com, or the README files that ship with the Client 32 for DOS/Windows and Windows 95.

Using NetWare 4's Bindery Services

NETWARE 4's BINDERY SERVICES allow NetWare 3 bindery-based applications and users to continue to operate on a NetWare 4 server. This feature provides several useful benefits:

- Because applications that must run with a bindery can still be used, your investment in your applications is preserved.

- If you cannot upgrade your NetWare NETX.COM clients to the newer VLM client just yet, those users can still connect to a NetWare 4 server (although they will not enjoy all the benefits of a VLM client).

Bindery-Based Applications

NDS has the capability to allow bindery-based applications to function as if they were still running on a NetWare 3 server. In order for those applications to run, your NetWare 4 server must have a bindery context set. This context tells the NetWare 4 server the location or context of the bindery-based users.

Many Novell and third-party applications are being modified to take advantage of NDS. However, Bindery Services will continue to be included with NetWare 4 until all applications are NDS-aware.

In versions of NetWare 4 prior to 4.1, you could only set one bindery context for each NetWare 4 server. This meant that your bindery users all had to reside in a single container object if you had a bindery-based application that they all needed to use.

NetWare 4.1 allows you to set up to 16 bindery contexts per server, giving you greater flexibility in where to place your users. Because you are no longer restricted to a single container object, you are not limited in where in your tree you place users who need to access a bindery-based application on a particular server.

Setting the bindery context can be accomplished in three different ways:

- You can use the SET command at the NetWare 4 server prompt by typing:

    SET BINDERY CONTEXT=<server object context>

- Figure 7.15 shows an example of how a server's bindery context is set.

FIGURE 7.15

Setting a bindery context for server ATL-MKTG-001

```
CSI1:set bindery context
Bindery Context:  OU=SYS_LAB.O=NCS
Maximum length:  255
    Can be set in the startup ncf file
    Description: The NetWare Directory Services container where bindery
                 services are provided.  Set multiple contexts by separating
                 contexts with semicolons.
CSI1:SET BINDERY CONTEXT = OU=MKTG.OU=ATL.O=WWW
```

- You can place the SET BINDERY CONTEXT= <server context> command in your STARTUP.NCF file so that it is set every time the server is booted.

- You can use the SERVMAN utility to set up to 16 bindery contexts for a single server. (See Chapter 12 for more information about the SERVMAN utility.)

Bindery-Based Users

Any user who is running the older NETX.COM client from Novell and logs in to a NetWare 4 server will be logging in using Bindery Services. In order to log in to a NetWare 4 network as a full NDS user, you must be running Novell's VLM requester technology at your workstation.

VLM-based users may also log in to a NetWare 4 server using Bindery Services by specifying the /b option during their login. For example, user Sally could log in as a bindery client by entering:

```
Sally/b
```

Bindery-Based Login Scripts

Login scripts that are used in NDS are different than scripts used from a NetWare 3 bindery. Bindery-based login scripts are stored in the user's SYS:MAIL subdirectory. If you migrate from NetWare 3 to NetWare 4.11, the bindery-based login script will be copied over to the user's SYS:MAIL directory. If you want the user to execute this script as an NDS user, you must copy it from a control file on the NetWare 4 server and place it into NDS using the UIMPORT utility.

The system login script from NetWare 3 is not copied during an Across-the-Wire migration (see Chapter 8). If you want users to execute this script, you must copy the NET$LOG.DAT file from the NetWare 3 server to the PUBLIC subdirectory on the SYS volume of NetWare 4. You then must use the INCLUDE statement in the container login script to call the NetWare 3 login script. (See Chapter 13 for more information about the UIMPORT utility.)

Accessing NDS with Other Clients

OS/2 CLIENTS WILL log in to a NetWare 4 server as NDS users. They will execute either their personal login script or an OS/2 default login script.

Macintosh clients in NetWare 4.11 can log in to the network as NDS users. However, there are no NDS utilities currently available that run on the Macintosh. The user's activity will be bindery-based after the NDS login.

UNIX clients running Novell's UnixWare client will log in to the network as bindery-based clients and will not execute a login script of any kind.

For more information about the various types of NetWare clients, see Chapter 10.

NetWare 4.11 provides flexibility for users to execute from one to three login scripts. Keep in mind that the more scripts the users execute, the more administration is required. Avoid the use of user login scripts if possible, because they are difficult to maintain. The more you know about creating login scripts, the more automated you can make the network environment.

Installation and Migration to NetWare 4.11

PART

2

Preparing for a NetWare 4.11 Migration

QuickTips: Migration Preparation

▨ Create an implementation schedule and task list   148

to manage and track the status of the NetWare 4.11 implementation project. Include the following information:

- Task description

- Start date

- Target end date

- Person assigned

- Percentage of completion

▨ Schedule installation of the workstation software for NetWare 4.11   149

by allotting about fifteen minutes per workstation. Some considerations are:

- Plan the contents of the NET.CFG file.

- Swapping disks takes time; load the client from a server if possible.

- Migrate the network staff workstations first. This way, administrators can acquire some experience before the users are transferred to the new system.

- Workstations with host connections or other dial-out software may require special adjustments, so they may require more time to migrate.

- Plan your workstation migration for a weekend, if possible.

Clean up your binderies 152

so that only the necessary files and objects are transferred during the migration process. Here are some bindery tasks to consider:

- Novell's migration utility does not migrate the second occurrence of a duplicate object name. Use Novell's DupBind utility, available from NetWire, to find duplicate object names on your NetWare 3 server.

- Delete any users, objects, and user access privileges that are no longer in use.

- Delete unused files and applications on your NetWare 2 or 3 server.

- Decide which Ethernet frame type to use (NetWare 4's default type is 802.2 and is recommended).

- Back up your NetWare 2 or 3 server, then run the BINDFIX utility to clean up your bindery. Be sure to run your backup again.

Decide which utility you will use to migrate 154
or upgrade servers

to NetWare 4.11. Novell provides two utilities for this purpose:

- The In-Place migration method (INSTALL.NLM) is recommended for upgrading an existing NetWare 3 server to NetWare 4.11 on the same hardware device. This method is fast and efficient because it does not move any data files.

- The Across-the-Wire method (MIGRATE.EXE) is recommended when you want to migrate a network server from either a different network operating system or when you are replacing the server hardware.

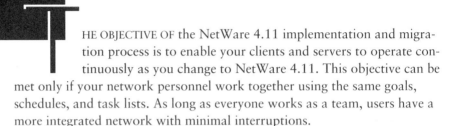

THE OBJECTIVE OF the NetWare 4.11 implementation and migration process is to enable your clients and servers to operate continuously as you change to NetWare 4.11. This objective can be met only if your network personnel work together using the same goals, schedules, and task lists. As long as everyone works as a team, users have a more integrated network with minimal interruptions.

In order to accomplish this objective, you should first define an implementation schedule and task list. The schedule provides you with a time-line for the implementation. It describes the individual implementation tasks that need to be completed.

This chapter explains how to prepare for installing or upgrading your network servers to NetWare 4.11. It provides guidelines for developing an implementation schedule, for developing a task list, and for preparing your workstations and servers for migration.

Developing an Implementation Schedule and Task List

A WELL-PLANNED IMPLEMENTATION schedule will help you manage and track the status of the NetWare 4.11 implementation project. For each implementation task, the schedule should include a task description, a start date, a target end date, the person assigned, and the percentage of completion. The schedule can then be used to set deadlines, measure the progress of tasks, review the work, and produce reports for management and staff.

You should consider the following tasks when you are preparing for a migration to NetWare 4.11:

- Installing client software on your workstations

- Cleaning up NetWare 2 and 3 binderies before migration

- Installing and configuring the NetWare 4.11 servers

The chart shown in Figure 8.1 defines some of the most common implementation tasks associated with NetWare 4.11. You can use this outline as a starting point for your own schedule. In your own schedule, include the tasks that correspond to the needs of your company and staff.

NDS Implementation Schedule

Task Description	Begin Date	Target End Date	Person/Team Assigned	% Complete
Educate Team	11/15/96	Ongoing	Steve Jones	50
Design Naming Standard	11/20/96	12/1/96	Mike Smith Phil Johnson	100
Design NDS Tree	12/5/96	12/20/96	Phyllis Franks Pete Lynn	100
Install Client Software on IS Group	1/5/97	1/5/97	Joe Michaels	100
Clean Up NetWare 3 Bindery	1/10/97	1/15/97	Susan Smith	90
Migrate 100 Clients to VLMs	1/20/97	1/30/97	Client Team	100
Migrate First Server to NetWare 4.11	2/5/97	2/6/97	NetWare 4.11 Server Team	100

The rest of this chapter describes the implementation tasks in detail. It focuses on points you need to consider and offers suggestions for making the migration process go more smoothly.

Tasks Involving the Installation of Client Software

NE OF THE first tasks on your schedule should be installing the workstation software for NetWare 4.11. We recommend installing the client software regardless of your time frame for installing NetWare 4.11 servers. You can begin to realize the benefits of the client software before installing your first NetWare 4.11 server.

For more information about installing the client software, see Chapter 10.

Benefits of Client Software

The DOS/Windows client should be upgraded as soon as possible so that users can take advantage of the following:

- Full NDS connection to NetWare 4.11 servers and single login capability through background authentication, as well as full backward compatibility with existing NetWare 3 servers.

- Optimized memory capabilities gained by loading the VLM Requester or Client32 for Windows/Windows 95 into high memory, which can provide the workstation with more conventional memory.

- Increased client performance through the use of Packet Burst and Large Internet Packet (LIP) features.

- Increased security through RSA encryption when you log in to NetWare 4 servers.

- Ability to select which VLM modules you want to load at each workstation and other configuration options found in Novell's 32-bit clients.

Other workstation types can also be migrated without difficulty. The OS/2 Requester for NDS provides many of the same benefits as the DOS/Windows Requester and is fully backward compatible. The Macintosh client for NetWare 4.11 also provides the benefit of single login to any NetWare 4 servers in the same tree.

Tips on Workstation Tasks

Your migration schedule should allot about fifteen minutes per workstation for the initial upgrade to the NDS client software. For example, if each workstation takes fifteen minutes to migrate and ten people are assisting with the migration, you can migrate approximately 320 workstations in 8 hours.

Determine beforehand all the changes that must be made to each workstation so that you only work with each workstation once.

We recommend that you use the INSTALL.EXE program from the DOSWIN client area under SYS:PUBLIC for VLM installation. INSTALL.EXE automates the workstation upgrade process and configuration. You can also run Novell's newer 32-bit client installs the same way.

Following are some suggestions to consider:

- Define the contents of the NET.CFG file to be implemented on all workstations and use a standardized NET.CFG file.

- To save time, load the client from a server rather than swap disks. Loading the client software from the server is much faster.

- Consider doing any other necessary workstation upgrading in conjunction with the client software installation. For example, you might need to install the latest version of DOS or upgrade the workstation hardware. Upgrades like these make installations take longer, but they save time in the long run.

- First, move your IS or network staff to the VLM or 32-bit clients so that administrators can get acquainted with the technology. This way, when you migrate the user community, you will have experienced personnel to guide the other users.

- Take into consideration the fact that workstations with host connections or other dial-out software may require special adjustments when loading the VLM client. These situations may take more than fifteen minutes at the workstation.

- Plan your workstation migration to take place over a weekend, so your normal network operations are not disrupted.

- Devise a strategy for automating future upgrades from the server. The first instance of the VLM installation does require you to visit each machine. Some suggestions for automation are:

  - Use Novell's WSUpgrade to distribute software.

  - Create .BAT files on the server that automatically check the client version and upgrade a workstation when the user logs in to the server. This can be accomplished by using Novell's Automatic Client Update (ACU) software.

  - Create a script using a third-party scripting language.

Cleaning Up Your Binderies

F YOU ARE migrating from NetWare 2 or NetWare 3, you should spend some time cleaning up your binderies so that only the files and objects that you need are transferred during the migration process. Following are some bindery tasks to consider:

- Review all bindery object names to see if they conform to your NDS naming standard. If any names do not conform, make the changes before migrating. Also look for duplicate object names, such as a print server and print queue with the same name. Novell's migration utility does not migrate the second occurrence of a duplicate object name. Use Novell's DupBind utility, available from NetWire (CompuServe), to display duplicate object names.

- Delete any users or objects that are no longer used. Also delete any user access privileges that are no longer needed on the NetWare 4 server. You can use SECURITY.EXE to obtain detailed security information about a NetWare 3 server.

- Check for users with accounts to multiple servers. If you plan to migrate all servers to NetWare 4.11 immediately, you should consider deleting all but one user account for that user. The Novell migration utilities migrate users and data into the same container in your NDS tree. If you do not delete the duplicate users, you will be given a choice of two options during migration to NetWare 4.11: you can change the user name on the second and subsequent servers, or you can merge the user objects that have the same name into a single NDS object with cumulative rights.

If the servers are migrated into different containers, the duplicate user name will be migrated to each container with the same name, but a different context. However, we recommend not using the same user name in different contexts. Having duplicate names complicates the use of electronic mail software and may not be allowed by your package.

- Clean up your NetWare 2 or 3 file system by deleting files and applications that are no longer in use. Do not transfer mountains of unused data in the NetWare 4.11 migration. Now is the time to do some spring cleaning on your file server.

- Upgrade your hardware if it is not sufficient for the new platform. In a multiple-server environment, your server should be at least a 486 machine with a minimum of 12MB of RAM (this depends on how many NLMs you load on your server). (A high-end 386 would be sufficient only in a single-server environment.) Disk capacity required by NetWare 4 is about 80MB for the operating system. Novell's online documentation requires an additional 80MB if you choose to install it.

- Determine if you will use the NetWare 4.11 default Ethernet frame type of 802.2. Novell's NetWare 4.11 also supports 802.3, but you must determine which frame type you want to run on your workstations. We recommend that you use 802.2 and begin phasing out 802.3 frame types. Most emerging technologies now use only 802.2. You can also eliminate additional traffic by standardizing to a single frame type.

- Run a complete backup of your NetWare 2 or 3 server, and then run the BINDFIX utility to clean up your bindery. You can then run the backup again on the "clean" system.

Tasks Involving Installing and Configuring Servers

S ERVERS CAN EITHER be new NetWare 4.11 servers "installed from scratch" or be migrated from a previous version of NetWare or other network operating system. In order to install a new NetWare 4.11 server from scratch, you simply run the installation program from the Net-Ware 4.11 CD-ROM and select the appropriate options.

If you have the resources, the best approach is to install a new NetWare 4.11 server, rather than upgrade an existing NetWare server, and move the users over to it. This approach allows you to maintain your existing NetWare 3 server while migrating to the NetWare 4.11 hardware.

Novell provides two utilities for migrating or upgrading servers to NetWare 4.11: the In-Place (INSTALL.NLM) and Across-the-Wire (MIGRATE.EXE) utilities. These utilities include support for migrating from versions 2 and 3 of NetWare, as well as from LAN Server and LAN Manager systems. Banyan Vines is migrated using a Novell utility called BMIGRATE.EXE. See Chapter 11 for information on Novell's latest migration utility for migrating the latest versions of LAN Manager, LAN Server, and NT to NetWare 4.11.

The In-Place migration method is recommended when you are upgrading an existing NetWare 3 server to NetWare 4.11 on the same hardware device. The Across-the-Wire method works best when you want to migrate a network server from a different network operating system than NetWare or when you intend to replace the server hardware.

The time required for upgrading a server to NetWare 4.11 depends on the amount of data on the server and method of migration. The upgrade can take anywhere from two to eight hours per server. The In-Place migration method is the fastest method for migration, because it does not move any existing data or files. The Across-the-Wire migration method is slower, because all the data must be migrated across the LAN or WAN.

The following sections provide an overview of the Across-the-Wire and In-Place migration methods.

For more information about migrating NetWare 3 servers to NetWare 4.11, see Chapter 11. For more information about migrating from other network operating systems, see Appendix C.

Migrating with Across-the-Wire (MIGRATE.EXE)

The Across-the-Wire (MIGRATE.EXE) utility allows you to migrate the bindery or bindery-like information and data files from both NetWare servers and non-NetWare servers to NetWare 4. The utility runs on a DOS workstation and is physically connected to both a source and destination server. The workstation reads the data and information from the source server and writes it to the destination server.

The MIGRATE utility option, called same-server migration, allows a migration to be performed when a concurrent connection to the source and destination server cannot be made. However, we recommend always using the concurrent connection method because it provides the highest level of functionality with the least risk of data loss.

Since the utility runs as a client program, it is important to choose a fast workstation (486 or better) with a 16- or 32-bit LAN card. Although a slower workstation with an 8-bit LAN card works, it requires more time to complete the migration. It is the workstation's responsibility to move all the data. In order for the program to log all of the events of the migration, the workstation needs a minimum working directory of 5MB. The operation fails if you attempt it with less then 5MB.

The Across-the-Wire utility is included on the NetWare 4.11 CD-ROM. To obtain the most recent version of the utility from NetWire (CompuServe) free of charge, download the file called MIGRATE.EXE from section 6 of NOVLIB.

Strengths of Across-the-Wire Migration

The strengths of the Across-the-Wire method include the following:

- Allows for migration from other network operating systems. The source servers can be NetWare 2, NetWare 3, LAN Server, or LAN Manager. The destination servers can be NetWare 3 or NetWare 4.11.

- Preserves the source server during the migration; the information and data remain the same. The DOS workstation where the program is running is simply reading from the source server. If there is a failure (such as a power outage or loss of connection), the source server is left unmodified.

- Provides the ability to migrate or consolidate multiple source servers (even with different network operating systems) into a single destination server. For example, the users, groups, and data files can be merged into a single NetWare 4.11 server.

- Gives you the chance to replace or upgrade the destination server to newer, more powerful hardware.

- Lets you select the information to be migrated. For example, you can select a volume from the source server to be moved to the destination server as a volume with directories. Specific volumes can be selected or rejected.

- Allows you to change the volume block size of the destination server. For the volumes in NetWare 4.11, we recommend that you always select a volume block size of 64KB for improved performance and the benefits of block suballocation.

- Allows you to turn on or set file suballocation and file compression. We have witnessed a 30 to 50 percent return of disk space from suballocation alone after the migration has been completed.

Across-the-Wire Method Considerations

Some special considerations for the Across-the-Wire migration method include the following:

- Connecting the DOS workstation to both the source and destination server could be a problem if you need to support different network operating systems (such as LAN Manager and NetWare 4.11), because you must load both protocol stacks for each server.

- The connection to the NetWare 4 destination server is as a bindery client. This can be a problem when you try to migrate information that needs to be placed in NDS, such as login scripts. You will have to run other utilities such as Novell's UIMPORT.

- The migration utility transfers the data being migrated across your network. This makes the Across-the-Wire method slower than the In-Place method for migration. Moreover, it could increase the network traffic. You may need to execute the migration process during off-peak hours.

Migrating or Upgrading with In-Place (INSTALL.NLM)

The In-Place migration program (INSTALL.NLM) lets you upgrade from both NetWare 2 and NetWare 3 servers to NetWare 4.11. Before you can upgrade a NetWare 2 server, you need to upgrade that server to NetWare 3. Then the NetWare 3 server can be upgraded by executing the NetWare 4.11 installation program, which runs as a NetWare Loadable Module (NLM).

See Chapter 11 for more information about running the migration utilities to migrate NetWare 2 and 3 servers.

You can use the In-Place migration method when your server hardware remains the same. For example, use it when you want to upgrade a NetWare 3 server to NetWare 4.11 and remain on the same physical device. The users and files on the server will not be moved or changed.

Strengths of the In-Place Method

The strengths of the In-Place migration method include the following:

- Uses the same or existing hardware. This eliminates the cost of having to acquire a new server system just to migrate, so it preserves your hardware investment. Make sure, however, that your existing hardware can support NetWare 4.11.

- Migrates the bindery information with full NDS compatibility. This means that files that were closely tied to the bindery can be written directly into NDS. For example, users' login scripts are placed directly into NDS. Passwords and trustee assignments are preserved as well.

- Preserves all print configuration databases. The PRINTCON.DAT and PRINTDEF.DAT databases are written directly into NDS on account of the full NDS compatibility.

- Migrates all the server information faster. Since all the data in the file system is in the correct format and in the right place, no data needs to be transferred. The volumes remain unmodified. The only information that needs to be reformatted is the bindery, which will be switched to NDS format.

In-Place Method Considerations

Considerations for the In-Place migration or upgrade method include the following:

- This method does not allow the volume block size to be changed. We recommend that each NetWare 4.11 server have 64KB volume blocks. However, because the file system is in place before the migration or upgrade remains intact, the original volume block size will initially be set for your server (probably 4KB blocks).

To change the volume block size, follow these steps: (1) back up the data to tape, (2) delete the volume, (3) create the volume using the correct volume block size, and (4) restore the data from tape. You can also use Novell's DSMAINT utility if you are replacing the SYS volume of a server.

- This method does not allow you to turn on suballocation for the file system. You can turn on suballocation after the upgrade, but it will affect only the subsequent file writes to the disks.

- This method may require a restoration from a tape backup if a failure occurs during the upgrade process. You can restart the In-Place process, but there is a possibility that you will have lost some data, which you will need to restore from your backup.

- The In-Place migration of NetWare 2.1*x* to NetWare 3.12 does not preserve passwords during migration.

- Trustee assignments are transferred for each user unless your SYS volume on the NetWare 2.1*x* server was not mounted prior to the migration. You can then go back and do a bindery migration, but it will not include the trustee assignments.

To achieve the implementation objective of seamlessly integrating NetWare 4.11 into your network environment, each server and its workstations should be upgraded to the latest release of NetWare 4.11. The guidelines presented in this chapter will assist you in starting the implementation process. You can customize these procedures to meet the needs of your organization. By following the implementation schedule and task list you developed, you will get a clear idea of how your installation and migration should progress.

Conducting Lab Testing and Setting Up a Pilot System

QuickTips: Lab Testing

Set up a lab for testing   165

if your NetWare network will contain thirty or more servers. Your lab should include at least three nodes: two servers and one workstation. The servers can be configured to test synchronization, partitions and replicas, and time synchronization. Following are suggestions for setting up your lab:

- Use hardware (server and workstation hardware, as well as LAN adapter cards) that is representative of your actual network environment.

- If possible, duplicate your network topology (such as Token Ring or Ethernet).

- If you are migrating from NetWare 3 to NetWare 4.11 and you have the hardware, consider doing an Across-the-Wire migration of a current NetWare 3 server to a lab server for practice.

- If you do not have the extra hardware, you can also do a tape backup of your NetWare 3 server, migrate the hardware to NetWare 4.11, and then do a tape restore of your NetWare 3 data. This allows you to create a lab server from an actual production server.

Evaluate all areas of your NetWare   166
implementation

in your lab testing, including the following areas:

- CD-ROM drivers and hardware. Make sure that you have the latest CD-ROM drivers for your hardware. If you are using a CD-ROM bay or other device to mount multiple CD-ROMs, test that device as well. Mount the CD to a NetWare volume, then log in to the server and map a drive to the NetWare volume.

- Install NetWare 4.11. Practice installing the NetWare 4.11 operating system and NDS. Also practice removing NDS from the server. These steps give you experience with the installation and removal of NDS using the INSTALL.NLM.

- Create the NDS tree based on your tree design. Design the appropriate container object levels and the objects as they will actually appear.

- Configure time synchronization. Install the servers with the default time synchronization configuration, and then modify the configuration by using the SERVMAN utility. Make adjustments to the time on the servers to get a feel for how this process works.

- Create partitions and replicas on your lab servers. Use the Partition Manager in the NWAdmin utility to add partitions in your NDS tree. The additional partitions can be stored on your lab servers.

- Test applications. Make sure your applications are compatible with Net-Ware 4.11. If any applications require the NetWare bindery, you must enable NetWare 4.11 Bindery Services on your server and place a read/write replica of the set bindery context.

- Practice using Novell and third-party utilities. Some utilities to test include NWAdmin, NWUser, SERVMAN, DSRepair, and NDSManager.

- Test backup and restore procedures. Use your specific backup software on an entire volume. Then restore that volume to ensure that your disaster-recovery procedures are working properly. You can back up NDS as well as your file system.

- Create a NetWare 4.11 pilot system. Duplicate a production server and place it as one of the servers in your lab. Migrate a current production server from your site as the first NetWare 4.11 server. Integrate other supporting systems, such as the printing infrastructure and the workstation LAN configuration. Finalize your client migration procedures.

FOR LARGE NETWARE 4 environments, one of the most important elements of a successful NetWare 4.11 implementation project is setting up a lab facility. By "large" environment, we mean any site in which more than thirty NetWare 4.11 servers will be installed or migrated. With this number of servers, you may need to customize some of the configuration options, rather than use all of the default settings of NetWare 4.11. A lab is helpful in this process.

Some sites already have a lab for testing new software and applications. Others are considering the creation of a temporary lab for this project. This chapter details the steps you should take for a successful lab and pilot system.

If your network consists of less than thirty servers and you do not have the resources to create a lab, you can skip this chapter and move to Chapter 10, which covers migrating NetWare 3 clients to NetWare 4.11. A lab is not as important in smaller network environments, where systems are configured with many of the default options.

Why Bother with Lab Testing?

SETTING UP A lab early in the NetWare 4.11 implementation process helps the project move forward more quickly and easily. Lab testing gives you time to work with the operating system, familiarize yourself with NDS, and run the Novell utilities and other third-party applications.

Setting up a lab and installing NetWare 4.11 helps instill confidence in a project team because the team learns how to use the many features of NetWare 4.11. The lab not only furnishes a place for a hands-on experience, but it also provides a place to make mistakes and become comfortable with NetWare 4.11.

Setting Up the Lab

A LAB NEED NOT be extensive or require months of activity. The intention is to provide you and your network administrators with an environment to install, configure, and test NetWare 4.11. Once you've set up the lab, you can move on to the installation of NetWare 4.11 in a production mode.

Your lab can be small—a minimum of three nodes, consisting of two file servers and one workstation. An even better configuration is to have two servers and two workstations. You should include at least one CD-ROM device for installing NetWare 4.11. You might also consider having a connection to your company's actual network backbone, so that you have access to NetWare 3 servers (if you have any). You can add more nodes as either workstations or servers, if needed.

Figure 9.1 illustrates a small lab setup with several servers, a CD-ROM drive, and several workstations. All are connected through a small concentrator.

Select hardware for your lab that is representative of your actual network environment. This includes the server hardware, workstation hardware, and LAN adapter cards used in your environment.

Try to duplicate your LAN topology when possible. For example, if you use a Token Ring topology, use a Token Ring concentrator in your lab.

If you are migrating from NetWare 3 to NetWare 4.11 and you have the hardware, consider doing an Across-the-Wire migration of a current NetWare 3 server to a NetWare 4 server in the lab. There are many advantages to this approach:

- It allows you to upgrade your hardware to a new platform for NetWare 4.11.

- It does not interrupt the operation of your current NetWare 3 server.

- You can migrate a test group of users to the NetWare 4.11 lab server, and they can run their applications as they do on the NetWare 3 server.

- When you are ready to switch over to NetWare 4.11, you can bring down the NetWare 3 server and migrate users to the new NetWare 4.11 server.

- You can leave the NetWare 3 server in place for a week or so while you make sure that the NetWare 4.11 server is fully operational.

FIGURE 9.1

An example of a small lab setup for installing NetWare 4.11, its utilities, and network applications

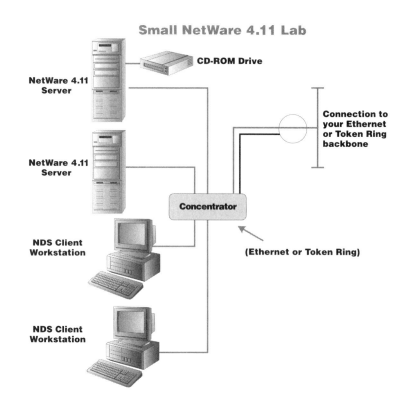

Small NetWare 4.11 Lab

 See Chapter 8 for a discussion of the advantages of using the Across-the-Wire (MIGRATE.EXE) utility and the considerations involved with this method.

Areas to Evaluate in Lab Testing

BY THIS POINT, you will have acquired the tools to begin the lab process. You can evaluate the following areas in your lab:

- Test CD-ROM drivers and hardware
- Install NetWare 4.11 and create the NDS tree

- Configure time synchronization

- Create partitions and replicas

- Test applications

- Run Novell and third-party utilities

- Test backup and restore procedures

- Create a NetWare 4.11 pilot system

The following sections describe each of these testing areas in detail.

Testing CD-ROM Drivers and Hardware

Before you begin testing, make sure that you have the latest CD-ROM drivers from Novell or from third-party manufacturers. You can avoid many problems when mounting your CD-ROMs by running the latest drivers for your hardware. Never assume that you can "get by" with an older version of a driver.

Most hardware vendors have bulletin boards that you can contact to obtain their latest drivers free of charge. Novell also offers a "Fax Back" number that you can call to obtain information about all hardware certified to run on NetWare 4. Novell's Fax Back number is (800)414-LABS.

If you are using a CD-ROM bay or other device to mount multiple CD-ROMs, be sure to test it with NetWare 4.

Mounting a CD-ROM as a NetWare Volume

Before you can mount a CD-ROM as a NetWare volume, you must first mount your CD-ROM as a DOS device and install NetWare 4. (See your CD vendor's documentation for instructions on mounting your CD as a DOS device.)

During NetWare 4.11 installation, the following files are copied to the SYS:\SYSTEM directory:

- AHA1640.DSK (or the appropriate driver for your server's adapter card)

- ASPITRAN.DSK

- ASPICD.DSK *or* CDNASPI.DSK

You can also return to the installation program and load these drivers. Note that if you have a disk, CD-ROM, or another device that uses ASPI, you should add the following line to your STARTUP.NCF file:

```
SET RESERVED BUFFERS BELOW 16MB=200
```

The following steps will help you install your CD-ROM as a NetWare volume:

1. Access the following directory on the NetWare 4.11 CD: NETWARE.40_____\DISKDRV.

2. Download the appropriate DSK files to your SYS:\SYSTEM directory. Then load one of the following (or an appropriate driver, depending on your hardware):

   ```
   ASPICD.DSK
   CDNASPI.DSK
   ```

3. From the server console, type the following (or your appropriate DSK driver; you may require the setting ABOVE 16=y):

   ```
   LOAD
   LOAD CDROM.NLM
   ```

4. After loading the previous drivers, type the following at the console to list the CD loaded and then to list the volume name and number for the CD that is currently loaded:

   ```
   CD DEVICE LIST
   CD VOLUME LIST
   ```

5. Issue a CD MOUNT *<volume name>* or CD Device #. The CD will mount as a NetWare volume.

With a NetWare volume mounted, you can then map a drive to this volume and access the CD-ROM device.

The LOAD AHA1640.DSK command may require ABOVE 16=Y, which tells the driver that it may need to look above 16MB in memory to load properly. The AHA1640.DSK driver autoloads ASPITRAN.DSK.

The first command lists the CD loaded. If it doesn't show your CD as a device, check your SCSI IDs or look for other hardware problems. The second command lists the volume name and number for that CD. If it doesn't display a volume, you may not have a volume name and number for that CD.

The CD will be mounted as a NetWare volume. With the CD mounted, you can log in to the server from a workstation and map a drive to the NetWare volume.

Installing NetWare 4.11

In the lab, practice installing the NetWare 4.11 operating system and NDS. Loading the software is not difficult, but you should familiarize yourself with the different installation options. You will need to add new NLMs or additional licenses. Both of these procedures are handled by the Install utility.

You should also practice removing NDS from the server. At some point, you may need to remove a server from the tree, perhaps because the server hardware needs to be repaired or because you plan to ship the server to another location. To avoid problems, be sure to follow the appropriate steps for removing a server from the tree.

See Chapter 11 for information about NetWare server installation procedures. See Chapter 15 for details on removing a server from the NDS tree.

Creating the NDS Tree

All the information you have garnered thus far from this book can be applied in the lab. The creation of an NDS tree in the lab should be based on the following:

- Your understanding of NDS objects (see Chapter 2)
- Your NDS naming conventions (see Chapter 3)

- Our guidelines for successful NDS tree design (see Chapter 4)

- Your understanding of time synchronization (see Chapter 6)

Configure the first lab server you install to be the first NetWare 4.11 server on the actual network. Create the NDS tree as it will actually appear for your user community. Design the appropriate container object levels and create the necessary objects for your tree. Do not make up names for your objects; use your naming standard document for the definitions of containers and other objects. Making up names adds additional work because you likely need to go back and change them.

Most of the work of creating your tree is done with the NWAdmin utility. Figure 9.2 shows NWAdmin being used to create an OU object. In the lab, you gain experience in using this utility to create objects such as containers and organizational role subadministrators. (You also use the NWAdmin utility for many NDS and file system rights assignments.)

FIGURE 9.2

Using the NWAdmin utility to create a new NDS object

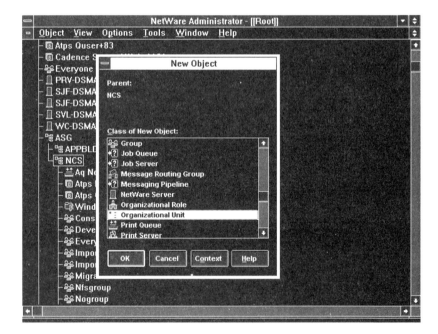

Configuring Time Synchronization

Initially, the servers in your lab should have the default time synchronization configuration. This means that your first NetWare 4.11 server is a Single Reference time server, and any other servers added to the tree are Secondary time servers (see Chapter 6).

Once you have operational servers with workstations logging in, you can modify the time synchronization parameters. Using the SERVMAN utility, you can change the Single Reference time server to a Reference time server and your Secondary time server to a Primary time server. To run this utility from the server console, type

        LOAD SERVMAN

Figure 9.3 shows the SERVMAN utility being used to change a server to a Reference server.

FIGURE 9.3

Using the SERVMAN utility
to change a server to a
Reference server

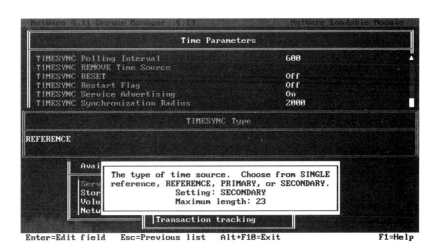

Your motive for testing time synchronization is to see the effects of setting time ahead on one of the servers. At a server console, type **TIME** and enter a value several hours ahead.

Monitor the other server(s) by typing the following at their consoles:

        SET TIMESYNC DEBUG = 7

Then watch them adjust their clocks forward.

You can also try the same operation by setting time back on one of your servers. We do not recommend doing this on an actual network, but doing it now gives you a feel for how time synchronization operates in a NetWare 4 environment. This lab exercise may take you only 30 minutes to complete. Again, your objective is to understand how time synchronization operates.

Creating Partitions and Replicas

Use your lab to learn how to create partitions and replicas. The size of your lab may limit how many partitions and replicas you can create, but you can still learn the process and gain some experience with the utilities.

The [Root] partition is the first partition automatically created when you install NetWare 4.11. Using the Partition Manager in the NWAdmin utility, you can add partitions for containers you have created in the tree. Even though all your new partitions may be stored on a single lab server, you will have gained the experience of creating them. Figure 9.4 shows an example of using the Partition Manager to create partitions. (See Chapter 13 for more information about using the NetWare 4 utilities, including NWAdmin and Partition Manager.)

You can also use Novell's NDS Manager Utility for partitioning operations. This Utility can work as a stand-alone or as a snap-in to Novell's 32-bit NWAdmin utility.

Testing Applications

After your lab is set up, you should test the production applications running on NetWare 4.11. Following are the major compatibility issues for applications:

- Does the application require the NetWare bindery? If so, you must enable NetWare 4 Bindery Services on your server (see Chapter 7).

- Will the applications run on NetWare 4.11 with the VLM or 32-bit client? Have several lab workstations test the applications that are installed on NetWare 4.11. Your testing may be extensive or minimal, depending on your needs. At a minimum (and this suffices for most companies), you should give the following three basic tests:

    1. Does the application run without interruption on NetWare 4.11?

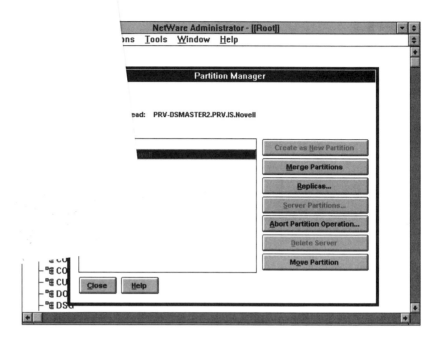

2. Can you print using the application (if applicable)?

3. Can you save your work to the server using the application?

Usually, you don't experience any problems with common applications, such as spreadsheets and word processors. In-house applications created by your company or group should be tested thoroughly.

- Will the applications run on NetWare 4.11 with the NETX shell?

- Does your tape backup system support NetWare 4.11 and NDS. A backup system that supports a NetWare 3 file system is not sufficient. Be sure to verify that your backup software also backs up NDS.

- Which server applications (NLMs) run on NetWare 4.11? Make sure that the service you need in your application runs on NetWare.

List your network applications in a table similar to the one shown in Figure 9.5. The table should reflect all of your production applications. Once the major categories are complete, you should review your network for any custom applications or utilities you plan to use.

| | | | | | TESTED | |
Applications Tested on NetWare 4	VLM Run	VLM Save	VLM Print	NETX Run	NETX Save	NETX Print
Word Processing	✓	✓	✓	✓	✓	✓
Spreadsheet	✓	✓	✓			
Database				✓	✓	✓
Payroll						
In-House Software						

Testing Novell and Third-Party Utilities

All NetWare 4.11 utilities should be installed and run in your lab, mainly so that you can gain some experience with them. You may also want to install and run third-party utilities that work with NetWare 4.11. Table 9.1 lists some of the NetWare 4 utilities with which you should familiarize yourself.

TABLE 9.1

Some NetWare 4 Utilities
to Test in Your Lab

UTILITY	FUNCTION
AUDITCON.EXE	DOS-based utility for setting up auditing for NetWare 4 servers.
DSMaint	A utility used to temporarily back up a SYS volume during replacement or repair.
DSREPAIR.NLM	NLM-based utility, run from a server console or through RCONSOLE, for repairing replica lists and other parts of NDS.
DSStandard	A utility from Preferred Systems, Inc., that is used for modeling and maintaining Directory Services.
DSTRACE	NDS server SET command that displays NDS activity and status information.
NDSManager	Workstation utility used to track the status of NDS partitions for monitoring and maintaining a network.
NetWare Application Launcher	An administration utility used to supply applications via NDS to the user's desktop. The NAL is part of the NetWare Application Manager family of products.
NWUser	User-based utility for mapping drives and capturing to printers.
Partition Manager	Windows-based option within NWAdmin used to create and view partitions and replicas.
PARTMGR.EXE	DOS-based utility for creating and viewing partitions and replicas (it allows you to do the same things as the Windows-based Partition Manager).
SERVMAN.NLM	Server-based utility for defining server parameters (such as time synchronization), storage statistics, volume information, and network information.

Testing Backup and Restore Procedures

Carefully and thoroughly test the backup and restore operations for your NetWare 4 environment. Performing a quick backup operation on some files is not sufficient. You should put your backup software through its paces on an entire volume. You should also restore that volume to ensure that your disaster-recovery procedures are working properly.

Back up NDS as well as your file system. Keep in mind that replicas provide the first and safest means of disaster recovery for your network. Because objects are time-stamped, only restore NDS from a tape backup as a last resort because the restored objects have old time-stamps on the tape.

Creating a NetWare 4.11 Pilot System

The best method for testing all your production applications in the lab is to duplicate a production server and place it as one of the servers. This way, each application that runs in production on that server can be tested in a more real-time fashion for compatibility with NDS and Bindery Services.

After you have completed your application testing and completed a "mock" migration of a production server in the lab, the next step is to choose a production server and migrate it as the first NetWare 4.11 server. The pilot system is the procedure of installing your first production NetWare 4.11 server. A pilot system is the bridge between the lab and a full implementation of NetWare 4.11 in your user community.

The purpose of a pilot system is to stage NetWare 4.11 in full production on your network. The pilot system enables you to complete the final application testing and to integrate the supporting systems. For example, you can establish or migrate the printing infrastructure and optimize the workstation LAN configuration. The pilot system is also an excellent time and place to refine troubleshooting procedures for your NetWare 4.11 system. Other tasks that could be finalized are security access and the user interface for DOS and Microsoft Windows.

During the pilot phase, you should finalize the steps you want to take for the client migration. Three methods can be used to copy or load the client files: floppy disk, CD-ROM, or over the network from a NetWare 4.11 server. Determine which media works the best in your environment.

As the pilot system, we recommend choosing a server that is the home server for your central IS staff. The IS staff should understand the responsibilities and possess the skills to resolve most issues surrounding the first server migrations. Therefore, the IS staff is generally the first group to be migrated. The IS staff will gain a better understanding of NetWare 4.11 in production. This pilot system provides a foundation upon which to build the rest of the NetWare 4.11 network.

The lab should provide you with good hands-on experience before you begin the actual migration to NetWare 4.11. The lab process should be short and well-defined. If you follow the steps outlined in this chapter, you will gain a lot of first-hand experience with NetWare 4.11. Your lab tests will pay dividends later, when you migrate many servers to NetWare 4.11.

Migrating Workstations to the NetWare DOS Requester

CHAPTER

10

QuickTips: Client Migration

■ **Use the client software appropriate**   **177**

to the type of workstation you are upgrading. Novell provides the following client software for the different types of workstations:

- NetWare VLM Client

- NetWare Client for OS/2

- NetWare for Mac OS

- NetWare Client for Windows NT

- NetWare UNIX Client (NUC)

- NetWare Client 32 for DOS/Windows 3.1*x*

- NetWare Client 32 for Windows 95

■ **Load the NetWare DOS Requester on**   **180**
workstations

using the *client* software INSTALL.EXE utility. You can use the *client* INSTALL utility in the following ways:

- Disk installation. Although it's the slowest method, you may need to load the client software from disks if the workstation does not have the NETX shell (such as when you are upgrading from another network operating system). You can create the client installation disks from a NetWare 4.11 CD, mounted as either a DOS device or a NetWare volume. Run INSTALL.EXE and choose the option to create disks.

- Server installation. To install from a server, you must have a client running the NETX shell or an earlier version of the NetWare DOS Requester. The workstation logs in to the NetWare 4.11 server and runs the INSTALL.EXE utility.

- CD-ROM installation. This is similar to server installation, except that you access the INSTALL.EXE utility from a CD-ROM. The CD-ROM must be mounted as a NetWare volume for this method to work.

Automate the client installation process   187

by using batch files instead of INSTALL.EXE. This method is recommended when your network has hundreds or thousands of workstations, which are configured similarly. You can create a container login script that will launch a set of batch files to install the client software automatically. This method uses the following files:

- An instruction document file, with information about new user IDs and a checklist for the client installation procedure

- A batch file to copy the VLMs

- A batch file to upgrade the workstation's version of DOS (optional)

- A batch file to add the Windows Workstation Utilities group (optional)

- An INSTALL.CFG file with installation configuration settings

- A standardized AUTOEXEC.BAT file

- A standardized CONFIG.SYS file

- A batch file to run SCANDISK and DEFRAG

- A standardized LAN.BAT file

- A standardized NET.CFG file

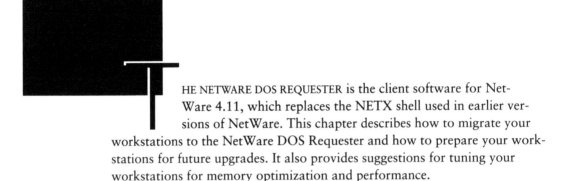

THE NETWARE DOS REQUESTER is the client software for NetWare 4.11, which replaces the NETX shell used in earlier versions of NetWare. This chapter describes how to migrate your workstations to the NetWare DOS Requester and how to prepare your workstations for future upgrades. It also provides suggestions for tuning your workstations for memory optimization and performance.

Retaining Workstation Connectivity

WITH THE CLIENT software, you can upgrade network clients without modifying your existing server configurations. Your users will retain connectivity to all versions of NetWare. Once your client workstations are migrated to the NetWare DOS Requester, your NetWare servers can be migrated to NetWare 4 systematically without interrupting user access to any server on the network.

With the NetWare DOS Requester, you can install only the connectivity options needed on any workstation. For small networks, users can choose their optimal configuration to minimize memory use and maximize performance. For large network environments, you can establish a common configuration for multiple workstations.

Types of Workstations Supported

CLIENT 1.2 FOR DOS/Windows, supplied with NetWare 4.11, allows DOS and Microsoft Windows users to access all NetWare services, including NetWare 4, NetWare 3, NetWare 2, and Personal NetWare. NetWare client software is also available for OS/2, Macintosh, Windows NT, and UNIX workstations. These other software packages are discussed in the following sections.

NetWare Client for OS/2

NetWare Client for OS/2 version 2.12 is available with IntranetWare/NetWare 4.11. It provides OS/2 users with reliable connectivity to all the features of NetWare 4.11.

OS/2 users can now run enhanced mode Microsoft Windows applications that take advantage of NetWare client services. This gives OS/2 users access to an expanded variety of applications on their network.

NetWare Client 2.12 for OS/2 also enables NetWare 4 server management through WinOS/2, so OS/2 users can run the GUI-based NetWare administrative application, NWAdmin. This means OS/2 users no longer require a DOS or Windows machine to manage their NetWare network through NDS.

NetWare Mac OS

Beginning with the NetWare 4.11 release, NetWare 4 includes full Macintosh services. NetWare for Macintosh 4.11 gives Macintosh users full access to NDS and includes the familiar and easy-to-use interface to NetWare file and print services. It also allows non-Macintosh clients to access AppleTalk-based network resources, such as Apple LaserWriter printers and HFS-formatted CD-ROM volumes.

NetWare for Macintosh 4.11 includes system software for NetWare 4.11 servers and client software for Macintosh workstations. Through new Macintosh client software, including MacIPX and MacNDS, users can now take advantage of NDS. Macintosh users get a single secure login to their NetWare network. Network administrators can now maintain a single user profile on the network for their Macintosh users, rather than having a separate user profile on every server.

An updated version of NetWare Tools, a Macintosh workstation application, is now available from CompuServe. The NetWare Tools application is located in NOVLIB Library 8. The file name is TOOLS.HQX. Users running NetWare for Macintosh 3 or NetWare for Macintosh 4 will want to download this utility update.

NetWare Client for Windows NT

The NetWare Client for Windows NT allows Windows NT workstations to integrate into NetWare networks. Users can log in to their NT workstation once and access all the services on their NetWare network. The NT client includes support for NDS, enabling NT clients to take advantage of all of NDS's features, including transparent access to all the resources on the network, regardless of where they are physically located. The product runs on both Windows NT 3.5 and 4.0 and includes the following features:

- Full NDS support including login script execution.

- Access to NetWare file and print services through NT File Manager and NT Print Manager

- Support for both ODI and NDIS 32-bit server LAN drivers (all NetWare 4.11 certified server LAN drivers are supported)

- Support for both IPX and NetWare IP transport protocols for accessing NetWare services

- Compatibility with any DOS or Win16 application for backward-compatibility

- NetWare support for NT long file naming through Novell's HPFS name space

- Lower cost and complexity of installations by dynamically installing and refreshing client software across the network with ACU capabilities.

- Ability to centrally manage user access to network applications with Novell's Application Manager utility (NAM)

NetWare UNIX Client

Novell also offers software for UNIX clients, called NetWare UNIX Client (NUC). It runs in bindery mode, and users log in as bindery users.

You must use NUC version 3.05d. Running a previous version will cause problems with the NetWare 4.11 server.

How the NetWare DOS Requester Operates

THE NETWARE DOS Requester operates differently than the NETX shell client in previous NetWare versions. The most significant difference is in how the DOS Requester handles network requests from a workstation or server. The older NetWare shell intercepts calls and determines which requests are for DOS and which are for the network, and then responds accordingly.

The DOS Requester receives all requests from the DOS Interrupt 2Fh, which is known as the *DOS redirector*. The DOS redirector determines whether the request should be handled by DOS or by the network. If the request is for the network, the DOS redirector hands the request to the NetWare REDIR.VLM for processing. The REDIR.VLM then returns the response to the DOS redirector.

The DOS Requester consists of a group of modules known as Virtual Loadable Modules (VLMs). Each VLM consists of three parts:

- Startup segment, which is used to determine the module's relationship to other modules and the load order of these modules.

- Global segment, which performs the functionality of the module. The global segment is used to create an area of memory, which is known as the *global block*, used to store all of the loaded module's global segments.

- Transient segment, which is used to move modules into a temporary area of memory for execution. Therefore, the largest module being loaded will be the size of the transient swap block.

The VLM.EXE is a terminate-and-stay resident (TSR) memory manager that has the ability to sense other memory managers loaded on your workstation. It will work with these memory managers to load portions of the VLMs into upper or extended memory to provide the workstation with greater conventional memory. If no memory manager is available, the DOS Requester and its components are loaded into conventional memory.

Loading VLMs

THE VLMS ARE loaded by the DOS Requester when you type VLM. The VLM.EXE will try to load itself into upper memory if possible. The VLM.EXE then loads each module you have specified in your NET.CFG to determine the module's size and the module's relationship to other modules being loaded.

You can decide which modules should be loaded and which can be excluded to use less memory or improve workstation performance. Table 10.1 lists each VLM, its memory requirements, and whether it is required or optional.

TABLE 10.1

NetWare Client VLMs

VLM NAME	PURPOSE	MEMORY REQUIREMENTS	REQUIRED OR OPTIONAL
AUTO.VLM	Auto-Reconnect; Auto-Retry	2336 bytes	Optional
BIND.VLM	NetWare Bindery Module	3008 bytes	Required if you are connecting to a NetWare 3.1x or earlier version server
CONN.VLM	Connection Table Manager	3248 bytes	Required
FIO.VLM	File Input/Output	7104	Required

TABLE 10.1			MEMORY	REQUIRED OR
NetWare Client VLMs (continued)	**VLM NAME**	**PURPOSE**	**MEMORY REQUIREMENTS**	**OPTIONAL**
	GENERAL.VLM	Miscellaneous Functions: NETX.VLM and REDIR.VLM	1760 bytes	Required
	IPXNCP.VLM	IPX Transport Module	4976 bytes	Required
	MIB2IF.VLM	Used for SNMP services	2608 bytes	Optional
	NDS.VLM	NDS Protocol Module	6112 bytes	Required to run NDS
	NETX.VLM	NetWare Shell Compatibility	10,064 bytes	Optional
	NMR.VLM	NetWare Management Responder	1728 bytes	Optional
	NWP.VLM	NetWare Protocol Multiplexer	3040 bytes	Required
	PNW.VLM	Personal NetWare Module	5680	Required if you are running Personal NetWare
	PRINT.VLM	Printer Redirector	3952 bytes	Required if you need to print
	REDIR.VLM	DOS Redirector	10,256 bytes	Required
	RSA.VLM	RSA Encryption for NDS	15,408 bytes	Optional
	SECURITY.VLM	NetWare Enhanced Security	4192 bytes	Optional

VLM NAME	PURPOSE	MEMORY REQUIREMENTS	REQUIRED OR OPTIONAL
TRAN.VLM	Transport Protocol Multiplexer	311 bytes	Required
WSASN1.VLM	Used for SNMP services	9712 bytes	Optional
WSREG.VLM	Used for SNMP services	6832 bytes	Optional
WSSNMP.VLM	Used for SNMP services	11,968 bytes	Optional
WSTRAP.VLM	Used for SNMP services	7024 bytes	Optional

The best way to prevent an optional VLM from loading is to add the following line under the NetWare DOS Requester heading in the NET.CFG file:

```
EXCLUDE VLM = <vlm>
```

where *<vlm>* is the name of the module you do not want to load.

You can also rename a VLM that you do not want to load, giving it a different extensions (such as .SAV). Deleting the VLM will work, too, but this is not recommended.

A particular load order for BIND.VLM, NDS.VLM, and PNW.VLM is necessary for workstation optimization. Use the following guidelines for the NetWare Protocol entry in the workstation's NET.CFG file:

- If the workstation user usually logs in to a NetWare 3 server first, load BIND.VLM, then NDS.VLM, then PNW.VLM (if you use Personal NetWare):

```
NetWare Protocol=BIND,NDS,PNW
```

- If the workstation user usually logs in to a NetWare 4 server first, load NDS.VLM, then BIND.VLM, then PNW.VLM (if you use Personal NetWare):

```
NetWare Protocol=NDS,BIND,PNW
```

Using INSTALL.EXE

Y OU CAN USE the client INSTALL.EXE utility to load the NetWare DOS Requester on your workstations. This utility handles the installation of your VLM files by creating the C:\NWCLIENT directory and other directories for multi-language support.

Instead of using INSTALL.EXE to load the client software, you can create your own custom design batch files for installation. These batch files can be called from a container login script to automatically update each workstation that logs in to the server. The batch file method is discussed later in this chapter.

The INSTALL utility modifies the workstation's CONFIG.SYS and AUTOEXEC.BAT files. In the CONFIG.SYS file, INSTALL changes the LASTDRIVE= entry to Z (LASTDRIVE=Z), so that you can have search drive mappings that are assigned backward from Z. In the AUTOEXEC.BAT file, INSTALL adds one line at the top of the file:

```
C:\NWCLIENT\STARTNET.BAT
```

The INSTALL utility also creates a file named STARTNET.BAT, which allows you the option of running this file to run the client software on a DOS workstation. The file will be placed in the NWCLIENT directory. It will be similar to the listing shown here:

LSL	Loads the link support layer software
NE2000	Network interface driver (depends on the NIC you are using)
IPXODI	Loads the ODI software
VLM	Loads the Virtual Loadable Modules
F:	Changes to the network drive letter F
LOGIN	Logs in to the network

The installation process is extremely straightforward. After you complete the initial screen to specify installation parameters, the upgrade will proceed automatically.

If you have many different hardware types, you may need to do some special modifications on workstations. As mentioned earlier in the book, the best approach is to design your installation generally, and then revisit special-case situations.

The utility will pause only if it encounters duplicate files on the workstation that are newer than the files that the utility is trying to load. This may occur with duplicate DLL (Data Link Library) files that you may have previously updated from another source, such as NetWire. In most cases, newer DLL files will be backward-compatible, so you can say No to overwriting the files from the utility.

If you encounter problems with the VLMs (such as loading a NetWare utility like NWAdmin), you may need to reinstall the client software. Be sure to test a few of the workstations and the NetWare utilities before beginning a full-scale client migration.

You can use the INSTALL utility from disks, a file server, or a mounted CD-ROM. These methods are described in the following sections.

Installing from Disk

If you do not have access to a NetWare 4.11 server from the workstation you are upgrading, you will need to load the client software from disks. The disk installation method is the slowest method for installing the client software at each workstation. However, it may be necessary if the workstation does not have the NETX shell, as is the case when you are upgrading from another network operating system.

Installation will take approximately 15 to 20 minutes per workstation to load the client software from disks. This does not take into account the time for special requirements, such as loading dual protocol stacks on the same workstation for a migration to NetWare 4.11.

To create the client installation disks from a NetWare 4.1 CD, follow these steps:

1. Mount the NetWare 4.11 CD-ROM as either a DOS device or NetWare volume. You can also have the complete NetWare 4.11 CD-ROM stored on a file system of a server.

2. Change to the drive letter specified for your mounted CD-ROM or the directory where your NetWare 4.11 files are stored and run INSTALL.EXE (the NetWare 4.11 installation utility, not the client utility with the same name). You will see the screen shown in Figure 10.1.

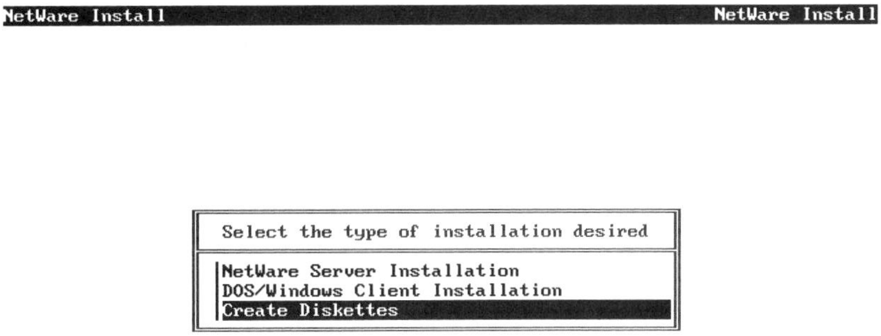

FIGURE 10.1

The NetWare 4.1 INSTALL utility has an option to create client disks.

```
NetWare Install                                    NetWare Install




                ┌─────────────────────────────────────┐
                │  Select the type of installation desired │
                ├─────────────────────────────────────┤
                │ NetWare Server Installation          │
                │ DOS/Windows Client Installation      │
                │ Create Diskettes                     │
                └─────────────────────────────────────┘
```

3. Choose the option to create disks and press Enter. You will see the screen for selecting the media size, as shown in Figure 10.2.

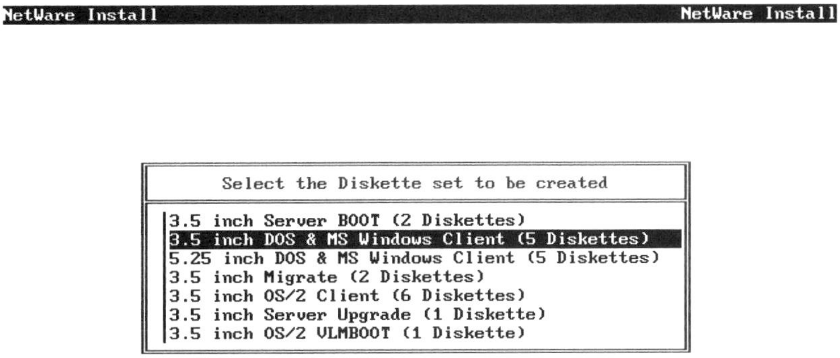

FIGURE 10.2

This screen displays the media sizes available for creating the client disks.

```
NetWare Install                                    NetWare Install




             ┌──────────────────────────────────────────┐
             │     Select the Diskette set to be created │
             ├──────────────────────────────────────────┤
             │ 3.5 inch Server BOOT (2 Diskettes)        │
             │ 3.5 inch DOS & MS Windows Client (5 Diskettes) │
             │ 5.25 inch DOS & MS Windows Client (5 Diskettes) │
             │ 3.5 inch Migrate (2 Diskettes)            │
             │ 3.5 inch OS/2 Client (6 Diskettes)        │
             │ 3.5 inch Server Upgrade (1 Diskette)      │
             │ 3.5 inch OS/2 VLMBOOT (1 Diskette)        │
             └──────────────────────────────────────────┘
```

4. Choose the appropriate media size and the client software you want to load, and then press Enter.

5. As prompted, insert the disks. You will need several disks, depending on the client type (DOS or OS/2).

You can now load Disk 1 and run INSTALL.EXE, which is the client installation utility.

If you are migrating a workstation from another operating system, you will need to prevent the other operating system from loading at start up. Once the other operating has been disabled, you can run the client installation utility and begin your upgrade process.

Installing from a Server or CD-ROM

The server installation method requires that you have a client running the NETX shell or an earlier version of the NetWare DOS Requester so that the workstation can access a NetWare 4.11 server. The workstation simply logs in to the NetWare 4.11 server and runs the utility from this subdirectory:

```
F:\PUBLIC\CLIENT\DOSWIN\INSTALL.EXE
```

This option is faster than loading disks and can be accomplished by some of your users with little assistance. After you answer the questions on the initial installation parameter screen, the process will continue to completion unassisted. It will pause only if it encounters duplicate files on the workstation that are newer than the files the utility is trying to load.

The CD-ROM installation option is similar to the server option, except that you are accessing the installation utility from a CD-ROM. The CD-ROM must be mounted as a NetWare volume so that you can access the utility from a CD. See Chapter 9 for instructions for mounting a CD-ROM as a NetWare volume.

Automating Client Installation through Batch Files

NSTEAD OF USING the INSTALL.EXE utility to copy and modify files, you can use your own batch files to install the client to meet your specific needs. You can create a set of batch files that not only replace the installation utility, but also automate the process. In order for this to work, your batch file must know where to place all the files and be able to take into account the changes that must be made in a Microsoft Windows environment.

This method is recommended for large installations that have many hundreds or thousands of workstations, which are configured similarly. You can run the VLM upgrade batch file from a container login script if you cannot visit each individual workstation.

If you can visit each workstation, you should consider performing other maintenance on your workstations as long as you are there. For example, you can upgrade the workstation's DOS version at the same time you install the NetWare client software. The examples presented in the following sections include a batch file for upgrading to DOS 6.

During VLM installation, you will not be able to change any options on the installation program screen, except to select the MLID driver. The workstation NIC's MLID driver might not be listed in the standard VLM client installation program. To allow the installation program to find a particular MLID, copy it and its .INS and .BIN files to the following location:

```
SYS:PUBLIC\CLIENT\DOSWIN\DOS
```

Instruction Sheets for Batch File Installation

In order to ensure that the batch file installation process works properly, you should prepare instruction sheets that contain information about new user IDs and a checklist for the client installation procedure. Figure 10.3 shows an example of an instruction sheet.

FIGURE 10.3

Instruction sheet for client installation through batch files

User Information

Your Old Login ID was:
BJONES

Your New Login ID is:
BJONES

Your New Home Directory is:

F:\USERS\BJONES

Installation Checklist

___ CHKDSK (check for adequate disk space)
___ Z:VLMUP.BAT (install VLMs)
___ Z:DOS6UP.BAT or Z:STEPUP.BAT (install 6.22 or step up from 6.2)
___ Reboot with DOS 6 diskette (transfers SYS)
___ Modify AUTOEXEC, CONFIG.SYS, LAN.BAT, NET.CFG
___ Reboot from C:\; LAN.BAT; LOGIN to network
___ Run Windows (check startup, personal group icons, new groups)
___ Z:FIXUP.BAT (scandisk and defrag)

Installer Name:_____ Date: _____

The instruction sheets can be taped outside the office or cubicle for each workstation to be upgraded. Instruction sheets do *not* need to be posted on those workstations that have special configurations and don't fit your standard setup. They must be done separately by the upgraders that are familiar with the workstation.

Batch Files and Other Files Required for Client Installation

To use the batch file process to upgrade workstations, you need the following files:

- VLMUP.BAT

- DOS6UP.BAT (optional)

- DOSGRP.BAT (optional)

- INSTALL.CFG

- Standardized AUTOEXEC.BAT

- Standardized CONFIG.SYS

- FIXUP.BAT

- Standardized LAN.BAT

- Standardized NET.CFG

The following sections provide examples of these files.

The VLMUP.BAT File to Install VLMs

The VLMUP.BAT file shown in Figure 10.4 can be run from the PUBLIC directory (Z:\) to install the VLMs. Keep in mind that your version of DOS may differ. These files can be used to update any version of DOS.

FIGURE 10.4

The VLXMUP.BAT file for installing client VLMs

```
REM @echo off
ECHO RUNNING VLM INSTALLATION...
IF EXIST C:\WINDOWS\WIN.COM SET WIN_THERE=YES
IF NOT EXIST C:\WINDOWS\WIN.COM SET WIN_THERE=NO
IF NOT EXIST C:\NWCLIENT\VLM.EXE GOTO UPDATE
ECHO SAVING OLD NET.CFG

REM If they already have vlm installed, update drivers, etc.
ATTRIB -R C:\NWCLIENT\*.*
MD C:\NWCLIENT\SAVE
REM Save a copy of the net.cfg in case we need to look at it.
COPY C:\NWCLIENT\NET.CFG C:\NWCLIENT\SAVE

REM update vlm.exe, *.vlm, lsl.com, ipxodi.com
REPLACE Z:\WSUP1\VLM11\*.* C:\NWCLIENT /U
ECHO C:\NWCLIENT ALREADY EXISTS, UPDATED VLMs.
REPLACE Z:\WSUP1\DRIVERS\TOKEN.COM C:\NWCLIENT /U >NUL
REPLACE Z:\WSUP1\DRIVERS\OSH39XR.COM C:\NWCLIENT /U >NUL
REPLACE Z:\WSUP1\DRIVERS\PRORAPM.DWN C:\NWCLIENT /U >NUL
REPLACE Z:\WSUP1\DRIVERS\CPQTOKNW.COM C:\NWCLIENT /U >NUL
IF EXIST C:\NWCLIENT\CPQTOKNW.COM COPY Z:\WSUP1\DRIVERS\
CPQTOKNW.BIN C:\NWCLIENT >NUL
```

FIGURE 10.4

The VLXMUP.BAT file for installing client VLMs (continued)

```
PAUSE
MD C:\NWCLIENT\SAVE
REM if they have a lan.bat in c:\, then delete it. We will run it out of c:\dos
COPY C:\LAN.BAT C:\NWCLIENT\SAVE
DEL C:\LAN.BAT
COPY Z:\MSDOS6\NET.CFG C:\NWCLIENT
CD Z:\
CD C:\
ECHO C:\NWCLIENT ALREADY EXISTS, UPDATED VLMs AND DRIVERS.
GOTO ICLIENT

PAUSE

:UPDATE
REM if they don't already have vlm, then lan drivers will be in C:\LANWS
MD C:\NWCLIENT >NUL
MD C:\NWCLIENT\SAVE >NUL
COPY C:\LANWS\NET.CFG C:\NWCLIENT\SAVE
COPY C:\LANWS\SHELL.CFG C:\NWCLIENT\SAVE
COPY C:\DOS\LAN.BAT C:\NWCLIENT\SAVE
COPY C:\LAN.BAT C:\NWCLIENT\SAVE
ATTRIB -R C:\LAN.BAT
DEL C:\LAN.BAT

REM allow the upgrader to stop the process if something went wrong
ECHO READY TO RUN VLM INSTALL?
PAUSE
Z:
CD \CLIENT\DOSWIN
INSTALL
CD Z:\
C:
CD \
REM delete all the old lan drivers
ATTRIB -R C:\LANWS\*.*
DEL C:\LANWS\*.* <Z:\YES.TXT
RD C:\LANWS
ECHO OLD C:\LANWS REMOVED

PAUSE
REM copy the standard net.cfg file to the user's NWCLIENT directory.
COPY Z:\MSDOS6\NET.CFG C:\NWCLIENT
ECHO NEW NET.CFG COPIED
```

FIGURE 10.4

The VLXMUP.BAT file for
installing client VLMs
(continued)

```
PAUSE

:END
ECHO COPYING NETWARE.INI
IF EXIST C:\WINDOWS\WIN.COM COPY Z:\MSDOS6\NETWARE.INI C:\WINDOWS

ECHO VLM UPDATED.
```

Keep in mind you will need to modify this file (and the other examples shown in this chapter) to suit your own requirements, and then test it to ensure that it will work properly in your environment.

The DOS6UP.BAT File to Upgrade to DOS 6.22

The DOS6UP.BAT batch file can be run from \PUBLIC to upgrade to DOS 6.22. If you must visit each workstation individually, you may want to take the time to upgrade your DOS level also. You can use the batch file shown in Figure 10.5 for this upgrade.

FIGURE 10.5

The DOS6UP.BAT file
for upgrading to
DOS 6.22

```
REM @echo off

REM test for what's out there.
IF EXIST C:\LANWS\*.* SET LANDIR=LANWS
IF EXIST C:\NWCLIENT\*.* SET LANDIR=NWCLIENT
IF EXIST C:\WINDOWS\WIN.COM SET WIN_THERE=YES
IF NOT EXIST C:\WINDOWS\WIN.COM SET WIN_THERE=NO
IF EXIST C:\DOS\XCOPY.EXE IF NOT EXIST C:\DOS\MEMMAKER.EXE SET
OLD_DOS=DOS
IF EXIST C:\DRDOS\*.* SET OLD_DOS=DRDOS
IF EXIST C:\NWDOS\*.* SET OLD_DOS=NWDOS
ECHO WINDOWS: %WIN_THERE%    OLD DOS: %OLD_DOS%

PAUSE

ECHO BACKING UP OLD CONFIG.SYS & AUTOEXEC.BAT & NET.CFG
MD C:\DOS
MD C:\DOS\SAVE
COPY C:\%OLD_DOS%\*.BAT C:\DOS\SAVE
COPY C:\CONFIG.SYS C:\DOS\SAVE
COPY C:\AUTOEXEC.BAT C:\DOS\SAVE
REM COPY C:\%LANDIR%\NET.CFG C:\DOS\SAVE

PAUSE
```

FIGURE 10.5

The DOS6UP.BAT file
for upgrading to
DOS 6.22
(continued)

```
IF %WIN_THERE%==YES COPY C:\WINDOWS\WIN.INI C:\DOS\SAVE
IF %WIN_THERE%==YES COPY C:\WINDOWS\SYSTEM.INI C:\DOS\SAVE
IF %WIN_THERE%==YES COPY C:\WINDOWS\PROGMAN.INI
C:\DOS\SAVE
MD C:\WINDOWS\TEMP

PAUSE

ECHO REMOVING OLD DOS
ATTRIB -R C:\%OLD_DOS%\*.*
IF EXIST C:\DOS\*.* DEL C:\DOS\*.* <Z:\YES.TXT
DEL C:\%OLD_DOS%\*.* <Z:\YES.TXT
DEL C:\%OLD_DOS%\TMP <Z:\YES.TXT
RD C:\%OLD_DOS%\TMP
RD C:\%OLD_DOS%
IF EXIST C:\%OLD_DOS%.386 DEL C:\%OLD_DOS%.386

PAUSE

ECHO COPYING MS-DOS 6.22 FILES...
COPY Z:\MSDOS6\*.* C:\DOS
COPY C:\DOS\CONFIG.SYS C:\
COPY C:\DOS\AUTOEXEC.BAT C:\

PAUSE

ECHO RUNNING DOSGRP.BAT..
@CALL Z:\DOSGRP.BAT

PAUSE
:END
LOGOUT
```

We have placed many PAUSE statements in the batch files so that the operator can stop the installation if any unusual error messages show up. We also removed the ECHO OFF command so that the upgrader can see which command caused the error message.

The DOSGRP.BAT File to Add Windows Workstation Utilities Group

If you are planning to add the Workstation Utilities group to the Windows Desktop, you can use the DOSGRP.BAT file. This batch file is shown in Figure 10.6.

```
@ECHO OFF
ECHO OFF
:MSDOS6
REM copy the msdos6.grp windows file and add to the progman.ini file

REM if windows is not installed on this machine, skip it
IF NOT EXIST C:\WINDOWS\WIN.COM GOTO ENDAPPS

REM if they've already been updated, skip it.
IF  EXIST  C:\WINDOWS\MSDOS6.GRP  IF  EXIST  C:\WINDOWS\MSDOS6.1
GOTO ENDAPPS

COPY Z:\MSDOS6\MSDOS6.GRP C:\WINDOWS >NUL
DEL C:\WINDOWS\MSDOS6.?

REM add a line to the progman.ini file so that the msdos6 group will appear
C:
CD \WINDOWS
COPY PROGMAN.INI PROGMAN.BK1 >NUL
COPY PROGMAN.BK1+Z:\WSUP1\PROGMAN.DOS PROGMAN.INI >NUL
ECHO MSDOS6 GROUP FILE COPIED AND ADDED TO PROGMAN.INI
>>C:\WINDOWS\MSDOS6.1
ECHO MSDOS6 GROUP FILE COPIED.
CD \
:ENDAPPS
Z:
```

The INSTALL.CFG File

INSTALL.CFG is a configuration file found in the SYS:PUBLIC/CLIENT/ DOSWIN directory. The VLM installation program reads this file for installation settings. Figure 10.7 shows an example of this configuration file.

You can modify the INSTALL.CFG file to add non-English unicode files (the default is English if your Language variable is set to English in NET.CFG). You can also edit INSTALL.CFG so that it does not add this line to the AUTOEXEC.BAT file:

```
CALL C:\NWCLIENT\STARTNET.BAT
```

nor install the NWUSER Windows group to the workstation's Windows Desktop.

FIGURE 10.7

A sample INSTALL.CFG file

[FILES]
WSDOS_1:CLIENT:DW:AUTO.VLM
WSDOS_1:CLIENT:DW:BIND.VLM
WSDOS_1:CLIENT:DW:CONN.VLM
WSDOS_1:CLIENT:DW:FIO.VLM
WSDOS_1:CLIENT:DW:GENERAL.VLM
WSDOS_1:CLIENT:DW:IPXNCP.VLM
WSDOS_1:CLIENT:DW:IPXODI.COM
WSDOS_1:CLIENT:DW:LSL.COM
WSDOS_1:CLIENT:DW:NDS.VLM
WSDOS_1:CLIENT:DW:NETX.VLM
WSDOS_1:CLIENT:DW:NMR.VLM
WSDOS_1:CLIENT:DW:NWP.VLM
WSDOS_1:CLIENT:DW:PRINT.VLM
WSDOS_1:CLIENT:DW:REDIR.VLM
WSDOS_1:CLIENT:DW:RSA.VLM
WSDOS_1:CLIENT:DW:SECURITY.VLM
WSDOS_1:CLIENT:DW:TRAN.VLM
WSDOS_1:CLIENT:DW:VLM.EXE

WSDOS_1:CLIENTLANG:DW:DOSRQSTR.MSG
WSDOS_1:CLIENTLANG:DW:IPXODI.MSG
WSDOS_1:CLIENTLANG:DW:NMR.MSG
WSDOS_1:CLIENTLANG:DW:READVLM.TXT

WSDOS_1:WINNLS:W:1252_UNI.001
WSDOS_1:WINNLS:W:UNI_1252.001
WSDOS_1:WINNLS:W:UNI_COL.001
WSDOS_1:WINNLS:W:UNI_MON.001

WSDOS_2:CLIENT:DW:TSASMS.COM
WSDOS_2:CLIENTLANG:DW:STPIPX.MSG
WSDOS_2:CLIENTLANG:DW:STPUDP.MSG

WSDOS_2:WINDOWS:W:ET.INI
WSDOS_2:WINDOWS:W:NWADMIN.INI
WSDOS_2:WINDOWS:W:NWRCON.PIF

WSDOS_2:WINSYS:W:NWCALLS.DLL
WSDOS_2:WINSYS:W:NWGDI.DLL
WSDOS_2:WINSYS:W:PNW.DLL
WSDOS_2:WINSYS:W:NWIPXSPX.DLL
WSDOS_2:WINSYS:W:NWLOCALE.DLL
WSDOS_2:WINSYS:W:NWNET.DLL
WSDOS_2:WINSYS:W:NWPSRV.DLL
WSDOS_2:WINSYS:W:NWUSER.EXE
WSDOS_2:WINSYS:W:TASKID.COM
WSDOS_2:WINSYS:W:TBMI2.COM

FIGURE 10.7

A sample INSTALL.CFG
file (continued)

WSDOS_2:WINLANG:W:NETWARE.HLP
WSDOS_2:WINLANG:W:NETWARER.DRV
WSDOS_2:WINSYS:W:NETWARE.HLP
WSDOS_2:WINLANG:W:TASKID.MSG
WSDOS_2:WINLANG:W:TBMI2.MSG

WSDOS_2:WINSYS:W:NETWARE.DRV
WSDOS_2:WINSYS:W:VIPX.386
WSDOS_2:WINSYS:W:VNETWARE.386
WSDOS_2:WINSYS:W:NWPOPUP.EXE

WSDRV_2:CLIENT:DW:STPIPX.COM
WSDRV_2:CLIENT:DW:STPUDP.COM

[WINDELETE]
NWPOPUP.EXE
NETWARE.DRV
NWCALLS.DLL
NWLOCALE.DLL
NWNET.DLL
NWPSRV.DLL
NWIPXSPX.DLL
VIPX.386
VNETWARE.386
NETWARE.HLP
TASKID.COM
TBMI2.COM
NWGDI.DLL
PNW.DLL

[REQUESTER]
FIRST NETWORK DRIVE=F
NETWARE PROTOCOL=NDS BIND

[TITLES]
WSDOS_1:NetWare Client for DOS and MS-Windows Installation Diskette #1
WSDOS_2:NetWare Client for DOS and MS-Windows Installation Diskette #2
WSDRV_2:NetWare LAN Drivers for DOS Clients diskette

[DISKSPACE]
LOWSPACE=5
INSTALLDOSSPACE=1
INSTALLWINSPACE=3

[WINGROUP]

[INSTALL]
INSTALLNWCLIENT

VERSION=1.11

Standard AUTOEXEC.BAT and CONFIG.SYS Files

For the batch file installation process to work, you also need standard AUTOEXEC.BAT and CONFIG.SYS files. Figures 10.8 and 10.9 show examples of these files.

FIGURE 10.8

Sample AUTOEXEC.BAT file

```
@ECHO OFF
VERIFY OFF
PATH C:\;C:\DOS;C:\WINDOWS
PROMPT $P$G
SET TEMP=C:\WINDOWS\TEMP
SET MOUSE=C:\DOS
LH /L:1,6384 C:\DOS\DOSKEY.COM
LH /L:1,47216 C:\DOS\MOUSE.COM
LH /L:1,16944 C:\DOS\SHARE /L:500 /F:5100
LH /L:0;1,45520 /S C:\DOS\SMARTDRV

REM call c:\dos\lan.bat
```

FIGURE 10.9

Sample CONFIG.SYS file

```
DEVICE=C:\DOS\HIMEM.SYS
DEVICE=C:\DOS\EMM386.EXE NOEMS HIGHSCAN X=C700-C7FF
WIN=F500-F7FF WIN=F200-F4FF
BUFFERS=10,0
FILES=100
DOS=UMB
LASTDRIVE=Z
DEVICEHIGH /L:1,12048=C:\DOS\SETVER.EXE
DOS=HIGH
SHELL=C:\DOS\COMMAND.COM C:\DOS\ /E:1024 /p
BREAK=OFF
DEVICEHIGH /L:1,9072=C:\DOS\ANSI.SYS
```

The FIXUP.BAT File to run SCANDISK and DEFRAG

You can use another batch file to run SCANDISK and DEFRAG. The FIXUP.BAT file for this purpose is shown in Figure 10.10.

FIGURE 10.10

The FIXUP.BAT file to
run SCANDISK and
DEFRAG

```
REM this batch file runs scandisk & defrag
REM
C:\DOS\SCANDISK C: /AUTOFIX /NOSAVE /NOSUMMARY
C:\DOS\DEFRAG C: /F /S:N
LOGOUT
```

A Standard LAN.BAT File

Another file you will need is a standardized LAN.BAT batch file. Figure 10.11 shows an example of this file.

FIGURE 10.11

Sample LAN.BAT file

```
@ECHO OFF
C:
CD \NWCLIENT
LH /L:1,23280 LSL
REM token ring
CPQTOKNW
LH /L:1,30768 IPXODI
REM c:\nwclient\iclient
LH /L:0;1,50624 /S VLM
CD \
F:
LOGIN %1
```

A Standard NET.CFG File

You should also create a standard NET.CFG file for the workstations that will be upgraded. Figure 10.12 shows an example of this file.

FIGURE 10.12

Sample NET.CFG file

```
NETWARE DOS REQUESTER
 FIRST NETWORK DRIVE=F
 NETWARE PROTOCOL=NDS,BIND
 PREFERRED SERVER=UTSTDP01
 NAME CONTEXT "OU=ATL.OU=REG1.O=WWW"
 SHOW DOTS=ON
 USE DEFAULTS=ON
 VLM=AUTO.VLM
 VLM=RSA.VLM
 ;Pburst Write Window Size=5
```

FIGURE 10.12

Sample NET.CFG file
(continued)

```
LINK SUPPORT
 BUFFERS 2 4216
 MEMPOOL 8432
 MAX STACKS 5

LINK DRIVER CPQTOKNW
 MAX FRAME SIZE 4216
 FRAME TOKEN-RING
 FRAME TOKEN-RING_SNAP
 PROTOCOL IPX E0 TOKEN-RING
 PROTOCOL TCPIP 8137 TOKEN-RING_SNAP

LINK DRIVER MADGEODI
 MAX FRAME SIZE 4216
 FRAME TOKEN-RING
 FRAME TOKEN-RING_SNAP
 PROTOCOL IPX E0 TOKEN-RING
 PROTOCOL TCPIP 8137 TOKEN-RING_SNAP

LINK DRIVER TOKEN
 FRAME TOKEN-RING_SNAP
 FRAME TOKEN-RING
 MAX FRAME Size 2048
 PROTOCOL IPX E0 TOKEN-RING
 PROTOCOL TCPIP 8137 TOKEN-RING_SNAP

LINK DRIVER CPQETHNW
 FRAME ETHERNET_II
 PROTOCOL IPX 8137 ETHERNET_II
 PROTOCOL TCPIP 8137 ETHERNET_II
 MAX FRAME SIZE 1518

LINK DRIVER OSH392R
 PORT 4A20
 INT 5
 DMA 0
 CABLE UTP
 SPEED 4
 FRAME TOKEN-RING
 FRAME TOKEN-RING_SNAP
 PROTOCOL IPX E0 TOKEN-RING
 PROTOCOL TCPIP 8137 TOKEN-RING_SNAP
 MAX FRAME SIZE 4216
```

For most sites, the easiest way to handle the NET.CFG file is to standardize configuration parameters for your general user community and distribute that file. You can set this up by providing a NET.CFG file that contains all the parameters available. Then you can simply comment out the parameters you don't need. If you later need to enable a parameter at a workstation, you can simply remove the remark from the NET.CFG file and reboot the system.

Making changes to the NET.CFG file affects the overall size of the global swap block, which is an area of memory that stores your VLMs.

Running the Batch File Installation

For batch file installation, the upgraders, equipped with DOS upgrade system disks, can be sent out to upgrade the workstations that have instruction sheets. Before beginning, the upgraders must make sure that the workstation's hard drives have enough disk space to install the software (5MB is required). Then they could proceed to run the batch files, as described in the following sections.

If you cannot have upgraders visit each workstation, at a minimum, you can call VLMUP.BAT from a container login script, and not run DOS6UP.BAT or DOSGRP.BAT. If you are upgrading from another operating system, these procedures will work very well as a semi-automated method.

Remember, you may need to modify the batch files and procedures presented here to suit your specific environment and needs.

Running VLMUP.BAT

You can run the VLMUP.BAT file manually or call it from your container login script. To run it manually, log in to the server with your own login ID. Then execute VLMUP.BAT, which is in the PUBLIC directory (Z:\).

To run VLMUP.BAT from a container login script, add this statement to the end of the script:

```
EXIT VLMUP.BAT
```

If the workstation doesn't already have the VLMs installed, this batch file will run the VLM installation utility.

If the workstation already has the VLMs installed, VLMUP.BAT will just update the VLMs and NIC drivers to the C:\NWCLIENT directory using the DOS REPLACE /U command. Also, a standardized NET.CFG file will be copied to the NWCLIENT directory. The user's old NET.CFG file will be copied to a separate directory (in case you need to refer to it later).

As its last step, the VLMUP.BAT file copies a standardized NETWARE.INI to the Windows directory.

Running DOS6UP.BAT

After the VLMs are installed, you can run DOS6UP.BAT from the PUBLIC directory. This batch file performs the following tasks:

- Determines which directories the LAN drivers are in, what the old DOS directory was, and if Windows was installed.

- Sets environment variables equal to those directory names.

- Saves copies of the CONFIG.SYS, AUTOEXEC.BAT, NET.CFG, and Windows .INI files (just in case you encounter any problems).

- Deletes the old DOS files and copies the new DOS (in our example DOS 6.22) files to the C:\DOS directory.

- Copies standardized AUTOEXEC.BAT and CONFIG.SYS files to C:\.

Finally, the DOSGRP.BAT file is called from PUBLIC. This adds a Microsoft Windows Program Manager group, which contains NWUSER and some MS DOS 6 Windows utilities, to the Windows Desktop. (It does this by copying the group file and adding a GROUP= line to PROGMAN.INI).

After running DOS6UP.BAT, reboot from a system disk that will run SYS C: in its AUTOEXEC.BAT.

Updating System Files

After installing VLM and DOS 6, you should compare the old CONFIG.SYS, AUTOEXEC.BAT, NET.CFG, and LAN.BAT files with the newly installed standard ones. If the old files contain any custom lines that tailor the workstation for the particular user, move them from the old file to the new one so that the workstation will continue to function the way the user expects.

Reboot the workstation, log in, run Windows, and generally make sure the workstation is fully functional.

The CONFIG.SYS and AUTOEXEC.BAT files should be optimized with DOS MEMMAKER on a standard workstation before the upgrade is finished. You may need to rerun MEMMAKER on workstations that have differences in their configurations.

Running **FIXUP.BAT**

Last, you can run FIXUP.BAT. This batch file runs MS-DOS 6's SCANDISK and DEFRAG in unattended mode to optimize the workstation's hard drive.

After starting FIXUP, you can move on to the next workstation.

Using Workstation Performance and Memory Tuning Options

THIS SECTION DISCUSSES some of the parameters that affect workstation performance and memory usage. If necessary, you can adjust these settings to suit your needs. But keep in mind that there is usually a cost associated with making adjustments. You may sacrifice memory for performance or vice versa.

There are many performance and tuning options available for the NetWare DOS Requester. For more information, refer to Novell's DOS and Windows client documentation.

Adjusting Performance Parameters

Certain aspects of the NetWare DOS Requester will affect the performance of the workstation. For example, when you initially log in to NetWare 4, it takes a moment for the authentication process, LIP (Large Internet Packet) negotiation, and Packet Burst negotiation to be completed. (The latter two are default parameters that you can adjust.) This adds a slight delay for users immediately after they enter their password at the workstation. After the login process is completed, users should notice no delay in response to or from a file server. In fact, they should see an overall increase in performance.

The performance of the workstation can be affected by the hardware (286 and low-end 386 workstations will have slower performance).

Table 10.2 describes the NET.CFG file parameters, including LIP and Packet Burst, that affect workstation performance.

	PARAMETER	SETTINGS	DESCRIPTIONS
TABLE 10.2 NET.CFG File Parameters That Affect Workstation Performance	Checksum = 1 (Default)	0–3	Mandates additional IPX error checking beyond the normal NIC error checking. Leave this parameter at 1 unless your NICs or network are experiencing many errors. Using this parameter executes additional code on each packet transmitted and thereby reduces performance.
	LIP = ON (Default)	OFF/ON	LIP negotiation initially requires the client to negotiate the largest packet size for transmitting packets over bridges and routers. For best performance, leave this set to ON.
	PB Buffers = 3 or 8 (Default)	0–9	Packet Burst will buffer up to 8 packets and send them onto the network, requiring only one acknowledgment for all 8. This parameter should be left set to 3 or 8, which is ON (0 is OFF).
	Cache Writes = ON (Default)	OFF/ON	Fills a local cache buffer with data before writing it to the network. This parameter will offload data to the local cache, thus freeing the workstation for other activities. This parameter should be left ON.
	True Commit = OFF (Default)	OFF/ON	Verifies that a write request has been written to a server's hard disk before servicing another request. When enabled, True Commit first writes data to the server's cache; then, after 3.3 seconds, it writes the data to disk. Using this parameter slows the workstation's performance. Data integrity can best be handled with Novell's Transaction Tracking System (TTS), which is part of NetWare.

NET.CFG Parameters That Affect Memory

As mentioned earlier, there is a tradeoff between performance and memory. You must experiment and test a configuration that has the proper balance for your environment. Be sure to verify the largest executable file size so that you can provide your workstations adequate conventional memory.

Table 10.3 lists the parameters that can affect workstation memory.

TABLE 10.3	PARAMETER	SETTINGS	DESCRIPTION
NET.CFG File Parameters that Affect Workstation Memory	Cache Buffers = 5 (Default)	0–64	A cache buffer is assigned to each file opened, up to the number of buffers available, which can greatly improve workstation reads and writes to the server. You can set up to 64 cache buffers. The size is automatically determined by the protocol frame size.
	Cache Buffer Size = *protocol frame size* (Default)		This parameter is automatically adjusted to your frame size (less 64 bytes). Therefore, the larger the frame size and number of buffers, the larger your global block size.
	Print Buffer Size = 64 (Default)	0–256	The DOS Requester will wait until it has 64 (the default) characters before the FIO VLM writes a print file. Performance depends on the type of files you are printing. Graphics files do better if the Print Buffer Size is set up to 256. Regular documents do not print as quickly at 256 because they are double-cached.
	PBurst Read Windows Size = 16 (Default)	2–64	Sets the number of bytes read from the server before the workstation receives a reply. Adjust this setting only if you have multiple router hops or slow WAN links between a workstation and server.
	PBurst Write Windows Size = 64 (Default)	2–64	Sets the number of bytes written to the server before the workstation receives a reply. Adjust this setting only if you have multiple router hops or slow WAN links between a workstation and server.

TABLE 10.3	PARAMETER	SETTINGS	DESCRIPTION
NET.CFG File Parameters that Affect Workstation Memory (continued)	Load Low Conn = ON (Default)	OFF/ON	Allows you to load the CONN.VLM (connection table) into the global block area. This will improve workstation performance, but it will add about 3KB to your global block size.
	Load Low IPXNCP = ON (Default)	OFF/ON	Allows you to load the IPXNCP.VLM into the global block area. This will improve workstation performance, but it will add about 4KB to your global block size.
	Signature Level = 1 (Default)	0–3	Enables packet signing, but will slow performance a little if you use it. The default of 1 means enabled but not preferred. The setting of 0 will prevent SECURITY.VLM from loading. If you have an extremely secure environment, you may need to use this VLM at the expense of some performance.

Migrating to the NetWare DOS Requester can provide immediate benefits, even before you migrate your servers to NetWare 4. By following the steps outlined in this chapter, you can greatly reduce the amount of time and effort required to upgrade you workstations. You can plan your workstation migration so that it is efficient and causes little impact to your user community.

Other clients, such as OS/2 and Macintosh workstations, can also take advantage of using the NDS client technology for their operating systems.

For more information about Client 32 for DOS/Windows and Client 32 for Windows 95, see your Novell documentation or visit the company's Web site at http://www.novell.com.

Migrating NetWare Servers to NetWare 4.11

QuickTips: Server Migration

▦ Upgrade to NetWare 4.11 from a   **214** previous version of NetWare

by using the method that suits your needs:

- If you do not need to maintain an exact copy of all the server's information, you can simply copy files from your current system to the NetWare 4.11 file system. This method transfers only the files, not the users, trustee assignments, and other network data, such as group memberships and printing configurations.

- If you need to preserve most or all of the data and network information, use one of the NetWare migration utilities. For some companies, the copying approach either may not migrate enough information when moving to NetWare 4.11 or may be too disruptive. Use the migration method when you need to retain users, trustee assignments, group memberships, and printing configurations, with a minimum of downtime and training.

▦ Migrate users, trustee assignments, and   **214** other network data

from earlier versions of NetWare by using one of NetWare's migration utilities. There are two types of migrations:

- The Across-the-Wire migration method (using MIGRATE.EXE), which requires three computers: a NetWare 3.1x server, a NetWare 4.11 server, and a workstation to perform the migration. Choose Across-the-Wire if you are upgrading to new hardware and are coming from NetWare 2.x or 3.x. Passwords are not migrated. You can generate passwords randomly or allow users to access the NetWare 4.11 server without a password the first time they log in.

- Another process is used to upgrade the hardware on an existing NetWare 4.*x* server. A utility called DSMaint was written to facilitate a hardware change. To change the hardware of an existing NetWare 4.*x* server, upgrade the NetWare 4.11 server. Backup the existing files and trustees, run DSMaint, upgrade the hardware, run DSMaint, then restore files and trustees. DSMAINT is now part of the INSTALL.NLM utility.

- Use DSMIGRATE.EXE if you want to model an NDS tree and then migrate a bindery from NetWare 3 to NDS. DSMIGRATE, licensed from Preferred Systems, Inc., is bundled as part of Novell's latest 32-bit NWADMIN utility (found in NetWare 4.11). DSMIGRATE is a subset of Preferred Systems' DS Standard product.

Migrate from NetWare 4.x to NetWare 4.11   222

by using one of these methods:

- Install NetWare 4.11 over your NetWare 4.1 server by using the NetWare 4.11 INSTALL program's Installation option.

- Use the NetWare 4.11 INSTALL program's Upgrade option.

- Use RCONSOLE to copy the files.

Migrate from NetWare 3 to NetWare 4.11   226

by using either the across-the-wire (MIGRATE.EXE) or the in-place (INSTALL.NLM) method. For in-place migration, use the NetWare 4.11 INSTALL program's Upgrade option.

Migrate from NetWare 2 to NetWare 4.11   239

by first migrating your servers to NetWare 3.12. Use the in-place migration utility to upgrade to NetWare 3.12. Then you can use a migration utility to upgrade from NetWare 3.12 to NetWare 4.11. Users running older versions of NetWare need to upgrade to NetWare 2.10, then upgrade to NetWare 3.12, then upgrade to NetWare 4.11.

YOU CAN UPGRADE to NetWare 4.11 from earlier versions of NetWare, including versions 4.1, 4.*x*, 3.1*x*, and 2.*x*. This chapter covers the options available for upgrading servers to NetWare 4.11 from these earlier versions of NetWare.

For information about migrating from non-NetWare operating systems, see Appendix C, which covers migrating from LAN Server, LAN Manager, and Banyan VINES.

Upgrading Methods

WHICH METHOD YOU use to upgrade from a previous version of NetWare depends on the information that you need to transfer from your existing NetWare system to a NetWare 4.11 server. You have two basic choices:

- Copy the files only. If you do not need to maintain an exact copy of the server's information, consider the option of simply copying files from your current system to the NetWare 4.11 file system. This method transfers only the files, not the users, trustee assignments, and other network data, such as group memberships and printing configurations. The transition to the new system may disrupt users' work, but copying is the easiest and quickest way to update a network with files only.

- Migrate the files and the trustee assignments. If you need to preserve most or all of the data and network information, use one of NetWare's migration utilities. For a majority of companies, the copying approach doesn't migrate enough information when moving to NetWare 4 or it is too disruptive. Use the migration method when you need to retain users, trustee assignments, group memberships, and printing configurations, with a minimum of downtime and training.

In order to be upgraded, your server must meet the NetWare 4.11 hardware and memory requirements. Also, whichever method you decide to use, you should take some steps to prepare for the upgrade process before you begin. These preliminary steps are described after the following discussion of NetWare 4.11 server requirements.

NetWare 4.11 Server Requirements

N ORDER TO upgrade from earlier versions of NetWare, your server's hardware and memory must meet the NetWare 4.11 requirements:

- At least a 386 processor (preferably a 486)

- 50MB of free disk space on the SYS volume

- At least 10 percent of free disk space on each volume to accommodate the enlarged directory and file allocation tables (FATs)

- Sufficient server memory to run the migration utility and upgrade to NetWare 4.11

A minimum NetWare 4.11 server setup includes a 15MB DOS partition, a 50MB NetWare partition, and 8MB of RAM. However, that 8MB of RAM will get the server up but not allow for much else. A better minimum setting for required RAM is 16MB. Similarly, the 50MB for the NetWare partition is the bare minimum for disk storage.

Servers with large disks and a large number of directories may need more memory to complete the upgrade than they need to run the server after the upgrade.

Preparing to Upgrade to NetWare 4.11

B EFORE COPYING OR migrating takes place, take these steps to make the overall process work more smoothly:

■ Record information concerning your server hardware, AUTOEXEC.NCF, STARTUP.NCF, and so on. This information may be necessary to complete the migration or to restore a server to its original state should something go wrong. Include information about the disk drives and controllers, network interface cards, and addresses, server names and addresses, and any files you need to boot your server. Make hard copies of this information and have it handy when you begin migrating or copying.

■ Make sure your server has the necessary amount of memory (as discussed in the previous section).

■ Obtain the latest versions of disk drivers and LAN drivers for your server system. You may experience difficulty with the server if you use older drivers. Load the disk drivers in the order of the controller boards. (See "Testing LAN Driver Compatibility" for a method for testing your LAN driver.)

Load the driver for the internal controller first, the driver for the first disk controller board second, and so on. If you do not follow the correct order, the system messages about your hard disks will be incorrect. Remember, in NetWare 2.1x and 2.2, the interrupt number is decimal. In NetWare 3.x and 4.x, the interrupt number is hexadecimal.

■ Review the information you have stored on the old server. Usually, you will find quite a bit of outdated information or programs that can be deleted. Removing unnecessary files saves time and space when you upgrade to the new server.

■ If you have planned any changes to your file and directory structure, implement those changes before proceeding. Salvage any deleted files you want to keep.

■ Back up your source server by using your regular backup software. No matter which method you use to upgrade, doing a full backup is a good precautionary measure. Also, test the restoration capabilities of your backup software.

Running **BINDFIX**

As mentioned in Chapter 8, you should run BINDFIX before and after your backup. You need sufficient rights to the SYS:SYSTEM directory to run BINDFIX.

BINDFIX deletes the mail subdirectories and trustee rights of users who no longer exist on the network and fixes incorrect records in the bindery. It also deletes the mail subdirectories for users who no longer exist. You may want to copy the NET$BIND.OLD and NET$BVAL.OLD files to a diskette in case you need to recover the original bindery later.

Testing **LAN Driver Compatibility**

Before proceeding to upgrade servers, you may want to test LAN drivers for compatibility. You can load them by typing

```
LOAD A:LANdriver
```

and pressing Enter. *LANdriver* is the name of your NetWare 3.12 LAN driver. Answer the LAN driver configuration information prompts by entering the information you previously recorded. If the LAN driver loads, it can communicate with the network board and is compatible with NetWare 4.11.

If the LAN driver does not load, the following message appears:

```
Module xxx.LAN not loaded
```

If you see this message, either the LAN driver is incompatible with NetWare 4.11 or the configuration is wrong. Check the configuration and try again.

If you're sure the configuration is correct, find out if you have the correct driver version. Unload the third-party LAN drivers to free more memory for the upgrade by typing

```
UNLOAD LANdriver
```

and pressing Enter. If the LAN driver is left loaded and bound to a protocol, extra memory may be needed as the upgraded SYS volume is mounted. The bindery will grow to record all servers on the network.

Do not upgrade if the LAN drivers are not compatible. Call the manufacturer to get an updated version of the driver.

Upgrading by Copying the Files

THE SIMPLEST AND quickest way to move information from one
server to another is to copy it. However, copying is not the method
to use if you require other information besides the data.
This method works for those who need only to get the data from the old
system to the new. For example, if you are making significant changes to your
server's setup (perhaps you have implemented a new naming standard or
designed a new file system structure) you may decide to copy files only, and
then assign rights, create printing configurations, and so on.

Requirements for Copying Files

Here are the requirements for the copying option:

- An account with enough rights to read the data you want to copy must
  exist in the old environment.

- NetWare 4.11 must already be installed and running on the other server,
  with sufficient rights to create the locations and copy the data where you
  want it to go.

- A workstation with sufficient memory to log in to either server must be
  set up as well. This workstation must have the appropriate protocol
  stack(s) loaded to facilitate copying the data.

- Both servers must be visible to the workstation.

Copying Files to the New Server

When you are ready to begin copying, log in to both servers. Map a drive to
the source server (NetWare 3) and the destination server (NetWare 4.11).
Then issue a copy command with appropriate parameters. For example, if you
mapped the old server to the drive letter O: and the new server to the drive
letter N:, you could use the DOS XCOPY command, like this:

```
XCOPY O:*.* N: /S/E
```

The /S parameter copies files in subdirectories; the /E parameter allows empty subdirectories to be created. Figure 11.1 shows an example of copying the data from one server to another.

FIGURE 11.1

Copying the data from one server to another using the DOS XCOPY command

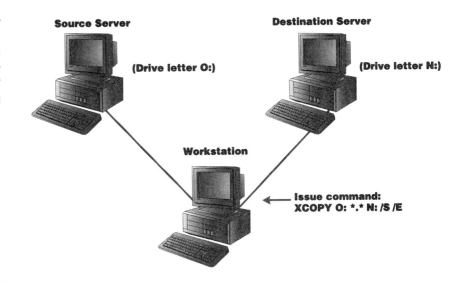

If you have problems seeing both servers from the workstation, check to see if both are using the same frame type. Novell changed the default frame type from 802.3 to 802.2.

If you cannot run both operating systems simultaneously or you want to use the existing hardware as the new operating system, you can use the following method:

1. Attach enough disk space to a workstation to hold the data, or add a tape backup device with enough capacity to hold the information you want to copy.

2. Copy the data from the old system to the appropriate media.

3. Bring up the new NetWare 4.11 system.

4. Copy the information back to your original hardware.

Figure 11.2 shows how this method works.

FIGURE II.2

Using a tape backup or workstation, you can temporarily store your server's data while you upgrade to NetWare 4.11.

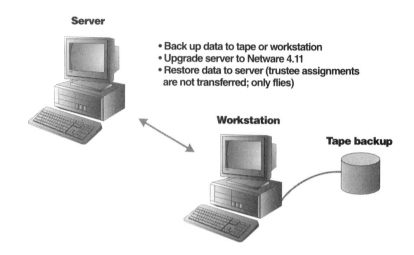

Server

• Back up data to tape or workstation
• Upgrade server to Netware 4.11
• Restore data to server (trustee assignments are not transferred; only flies)

Workstation

Tape backup

Remember, this upgrading method does not copy trustee rights, users, or any other network information. You should plan on spending time to assign appropriate rights and train the network users.

Using the Migration Utilities

F YOU NEED to preserve information during migration, and you do not want to disrupt the work of your network users, use a migration utility to upgrade your system. Novell provides several utilities for migrating user information as well as the server's existing data.

Choosing a Migration Utility

The upgrade method you use depends on what you plan to do with your existing hardware and the NetWare operating system version you're running.

- If you're running NetWare 3 or higher and you plan to maintain your existing hardware, use the Upgrade option in the NetWare 4.11 installation program (INSTALL.NLM).

- If you're planning to use new hardware, use the Across-the-Wire utility (AMU). This utility offers two options: across-the-wire (server-to-server) and same-server migration (which is not the same as the in-place migration method).

- If you're running NetWare 2.*x*, you can use either a special in-place method, 2XUPGRD, or AMU.

See Chapter 8 for a description of the across-the-wire and in-place migration methods, including their advantages and disadvantages.

Preparing to Use a Migration Utility

In addition to the procedures for preparing to upgrade to NetWare 4.11 described earlier in this chapter, you should complete these additional tasks before you use a migration utility:

- Check to see if you have a subdirectory depth of greater than 25 levels. The migration utilities do not migrate files deeper than 25 levels.

- Review your existing users and groups. Delete any unnecessary users or groups. Remove any users that no longer use the system or groups that are no longer being used.

- Review existing print queues and print servers. Delete or rename them as necessary. If you need additional queues or print servers, it is easier to create them in NetWare 4.11 after you migrate.

- Check for duplicate object names. When migrating, objects of the same name and type are merged. Consolidate names of users who exist under different names on different servers. For example, user Mark Peters might be MARK on one server and MPETERS on another server. If you upgraded both servers into the same context of an NDS tree, two User objects would be created for Mark Peters: MARK and MPETERS.

- Change the names of users with the same names on different servers that will be upgraded into the same context. For example, a user JANE might be on one server and a different user JANE on another server. Even though they are two different users, they would be merged into one NDS User object called JANE, and both users' access rights would merged as well.

- Change the name of objects with the same name, but different object types. Many sites have the same print queues and group names. Even though they are two different objects, NDS does not allow duplicate object names to exist in the same context. The first object is migrated; the second is not. In addition, check the destination server as well. You may find different objects with duplicate names if you are migrating into an existing context.

- Check your file-naming conventions. You may need to modify the length of directory and file names. Only files and directories that conform to the DOS naming convention (8+3) are migrated. You will also need to add name space support to any volume that contains files with long names. Macintosh and OS/2 files can still follow their respective naming conventions.

For more information about adding name space support, see ADD NAME SPACE in the Novell Utilities Reference.

- Obtain a copy of the NetWare 4.11 installation files. Usually this information is distributed on CD-ROM. You can obtain NetWare 4.11 on diskettes, but the installation or upgrade process with diskettes is much slower. The CD-ROM can be mounted as a NetWare volume, mounted as a DOS device, copied from the CD-ROM to a NetWare volume, or copied to a local hard disk. Mounting the CD-ROM as a NetWare volume or copying to a local hard disk makes the upgrade process run more quickly.

Migrating from Netware 4.x to Netware 4.11

F YOU ARE already running NetWare 4.x (NetWare 4.01, NetWare 4.02, or NetWare 4.1), you have three options for migrating to NetWare 4.11 (all variations):

- Install NetWare 4.11 over your NetWare 4.x server.

- Use the NetWare 4.11 installation program's Upgrade option.

- Use RCONSOLE to copy the files.

These options are described in the following sections.

Installing over Your NetWare 4.*x* Server

Use the following steps to install NetWare 4.11 over your NetWare 4.*x* server:

1. Down the NetWare 4.x server.

2. Load client software on the "downed" server. Attaching to NDS-only servers requires the latest VLM client or Client32 software on that server.

3. Log in to another server that contains the Netware 4.11 code, either on its hard drive or as a NetWare 4.11 CD volume that is mounted.

4. Map a drive to the NetWare 4.11 files and run INSTALL.BAT. You see the Netware 4 installation screen, as shown in Figure 11.3.

FIGURE 11.3

The NetWare 4.11 installation screen

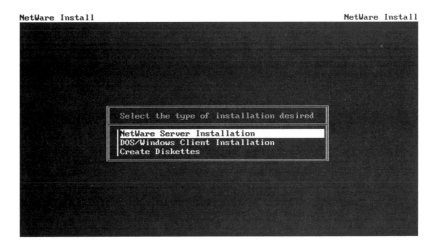

5. Select the NetWare Server Installation option. You see the screen shown in Figure 11.4.

FIGURE 11.4

Selecting the Net-
Ware 4.11 installation
option

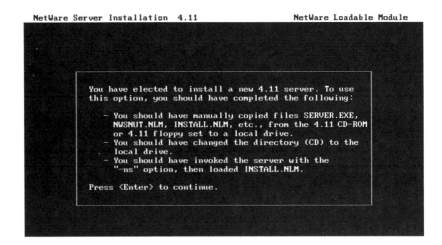

6. Proceed with the installation by following the directions on the screens.

Using the Upgrade Option to Migrate from NetWare 4.x

Another way to migrate from earlier NetWare 4 versions is to use the Net-
Ware 4.11 INSTALL program Upgrade option. This option copies new
NetWare 4.11 files onto the 4.x boot directory. It also copies SYSTEM
and PUBLIC files, SERVER.EXE, disk and LAN drivers, name space support modules, and other NLMs.

Follow these steps to use the Upgrade option:

1. Load the NetWare 4.11 INSTALL.NLM on the NetWare 4.x server that
you want to upgrade.

2. Choose Server Options. You see the screen shown in Figure 11.5.

3. Choose the Upgrade a 3.1x or 4.x server to 4.11 option.

4. Proceed with the installation by following the directions on the screens.

This method is similar to the one described in the previous section. However, NetWare 4.11 has a useful remote server login process that allows logins
to other servers to copy or install new files on the server.

FIGURE 11.5

To use the Upgrade option to NetWare 4.11, choose Server Options after running INSTALL.NLM.

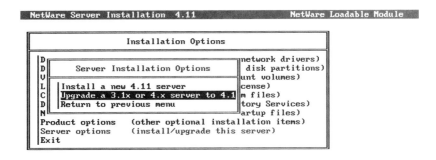

After running the upgrade, you may need to load RCONSOLE and copy files to the boot directory to update the boot files. You may need to copy or edit the following files:

- *.BAT (batch files)

- *.DSK (disk drivers)

- *.LAN (LAN drivers)

Using RCONSOLE to Migrate from NetWare 4.x

Another way to migrate from NetWare 4.x versions is to use RCONSOLE to copy the files. This method is similar to using INSTALL.NLM, but requires a few more steps.

Since you're using a DOS client, your NetWare 4.11 installation files should reside on the client. The REMOTE.NLM and RSPX.NLM need to be loaded on the server. RCONSOLE.EXE and associated files can be on the server or DOS client.

Run RCONSOLE and follow the steps in the previous section, but substitute the location of the installation files from the DOS client.

NDS and Mixed Server Environments

NDS in NetWare 4.11 is backward-compatible with NetWare 4.01, 4.02, and 4.10. However, the NDS schema has changed in NetWare 4.11. If you are running combinations of NetWare 4.01, 4.02, 4.10, and 4.11 in the same NDS tree, the NetWare 4.11 NDS schema must be distributed to all NetWare 4.*x* servers in your tree for NDS to run reliably.

You can distribute the schema in one of two ways:

- In your NDS tree, install NetWare 4.11 on a new server or upgrade an existing NetWare 4.*x* to NetWare 4.11. If all servers are running properly, the new schema will be automatically distributed to all current NetWare 4.*x* servers in your NDS tree.

- Run the DSREPAIR utility. If you are not installing or upgrading a new NetWare 4.11 server, or if any NetWare 4.*x* servers were not running properly when you installed the new NetWare 4.11 server, you can use the DSREPAIR utility to place the new schema on the designated NetWare 4.*x* servers.

If you are upgrading into a large context or have many objects to upgrade, placing objects into NDS may take a few minutes. Be patient!

Migrating NetWare 3.1x to NetWare 4.11

Y OU CAN UPGRADE from NetWare 3.1*x* to NetWare 4.11 by using the Across-the-Wire or In-Place migration method. The precise steps for migration vary, depending on your environment, hardware, and other factors. The following sections describe the general procedures for upgrading.

Refer to the NetWare 4.11 manuals and documentation for specific information about migrating from your NetWare 3.1x system.

Across-the-Wire Migration from NetWare 3.1x to NetWare 4.11

Three computers are needed to upgrade to NetWare 4.11 from NetWare 3.1x versions using the across-the-wire migration method:

■ A source server running NetWare 3.1*x*

■ A destination server already running NetWare 4.11

■ A DOS client workstation with NetWare client software loaded

The MIGRATE.EXE utility runs on the DOS client. The DOS client must be able to see both servers to perform a migration. An example of this setup is shown in Figure 11.6.

FIGURE 11.6

Three computers are needed to use the across-the-wire migration utility.

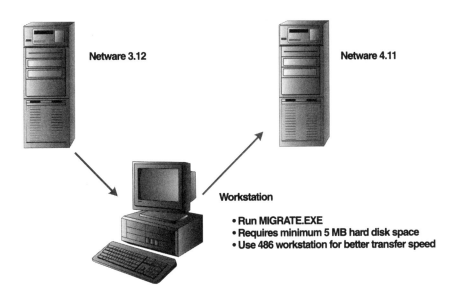

Netware 3.12

Netware 4.11

Workstation

• **Run MIGRATE.EXE**
• **Requires minimum 5 MB hard disk space**
• **Use 486 workstation for better transfer speed**

The across-the-wire method moves all the files through the DOS client. For this reason, the DOS client should be a very fast PC with a 486/33 CPU or faster, if possible. In addition, the DOS client needs to have at least 640KB of memory (with 480KB or more of free memory) and 5MB of free disk space on either a hard disk or another network drive that can attach to both the source server and destination server.

Network speed and packet sizes determine how quickly a migration occurs. Using a faster network reduces the time it takes for information to migrate. Larger packet sizes increase migration speed by allowing more data to pass through the network each time a packet is sent.

Before running the utility, make sure the workstation's CONFIG.SYS file includes the following line:

```
FILES = 20
```

Make sure as well that the NET.CFG file includes the following line:

```
PROTOCOL IPXODI IPX RETRY COUNT = 60
```

Load your LAN drivers on the DOS workstation and run the NetWare Client for DOS (VLMs).

A copy of NetWare 4.11 is needed to obtain the migration utility (MIGRATE.EXE). A subdirectory for migration exists on the destination Net-Ware 4.11 server if you selected that option during installation. You can copy the MIGRATE.EXE utility from the NetWare 4.11 subdirectory.

Make a subdirectory on the client workstation called MIGRATE, and then change to that subdirectory. The migration files are located in the MIGRATE subdirectory on the CD-ROM or destination server. Copy the files, including subdirectories, to the MIGRATE directory on the client workstation.

NetWare 3.x Migration Bindery Connection

A bindery connection from the DOS client to both servers is necessary. When you use the MIGRATE.EXE utility, it is imperative to have only bindery connections, because the utility depends on Bindery Services in order to work properly. To ensure only bindery connections, log in to the destination server by using the Bindery Services (/B when using VLMs) option. For example, you would type

```
LOGIN SRV1/SUPERVISOR /B
```

in bindery mode to log in. If you're running Client32, choose bindery connection from the Connection tab or use the MIGRATE utility to log in to the Net-Ware 4.11 server. Bindery mode is used when selecting the destination server through the utility.

The utility will not let you log in to the destination server if you are already logged in as an NDS client. If you are authenticated to the destination server as an NDS client, you must log in with a bindery connection or log out and use the MIGRATE utility to log in.

The MIGRATE utility places all objects being migrated into one single context. This context is set though the utility on the destination server. Each NetWare 4.11 destination server must have a read/write partition placed on it for Bindery Services to be enabled.

NetWare 3.x Migration Information Options

The MIGRATE utility allows you to select the information that will be migrated. The default is to migrate all the information. Table 11.1 shows the information that you can include or exclude, as well as comments about that information.

TABLE 11.1 Information Migrated with the MIGRATION Utility	**DATA TYPE**	**DESCRIPTION**	**COMMENTS**
	All Information	Migrates all the information listed in this table.	
	Data Files	Migrates all data files and the DOS and NetWare attributes for files and directories.	Will not overwrite a file or directory with one of the same name.
	Trustee Assignments	Migrates rights that are assigned to users and groups for directories and files (automatic conversion to NetWare 4.11 rights).	With this selection, you must also choose Users, Groups, and Data Files if they do not already exist on the NetWare 4.11 server.
	Users	Migrates user account names, user print job configurations (PRINTCON.DAT), and user login scripts.	Will not overwrite existing items on the NetWare 4.11 server.
	User Restrictions	Migrates user account restrictions.	Does not include user volume restrictions. If this type is chosen, Users must also be selected. Will not overwrite existing restrictions on the NetWare 4.11 server.

TABLE 11.1	DATA TYPE	DESCRIPTION	COMMENTS
Information Migrated with the MIGRATION Utility (continued)	Groups	Migrates the group members and group trustee rights for directories and files.	If a group from the source server already exists on the NetWare 4.11 server, the source and destination groups will be merged.
	Default Account Restrictions	Migrates default account restrictions.	Overwrites any existing information on the NetWare 4.11 server.
	Accounting Information	Migrates the accounting method chosen for charging network services to individual user accounts.	Overwrites any existing information on the NetWare 4.11 server.
	Print Queues and Print Servers	Migrates NetWare print queues and print servers and their corresponding setup information.	The source and destination information will be merged.

Migrating NetWare 3.x Directories

If you are migrating a file directory that has the same name and path as a directory that already exists on the destination server, the files from both directories are merged under the current destination directory name. The directory structure and files are migrated and become a part of the NetWare 4.11 file system. If necessary, modify the organization on the destination server after all the source servers are migrated.

Review directory security. Set any new directory and file attributes. If you have set up your login scripts so that users have drive mappings to directories in which they have no rights, those users will receive an error message when they log in.

Migrating NetWare 3.x Files

NetWare 3.x system files are not migrated to NetWare 4.11. Any file (newer or older) on a source server that has the same name as one that exists on the destination server is not copied to the destination server. An error message appears on the screen during the migration and is also written to the migration error report to let you know that a file by that name already exists on the destination server. You may want to overwrite the incoming file if it is older. You can also keep the file either by renaming it and copying it to the NetWare 4.11 server or by manually copying it over the old file after migration is completed.

Also, because all the data passes over the network, this process should be done during a weekend or late at night when the least amount of traffic is on the network. Large volumes may take three or four hours to migrate. If possible, choose a long weekend if you have large amounts of data to migrate (5GB or more).

User volume restrictions are not migrated. To set up the maximum amount of disk space a user can use, use the NetAdmin utility in NetWare 4.11 after you have finished the migration.

If your network includes workstations that use an operating system that supports long file names, make sure you have loaded the appropriate name space module. To ensure name space support each time the server is brought up, load the appropriate name space module in the NetWare 4.11 server's STARTUP.NCF file.

Migrating NetWare 3.x Login Scripts

The NetWare 3.x system login script is not migrated. If users are running in bindery mode or using NETX, you need to re-create the NET$LOG.DAT file. This can be done by copying the file from the source server or by re-creating the file with an ASCII text editor.

You can create a NetWare 4 container login script from a NetWare 3 system login script by using a Windows-type text editor. Copy the contents of the system login script onto the Clipboard, and then paste them into the container login script. Alternatively, you can use an INCLUDE statement to reference the NET$LOG.DAT file (if created), but make sure that the statement references an INCLUDE file located locally, not a remote file.

The majority of login commands work the same under NetWare 4.11 as they did under previous NetWare versions. External commands may not execute properly until all drive mappings have been completed. A work-around is to execute the external program from a batch file after executing the login script.

User login scripts are migrated to the destination server, but are not placed into the NDS database. The MIGRATE utility creates the UIMPORT.CTL and IMPORT.DAT files in SYS:SYSTEM on the destination server. These files are used by UIMPORT to place user login scripts into NDS.

The conversion of login scripts is not dynamic. If a reference is made to the server's name and that name has changed, you will need to edit each login script to change that reference. If the server name or directory path names have changed, examine each user login script after the migration and make any necessary corrections.

Migrating NetWare 3.x Passwords

Passwords are not included in the across-the-wire migration. The MIGRATE utility allows you to assign passwords that are generated randomly for all migrated users or to allow users to log in to the new system once without a password. During their first login, they are prompted to enter a password.

Randomly generated passwords are stored in a file called NEW.PWD in SYS:SYSTEM on the NetWare 4.11 server. They can be accessed only by the Admin user or equivalent. If you use random passwords, you need to find a way to distribute those passwords. For example, you might sort the passwords with a word processor into alphabetical order and give them to the users as they come into work. Then the users would change their passwords immediately upon logging in.

Migrating NetWare 3.x Printing

Even though you migrated all information or specifically included print queues and print servers, the MIGRATE utility does not migrate these items. This migration is done by another utility provided with NetWare 4.11 called MIGPRINT. If you copied all the files to the MIGRATE subdirectory on the DOS client, MIGPRINT.EXE was copied also.

The MIGPRINT utility allows you to migrate printers, print queues, print job configurations, and print servers from the source server into NDS. This utility has the following requirements:

- An NDS connection from the DOS client to the destination server

- A bindery connection from the source server

- The user must have Admin privileges to the context where the print services are to be migrated

- A search drive mapping to SYS:SYSTEM/NLS on the destination

Several command line parameters must be entered at the time of execution:

```
MIGPRINT /S=SrcSrvr /D=DstSrvr [/Vol=QueueVol] [/O=OutputFile]
```

where SrcSrvr is the source server and DstSrvr is the destination server. The other two parameters are optional. MIGPRINT takes advantage of Net-Ware 4.11's ability to locate print queues on a volume other than the SYS volume. If you don't want to migrate to the default SYS volume, replace the queue volume with the name of another volume. The /O parameter permits you to specify a different output file.

NetWare 4.11 no longer supports dedicated print servers separate from the file server. You need to move these services back onto the file server or find third-party solutions.

NetWare 4.11 has new remote printer software. NPRINTER replaces RPRINTER. Plan on updating remote printers as part of the upgrade. At some sites, the new remote printer software is found in the login subdirectory. This way, when remote printers attach to the network, they can run the new soft-ware. Also, keeping the software in one location makes it easier to manage.

Third-party printing solutions may need to be reconfigured after migration. Many third-party products store information about firmware in the printer's LAN card or memory. Upgrading may cause that information to be incorrect. Most of these products have utilities to take care of this type of situation. It's a good idea to test the ability of these printers to print after completing a migration.

See Chapter 12 and Appendix D for more information about configuring network printing.

Migrating NetWare 3.x Applications

Check third-party applications to see if they run properly. See if you can run the application, print from it, and save data within it. Some DOS applications don't work when installed on volumes that have more than 32MB of disk space. In some cases, you can make these applications work either by restricting the application's directory on the destination server with DSPACE or by using the MAP command to make the directory path a fake root. Appli-cations may not work properly because some of the files may not have been copied during migration.

NetWare 4.11 introduces new menu utilities. You may need to update or recompile menu applications to work in the new environment.

Other NetWare 3.x Migration Steps

The following are some other steps you may need to take for your migration from NetWare 3.x to NetWare 4.11:

- If the server's name is used in the users' NET.CFG files, you need to change it to the new NetWare 4.11 server name.

- If you have workstations that boot from diskettes, create new boot diskettes for each workstation.

- Copy the NetWare 4.11 utilities to other servers on the network. The NetWare 4.11 public utilities will run on servers running NetWare 3.x. Login scripts on the NetWare 4.11 server may not execute properly unless you copy the NetWare 4.11 login programs to all NetWare LOGIN directories on your network.

- Distribute your newly migrated objects to new containers. Migration places all objects into one container. This may not be the desired location for these objects. Use the NDS administration tools to move objects to their new locations.

- Check user account restrictions, time restrictions, and station restrictions to verify that they were properly migrated. Also, verify that the accounting charge rates are set up correctly if you plan to use the server accounting feature.

Running the MIGRATE Utility

When you are ready to run the MIGRATE utility, follow these steps:

1. If your client workstation does not have a CD-ROM device, create a MIGRATE directory on your client workstation and copy the MIGRATE files to your client workstation.

The BMIGRATE utility is a variation of the MIGRATE utility designed for migration of Banyan VINES systems. The steps in this section apply to running BMIGRATE.EXE as well as MIGRATE.EXE. See Appendix C for more information about migrating to NetWare 4.11 from Banyan VINES.

2. From the client workstation, start the MIGRATE utility. Change to the directory that contains the utility files, type **MIGRATE** (or **BMIGRATE** if you are migrating from Banyan VINES, as discussed in Appendix C), and press Enter. The Select the Type of Migration menu appears.

3. From the Select the Type of Migration menu, choose Across-the-Wire Migration.

4. From the Select the Source LAN Type menu, choose a source LAN type.

5. From the Select the Destination LAN Type menu, choose a destination LAN type.

Creating the MIGRATE Configuration Form

When selecting a source and destination, the MIGRATE utility does version checking according to the source type and destination type you selected.

1. Under Step 1, Configure the migration utility, press the ↓ key on the configuration form to accept the default working directory, or press Enter to specify another working directory. Follow the Quick Help to specify a different working directory.

The working directory is where the source directory information and the migration reports are stored. Data files are not stored here. You need 5MB of free disk space in this directory. Usually, the working directory is located on the hard disk drive of the workstation, but you can also put it on a network drive.

If you are using a network drive instead of a hard drive, you must have Create, Read, Write, and File Scan rights in this directory. If this directory doesn't exist, the utility creates it for you on your hard drive.

2. Under Step 1 on the configuration form, press Enter to select an error/ warning action. All errors are listed in the error report file, regardless of the option you select.

Choose Pause after warnings and errors if you want the utility to stop after each warning and error and prompt you to continue with the migration. Each time an error is reported and you are prompted, you can choose to discontinue the prompting. Choose Do not pause after warnings and errors if you do not want to be prompted after each warning and error.

Unless you plan to watch the entire migration process, it's best to choose not to pause after errors and warnings. This way, the migration process can run unattended. After the migration, you can review the report file, which shows each error generated during the migration (the error file is created regardless of which method you choose).

3. Under Step 2, Define the source server, on the configuration form, press Enter to display a list of source servers.

4. Choose the source server form which you want to migrate. This selection must match the source type you specified in step 5 of the previous procedure. When migrating multiple source servers, only one source server can be migrated at a time.

5. Under Step 2 on the configuration form, press Enter again to display categories of information you want to migrate. Only files that conform to DOS naming conventions (8+3) are migrated.

6. Using the F5 key, mark the information you want to migrate. Follow the Quick Help for details on how to select information. Mark as many categories as necessary. If you select All Information, all categories are migrated.

7. Under Step 2 on the configuration form, press Enter again to display a list of source volumes on the source server from which you want to migrate data. Mark source volumes to migrate only if you are migrating data files or trustee assignments on those volumes.

You must select a source volume to migrate if you select any of the following categories to migrate: All Information, Data Files, or Trustee Assignments.

8. Under Step 3, Define the destination server, on the configuration form, press Enter to display a list of servers on the network.

9. Choose the destination server that you want to migrate the source server to. This selection must match the destination type you specified in step 5 in the previous procedure.

10. Under Step 3 on the configuration form, press Enter to select a volume, and then press Enter again to specify the destination volume and directory on the NetWare 4.11 server. Destination volumes that match the source volumes are displayed as the default. Press the Ins key to see a list of available volumes and directories on the NetWare 4.11 server.

If you specify a directory that does not exist on the NetWare 4.11 server, you are prompted to create it. Volumes must already be created on the destination server before you can migrate data to them. The volume organization, as well as the directory structure, is migrated. You can modify the organization on the destination server after all the source servers have been migrated.

11. Press Enter when you complete the destination path of the source volume.

12. Continue to specify destination paths if you have multiple source volumes.

13. Press the F10 key when you finish filling out the Volumes' destination field.

14. Optionally, under Step 3 on the configuration form, press Enter and choose a password option.

If you choose Assign random passwords, new passwords are given only to users that had a password on the source server. Only users with rights to SYS:SYSTEM have access to this file. Users cannot log in until they are given their passwords from this list.

15. To proceed with the migration, press F10 to display the Select a Migration Action menu.

16. Choose a migration action, and then press Enter.

At this point, you can choose to migrate all the information you selected from the source server to the destination server, and the migration will start automatically. All information about the migration is displayed on the screen and entered into a report file, which you can review later, as described in the next section.

The NDS tree information you selected is copied to the working directory and translated into the NetWare 4.11 format; it is then copied to the NetWare 4.11 server. The data files are migrated directly to the destination 4 server.

When the migration is complete, the utility displays the following message:

```
Migration from the source server to the destination
     server is complete. Press <Enter> to continue.
```

Viewing the **MIGRATE** Migration Report

Once the migration process is completed, you can view the migration report by choosing View Migration Reports from the Select a Migration Action menu. Select the report for the migration you completed and press Enter.

The report resides in the working directory that you specified earlier. Use the report to help complete and customize definitions, attributes, and access privileges on the NetWare 4.11 server. If you find errors on your destination server after the migration, locate them in the migration report file and determine what actions to take on the destination server to correct the errors.

The report file is an ASCII text file that consists of the following:

- Summary information of the NDS tree import phase (migrating NDS tree data from the source server to the working directory)

- Summary information of the NDS tree export phase (migrating NDS tree data from the working directory to the destination server)

- Listing of each item in each category that was read from the source server

- Listing of each item in each category that was written to or created on the destination server

- The number of errors that occurred during the migration

To exit the report, press Esc once. To return to the Select a Migration Action menu, press Esc again. To exit the utility, choose Exit (return to DOS).

Verifying the Results and Completing the Migration

After the migration is complete, you can check the NetWare 4.11 server and perform the following completion and verification checks:

- Set up user login scripts.

- Run third-party applications.

- Examine the files in merged directories and reorganize them if necessary.

- Set up print queues and print servers.

- Check user restrictions and accounting charge rates to make sure your system is configured the way you want it.

- Set any new directory and file attributes.

If you chose to assign random passwords, you may want to print the NEW.PWD file and distribute the password information to your users. The users should change their passwords immediately.

The report, an ASCII text file, shows passwords sorted by date. If users were migrated from more than one server, the current password is the last one listed on the report.

In-Place Migration from NetWare 3.x to NetWare 4.11

For in-place migration from NetWare 3.x to NetWare 4.11, use the NetWare 4.11 INSTALL program Upgrade option. This procedure is the same as the one described for upgrading from earlier versions of NetWare 4. You load the NetWare 4.11 INSTALL.NLM on the NetWare server that you want to upgrade, choose Server Options, and then continue with the installation by following the directions on the screens.

After running the upgrade, you may need to load RCONSOLE and copy files to the boot directory to update the boot files. See "Using the Upgrade Option to Migrate from NetWare 4.x" earlier in this chapter for details.

Migrating NetWare 2.1x to NetWare 4.11

NOVELL NO LONGER sells the NetWare 2.1x product line, but there are undoubtedly sites still running this version. If you want to upgrade your 2.1x system to NetWare 4.11, two options are available, in-place and across-the-wire. If you need to do an in-place migration from NetWare 2.1x or 2.2 servers, you must first upgrade to NetWare 3.12.

Users running older versions of NetWare need to upgrade to NetWare 2.10, then upgrade to NetWare 3.12, then upgrade to NetWare 4.11.

In order to use the in-place utility, your NetWare 2.1x or 2.2 server must meet the hardware and memory requirements of NetWare 4.11, which are discussed at the beginning of this chapter.

Preparing for Migrating from NetWare 2.x to NetWare 3.x

Be sure to follow the general suggestions for preparing for migration given in Chapter 8 and at the beginning of this chapter. For example, you should back up your server, as well as do a full backup of the bindery and data files. You should also test the restore capability before continuing. To be safe, make several backups of the bindery and data files. Run BINDFIX before and after your backup.

Remember to obtain configuration information on the server. Make sure you have the server name, LAN configuration information (including the network address), and disk channel configuration information. Write it down and keep it near you. You'll refer to it later as you begin the migration or if you experience some difficulty and need to restore your configuration.

Assigning an IPX Internal Network Number

During the upgrade process, you will be asked to assign an IPX internal network number to your server. The IPX internal network number does not exist in a NetWare 2 network. In NetWare 3 and 4, it is a logical network number that identifies the individual server. This number must be different from other IPX external network numbers (for cabling systems) or IPX internal network numbers (for NetWare 3 or 4 servers).

The IPX internal network number for each server must be a unique hexadecimal (base 16, using numerals 0 through 9 and letters A through F), one to eight digits long. If your organization has adopted naming and numbering standards, obtain that information prior to migrating. See Chapter 3 for more information about naming standards.

Deciding which Upgrade Options to Use

Before starting the upgrade, you should decide which upgrade options you want to use. You have the following upgrade choices:

- Running the upgrade interactively or as a batch process

- Whether to create space for a DOS partition

- Whether to assign randomly generated or fixed passwords to users

- Whether to run the /BINDERY option

If you run the upgrade interactively, you are prompted to continue from one phase of the upgrade to the next, whether to create space for a DOS partition, and whether to have the NLM create and assign new passwords. All status messages and error messages are displayed. If you are a first-time installer, use the interactive method so you can follow each phase of the upgrade.

If you run the upgrade utility as a batch process, only error and status messages are displayed. The upgrade automatically proceeds through the phases without any input from the user. Use the parameters described in Table 11.2 to specify options, such as creating space for a DOS partition and creating and assigning new passwords to users. If you do not specify any options, the defaults are used. You are not prompted for these options later. If you are an experienced installer and have run several upgrades, use the batch process method, especially if you are upgrading several servers.

TABLE 11.2	**PARAMETER**	**EXPLANATION**
Parameters for Running the NetWare 2.x to NetWare 3.x Upgrade	B *or* BATCH	Runs the upgrade in batch mode.
	B2 *or* BATCH	Runs the upgrade in batch mode, not pausing for noncritical errors.
	BINDERY	Skips to Phase 4 to upgrade the NetWare 2 bindery only.
	F *or* FAST	Skips the lengthy memory and free disk space check.
	H, ?, *or* HELP	Shows a list of parameters.
	NORESTART	Does not save restart data to disk.
	PASSWORD=	Assigns a fixed password to all users.
	P0	Does not create a DOS partition.
	P*x*	Creates a DOS partition on the disk containing volume SYS (*x*=partition size in megabytes). The size range is 0 to 32MB. The default is 15MB.
	R+	Assigns randomly generated passwords.
	R-	Does not assign random passwords (default).

You should create a DOS partition if you do not have one. A 15MB DOS partition is recommended for NetWare 4.11. The upgrade utility can create the space (between 0 and 32MB) for a DOS partition on the disk that contains the SYS volume. Booting the server from a DOS partition is significantly faster than booting from a diskette. Many servers cannot access a DOS partition from an external hard disk.

If you use the /BINDERY option, you can restart the upgrade, skipping directly to the bindery phase. The NLM looks for the NetWare 2 bindery files (NET$BIND.SYS and NET$BVAL.SYS) in the SYS:SYSTEM directory and merges them into the NetWare 3 bindery (NET$OBJ.SYS, NET$PROP.SYS, and NET$VAL.SYS). If your NetWare 2 bindery files are corrupt, simply rename the NET$BIND.OLD and NET$BVAL.OLD files (created when you ran the BINDFIX utility) with the .SYS extension, and then restart the upgrade with the /BINDERY option.

When you use the /BINDERY option, trustee assignments for all users except SUPER-VISOR and GUEST are lost. Use the NetWare 3 GRANT utility or the NetWare 4.11 RIGHTS utility to restore trustee rights.

Running the Upgrade Process

Allow sufficient time to upgrade your server. Time requirements depend on the number of hard disks, not including mirrored disks and the amount of disk space in use. If you have several hard disks and a lot of disk space is in use, the upgrade can take several hours.

When you have completed your preparations, follow these steps for in-place migration:

1. Bring down the 2.1x or 2.2 server by typing **down** at the system console.

Do not down the server by simply turning off its power. This could add errors during the migration process. Use the DOWN command so that files are closed properly.

2. After the server responds that it is down, wait several minutes to be sure that all transactions to the system files are complete before turning the machine off. Once all disk activity has stopped, you can shut the server off.

3. Reboot the server from DOS and run the NetWare 2.1x or 2.2 VRE-PAIR utility on each volume.

4. Create an upgrade diskette from the NetWare 4.11 CD-ROM. You also need to copy the DOS FDISK and FORMAT utilities to the diskette. In addition, copy the needed upgrade files from the CD-ROM. The instructions on the CD are incorrect. Refer to the README file on the NetWare 4 for newer instructions. This diskette needs to be bootable.

5. Insert the bootable upgrade diskette into drive A:. Reboot the server. The computer now boots with the version of DOS on the upgrade diskette.

If you are creating a DOS partition on the hard disk, record the information you enter in the following steps. You will need to use this information again later.

6. With the upgrade diskette in drive A:, load the NetWare 3.12 operating system.

7. When you are prompted for the file server's name, type the server name and press Enter. You might want to use your NetWare 2.1x or 2.2 server name. That way, you do not need to change any login files, map statements, or batch files.

8. When you are prompted to assign an IPX internal network number to the server, type the IPX internal network number you defined for this server and press Enter.

9. When you see the server's disk drivers, replace the NetWare 2.1x or 2.2 disk driver with an appropriate one for NetWare 3.12. To decide which disk drivers to load, look at the configuration information you recorded.

10. If you used Macintosh name space, load the Macintosh name space support. Loading the Macintosh name space module ensures that all volumes are mounted properly during the migration.

11. You can now run the upgrade interactively or as a batch process. To run the upgrade interactively, type the following at the console prompt:

```
LOAD A: 2XUPGRDE
```

and press Enter. To run the upgrade as a batch process, type

```
LOAD A: 2XUPGRDE /B
```

and press Enter.

You can use the parameters listed in Table 11.2. For example, if you want to run the upgrade as a batch process, create a 20MB DOS partition on the disk containing volume SYS, assign randomly generated passwords, and type

```
LOAD A: 2XUPGRDE /B P20 R+
```

Remember, if you do not specify any options, the defaults are used. You are not prompted for these options later.

During the upgrade process, a calculation is made to determine if there is enough memory and disk space to complete the upgrade before the upgrade continues. After all the disks have been upgraded, volume SYS is mounted and the bindery is upgraded. The NetWare 2 bindery is merged into the newly created NetWare 3.12 bindery.

If the SYS volume cannot be mounted, the NetWare 2 bindery will not be upgraded. For example, if insufficient server memory is in the cache buffers memory pool, the SYS volume will not mount. This happens because the Permanent and Alloc memory pools do not release memory back to the cache buffers. It is remedied by rebooting the server or adding more memory.

If you chose to create a DOS partition and there is not enough space on your disk to create a DOS partition, the upgrade stops with the following message:

```
This NetWare server has insufficient free hard disk
space to complete the upgrade. The In-Place Upgrade pro-
cess is now being aborted.
```

Reboot the NetWare 2.1x server and delete unnecessary files to free more space on the disk. Then down the server and restart the upgrade process. After you create the DOS partition, the upgrade process proceeds.

Finishing Up the NetWare 2.x Migration

Once the server is upgraded, follow these steps to complete the migration process:

1. Down the server and use FDISK to create a DOS partition.

2. Leave the upgrade diskette in drive A and reboot the server.

3. Make the DOS partition bootable by formatting the disk with a /S parameter.

4. Copy an ASCII editor to the boot partition.

5. Make a directory on the server for a place to copy the NetWare files. Change to that directory and copy the 3.12 files there. These files can be obtained from the 4.11 CD-ROM. Run the INSTALL program from the 4.11 CD-ROM and choose the Create Diskettes option.

6. Select the option to upgrade from 2.*x* files in the size of floppy diskette you have. The files are copied onto diskette and then copied to the subdirectory on the server.

7. Boot the NetWare 3.12 server by typing:

   SERVER

   and pressing Enter.

8. Load the appropriate disk drivers and LAN drivers.

9. Load the INSTALL.NLM from the C drive and select System Options.

10. Choose Copy System and Public Files from the Available System Options menu. Insert diskettes as prompted. The following NetWare 2 files are not compatible with NetWare 4.11 and should be deleted:

LARCHIVE.EXE	NET$BIND.OLD
LRESTORE.EXE	NET$BVAL.OLD
MACBACK.EXE	NET$ERR.SYS
NARCHIVE.EXE	NET$OS.EXE
NRESTORE.EXE	NET$DOS.SYS
NET$BIND.SYS	NET$MSG.SYS
NET$BVAL.SYS	NET$REC.DAT
VAP files (*.VAP, *.HLD, *.VP?)	

Once the server is running NetWare 3.12, use the NetWare 4.11 installation program to move the server to NetWare 4.11. See "Migrating NetWare 3.1*x* to NetWare 4.11" earlier in this chapter for instructions.

Troubleshooting Migration Problems

A FTER MIGRATION, YOU may need to reinstall third-party programs that don't work so that they will work properly under NetWare 4.11. You may also need to enter new paths in the setup files for third-party applications. You may need to reinstall the application if it has an .EXE file that did not migrate or if the application is path-specific and you have changed the path structure during migration.

Some DOS applications don't work when installed on volumes that have more than 32MB of disk space. You may be able to make them work by restricting the application's directory on the destination server with Object Manager (which replaces DSPACE). You can also try making the directory a fake root with MAP.

Any directories that were merged may contain unrelated files. You may need to clean up those directories.

If you have menus set up, you may need to run a menu conversion program so your menus function properly under NetWare 4.11.

This chapter described the options and general steps for migrating to Net-Ware 4.11 from a previous version of NetWare. If you prepare for migration properly, you will be successful in your upgrade to NetWare 4.11. For more details on running the INSTALL and MIGRATE utilities, refer to Novell's NetWare 4.11 documentation. For information about migrating from other network operating systems, see Appendix C.

Day-to-Day
Operations

PART

3

Implementing Print Services in NetWare 4

QuickTips: NetWare Printing

at the highest possible container object (OU) level to support the most number of users. The three NDS print objects are Print Queue (or Queue), Print Server, and Printer. You must create at least one of each of these objects and assign the appropriate relationship between them to define the printing infrastructure in the network.

so that network printers are placed close to the people who will use them. Some printer configurations are more flexible than others. You can consider five printer configurations:

- Non-network workstation printer: A local printer, with the user sending print jobs from a stand-alone computer. The printer is not shared by other network users. Use this configuration only if you need to set up a special-purpose workstation and printer combination.

- Network workstation printer: A printer, designated as a NetWare printer, attached to a workstation. In this configuration, the workstation must always be powered on (but not necessarily logged in) and running the NPRINTER.EXE program.

- Network server printer: A printer that is connected to a server. In this configuration, the server must run the NPRINTER.NLM program. This configuration is not recommended if the printer cannot be placed close to the users (perhaps the server with the printer is in a locked room for security purposes) or when the printer will be subject to heavy use (because the processing the print jobs will slow the server's performance).

- Network-direct printer, remote printer mode: A printer that is connected directly to the network, through a hardware printer device. See Appendix D for instructions on setting up network-direct printing in remote printer mode.

- Network-direct printer, queue server mode: A printer that is connected directly to the network and acts like a special-purpose print server for the printer. See Appendix D for instructions on setting up network-direct printing in queue server mode.

We recommend that you configure the network printers as queue servers, because they are easy to manage and use. In many cases, queue server mode will place the least load on a NetWare server.

Set up NetWare print services for the first time   267

with the Quick Setup feature in the PCONSOLE utility. This feature creates the NDS print objects and makes all the necessary assignments automatically. Run PCONSOLE and select the Quick Setup option. Choose names for the print objects. Then load PSERVER.NLM at the server, using the new Print Server object's name. Finally, load NPRINTER.EXE at the workstation with the printer, or load NPRINTER.NLM at the server with the printer.

When you are migrating printing information from NetWare 3   269

consider the PRINTCON and PRINTDEF databases.

- With Across-the-Wire migration, you need to re-create the PRINTCON and PRINTDEF information in NDS after the migration. The PRINTCON and PRINTDEF databases are copied from their respective areas to the same areas on the destination server; they are not migrated directly to NDS.

- With In-Place migration, the PRINTCON and PRINTDEF information is migrated directly into NDS. After migration, you need to run PUP-GRADE.NLM (from INSTALL or from the server console) to convert the PRINTCON and PRINTDEF databases for NetWare 4.

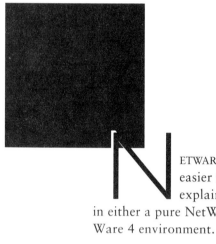

ETWARE 4.11 INCLUDES new printing features that make it easier to set up and use network print services. This chapter explains how to plan and implement NetWare print services in either a pure NetWare 4 environment or a mixed NetWare 3 and NetWare 4 environment.

New Print Features in NetWare 4.11

ETWARE 4.11 includes a number of new print features. The NetWare Administrator (NWADMIN) utility now includes a Print Services Quick Setup option under the Tools menu. This option provides functionality similar to the Quick Setup option in the PCONSOLE utility. The Print Services Quick Setup option enables you to easily create and associate Print Server, Printer, and Print Queue objects in the NDS tree.

You can use the new, graphical NPRINTER Manager (NPTWIN95.EXE) to enable network users to share a printer attached to a Windows 95 workstation. NPRINTER Manager (and its associated files) provides the same functionality that NPRINTER.EXE provides on a DOS or OS/2 workstation.

NetWare Distributed Print Services

NetWare Distributed Print Services (NDPS) is the next generation of print services. NDPS is designed to simplify access and administration of the network print services. As the name indicates, NetWare Distributed Print Services (NDPS) is a distributed service which consists of client, server, and connectivity software components to seamlessly connect the applications to the network printers.

NDPS gives users and administrators greater control over their printing. Bidirectional feedback, print job status, automatic driver downloading, and event notification for printer status are all features that simplify and streamline the usability and administration of network printing. For example, using NDPS, the user can get the characteristics for a selected printer before the print job is sent to ensure that the job will be printed correctly. The user also has the flexibility to know whether a printer is available or busy, and even copy or move print jobs between network printers as necessary.

The administrators use a snap-in to NWADMIN which provides a single comprehensive management utility to enable and control network printing for all major brands and models of printers. In the current print services, the initial setup requires creating print queues, printer objects, and print servers, and then establishing a relationship between them. NDPS eliminates the need to create and configure print queues, printers, and print server objects. In fact, NDPS doesn't require you to manage print queues at all. Instead, using NDPS a printer simply needs to be connected to the network to begin sending print jobs to it. The printer will indicate which driver it needs, and the driver will be automatically downloaded. This eliminates the need for users to configure their workstations with drivers for specific printers and other devices.

The NetWare Distributed Print Services product is currently an add-on product that can be easily integrated into your existing NetWare 4.11 networks. In the future, it will be included as the regular print services for the operating system. NDPS enables the following features and printing capabilities.

Simple Printer Access

When the client software is installed, a list of available printers, called a "short list," is immediately available. The printers are configured as NDS printers, which allows users to browse the NDS tree for new printers based on the printer's properties, such as location, type, and supported languages. Because NDPS supports bidirectional information to be passed between the client and printers, the users can match the print jobs with the printer's capabilities. The users can also query and receive the status of the individual printers. This enables users to know whether a printer is available, get information about the status of the print jobs, and receive notification that the paper tray is empty.

Users also have the flexibility to indicate that a print job or document needs to be printed on a special paper type. The printer will notify the user when the paper needs to be loaded or inserted and then will print only that document on the special paper. For example, the user specifies that a letter needs to be printed on a single sheet of letterhead. The printer will prompt the user to insert the letterhead and then print only that letter or document on the letterhead.

Easier Setup and Administration

The initial administrative setup and installation costs are reduced by having the new printers automatically register with NDPS. For example, using the current print services, a new printer immediately starts advertising its availability when it is added to the network, which results in increased network traffic. This advertising continues as long as the printer is on and active. Using NDPS, when a new printer is added to the network, it registers with a single registration agent. The agent will then notify all the appropriate clients of the printer's availability. This agent will take care of advertising all the printers. This greatly reduces the overall network traffic caused by network printers.

Using NWADMIN the administrators have a centralized, simplified, and common interface to manage the print services. Since NPDS is closely integrated with NetWare Directory Services, the administrator can create printer objects in the NDS tree and manage the printers regardless of whether they are from different vendors. Since, the printer objects appear as NDS objects, they can take advantage of NetWare security to control access to the printers and printer features for handling sensitive documents.

NDPS printing can be set up to have multiple redundant physical printers represented by a single printer object in NDS. This feature enables print jobs to be shared or distributed among several printers without user intervention. Printer chaining allows redundant backup printers to be accessed sequentially.

Any NDPS printer can be managed through a standard SNMP console using the standard printer Management Information Base (MIB).

NDPS Architecture

The components that comprise the NetWare Distributed Print Services architecture are independent of any single operating system. The architecture is designed to be portable to different environments. The major components of NDPS are: the virtual printer, print client, print service common facilities, communication service, print device subsystem, and physical printer.

Virtual Printer

The virtual printer (VP) performs all the tasks of the current print server, spooler, and print queue. These tasks are combined into a logical print management agent called the virtual printer. This logical print management agent maintains information about the specific physical printers, such as printer availability, status, and other property information in the NDS printer objects. The virtual printer accepts operations (queries, print jobs, etc.) from the print clients.

The virtual printer may reside several places in the system. For example, the VP may be running on the NetWare server, or in the physical printer device that is connected directly to the network. A virtual printer that has not been officially registered in NDS can advertise its presence and availability as a convenience printer. A convenience printer is a network printer that is available to anyone on the network but is not seen as an NDS object and thus does not take advantage of the ease of access and security.

Print Client

The print client is the agent for the service requester that resides on the workstation as part of the NetWare client software. The print client's responsibility is to send network print jobs from the workstation to the appropriate virtual printer on the network.

Print Service Common Facilities

The Print Service Common Facilities (PSCF) is an NLM loaded on the NetWare server that allows the virtual printer to accept and schedule print jobs sent from the client. The PSCF also receives information about the devices and resources it is managing. It validates security information, providing direct notification and feedback to the appropriate client or device. The PSCF is essentially the liaison between the virtual printers and the print clients.

The print clients communicate with the virtual printer using the NetWare Distributed Print Service Protocol (DPSP). The Novell implementation of a virtual printer supports the SNMP protocol, which enables the administrators to manage the virtual printer using ManageWise or any SNMP-based console.

Print Device Subsystem

The print device subsystem (PDS) is a driver that can be customized and implemented to control and send feedback to the physical print device. Normally, the print device subsystem is develop by original equipment manufacturers (OEMs), independent software vendors (ISVs), and others to take advantage of the functionality of each of the physical printer devices.

Physical Printer

The physical printer is the actual printer device that is attached to the network to service the print jobs sent by users. In order for the physical printer to be involved with the NetWare Distributed Print Services, it must either have the virtual printer component embedded or be enabled to communicate to a NDPS server. With the second option the server will support the printer and make it a full NDPS printer.

In addition NetWare 4.11 provides the following features:

- Support for up to 256 printers attached to one print server. This support can help you to reduce the number of print servers on your network and to consolidate the print infrastructure.

- A print layout page in the NWAdmin utility, which shows graphically the print layout relationship for a particular container object or print server. The print layout page for a print server shows all the printers attached to the print server, the queues serviced by those printers, and the print jobs in the queue.

- A feature that allows users to send their print jobs to a printer by simply specifying the printer name. The network takes care of all the print queue and print server activities.

- Support for an unlimited number of print job configurations.

Printing in NetWare 3 and NetWare 4

ABLE 12.1 PROVIDES a summary of the differences between NetWare 4 and NetWare 3 print services. The following list reviews the printing features in both versions in more detail.

TABLE 12.1	NETWARE 3 PRINTING	NETWARE 4 PRINTING
Differences between NetWare 3 and NetWare 4 Printing	Print objects (print queue and print server) are bindery objects.	Print objects (print queue, print server, and printer) are NDS objects.
	Print server's configuration information is stored in files in SYS:SYSTEM.	Print server's configuration information is stored as attributes of the NDS printer server object.
	PRINTCON information is stored as files in users' SYS:MAIL directories.	PRINTCON information is stored as attributes of the user object of the container object (such as an OU) in NDS.
	PRINTDEF information is stored as files in SYS:PUBLIC.	PRINTDEF information is stored as an attribute of the container object in NDS.

- In NetWare 3, the print queue and print server are the only objects offered to service printing. The users must send all of their print jobs to their specified print queue. In NetWare 4, users can specify either a printer (by name) or a print queue as the destination of their print job. This gives users more flexibility and control of the printing infrastructure.

- In bindery-based NetWare, print services and print queues are stored as objects in the bindery. Printers are attributes of the print server or configuration files in the print server directory in SYS:SYSTEM. In NetWare 4, the three print objects (Print Queue, Print Server, and Printer) are stored as NDS leaf objects in the tree.

- In NetWare 3, there can be printer configuration (PRINTCON) files for each user. These files are stored directly in the user's SYS:MAIL\ID# subdirectory. In NetWare 4, you can create configuration files for individual users or just one file for an entire container object (OU). The configuration files are stored as a property of the object in NDS.

- In NetWare 3, there can be a set of printer definitions for the entire system. The definition files are stored in SYS:PUBLIC. In NetWare 4, the printer definitions can be set per container object (OU). The files are stored in NDS.

The NDS Print Objects

THE BUILDING BLOCKS of NetWare print services are three NDS objects:

Print Queue (or Queue)

 **Print Queue**

Print Server

 **Print Server**

Printer

 **Printer**

The relationship between these objects establishes the NetWare print services, or infrastructure. To properly set up the NetWare print services, you must create at least one of each of these objects and assign the appropriate relationship between them. A Print Queue object is assigned to a printer. The Printer object is assigned to a Print Server object.

When a network user sends a print job to a network printer, NetWare temporarily stores the print job as a file in a file system directory on the server. This directory is called the *queue*. The stored print jobs wait in the print queue until the print server is able to send the print job to the printer. Figure 12.1 illustrates the relationship between the print objects.

In your NDS tree, place the Print Queue and Printer objects at the upper OU (or other container object) level to support the most number of users.

You can create the objects using either the Windows-based NWAdmin utility or the DOS-based PCONSOLE utility. If you are setting up NetWare 4 print services for the first time, we recommend that you use PCONSOLE, because it has the Quick Setup feature. See the section about setting up NetWare 4 printing, later in this chapter, for details.

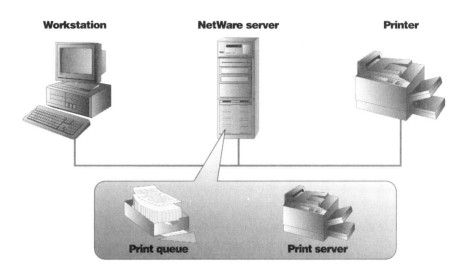

FIGURE 12.1

Relationship between
print objects

Print Queue Objects

Print Queue objects represent the directories where the print jobs are sent to be serviced.

In NetWare 3, the print queue subdirectory was located in SYS:SYSTEM and could not be moved. In NetWare 4, you can create the print queue subdirectory on any server volume. The queue is stored in a root subdirectory called QUEUES (which you can rename if desired) on the server volume.

We recommend that you place the print queue on a volume other than SYS, so that it is separate from the NetWare Transaction Tracking System (TTS) and other NDS data stored on the SYS volume.

Print Server Objects

A *print server* takes print jobs from the print queue and sends them to the assigned printer. Print Server objects represent the print servers that monitor print queues and printers.

Each print server is a software program loaded as a NetWare Loadable Module (NLM) on a NetWare server. In NetWare 3, the PSERVER.NLM program supports up to 16 attached printers. In NetWare 4, PSERVER.NLM supports up to 256 printers. PSERVER.EXE, a print server program run from a DOS workstation, is no longer available.

Printer Objects

Printer objects represent network printers attached to either a DOS or OS/2 workstation, to a NetWare server, or directly to the network. Each printer requires the NetWare printer program, NPRINTER, in order to attach to the print server and to service print jobs.

You can load NPRINTER in one of three ways, depending on your printer configuration:

- Printers cabled to the workstation on the network (through the workstation's parallel or serial port) use NPRINTER. EXE. This is called *remote printer mode.*

- Printers cabled to a NetWare server (through the server's parallel or serial port) use the NPRINTER.NLM program.

- Printers attached directly to the network store the NPRINTER code inside the printers themselves. The NPRINTER program resides in the firmware or flash memory of the printer device.

As mentioned at the beginning of the chapter, a new feature in NetWare 4.11 allows users to specify a printer device directly by printer name.

Do not confuse NetWare printers with printer drivers. Printer drivers are the software that allows applications to format print jobs for specific printers.

Configuring Printers

OU CAN CONSIDER five printer configurations, or relationships, when planning the printing infrastructure for your network:

- Non-network workstation printers
- Network workstation printers
- Network server printers

- Network-direct printers, remote printer mode

- Network-direct printers, queue server mode

The following sections explain the configuration considerations in more detail.

Configuring Non-network Workstation Printers

Without NetWare, users can print only to a printer cabled directly to their personal computers. This is defined as a *local printer*. The user sends print jobs from a stand-alone computer to the attached printer, as illustrated in Figure 12.2.

F I G U R E 12.2

Non-network workstation printing

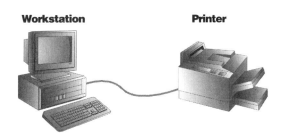

Workstation　　　　　　　**Printer**

This configuration is simple to set up but is extremely limited in a network environment. The printer is not shared by other network users; the only person who can use that printer is the user sitting at the workstation. However, if you need a special-purpose workstation and printer combination, you might set up a non-network workstation printer.

Configuring Network Workstation Printers (Remote Printer)

Network users can redirect their print jobs to printers designated as NetWare printers, attached to network workstations. The user's data is not sent directly from the workstation to the printer. Instead, the data is captured and redirected to a file in a print queue, where it waits to be sent to the printer. The data is first sent to the queue so that multiple print jobs are not contending for the same shared printer.

The print jobs wait in the print queue until the print server is able to send them to the printer. The print server will service the print jobs in the order in which they are received, unless a higher priority for a particular print job is stipulated by the user (for his or her own jobs) or administrator.

The network workstation printer configuration requires that the workstation always be powered on (but not necessarily logged in) and run the NPRINTER.EXE program. NPRINTER.EXE connects the workstation printer to the NetWare print server and waits to receive the print jobs passed to it. The server must run the print server program. This configuration is illustrated in Figure 12.3.

FIGURE 12.3

Network workstation printing

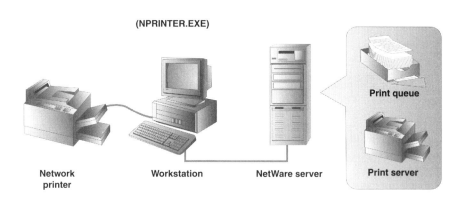

With this configuration, printing resources can easily be distributed across the network, close to the users that need them.

If the workstation that has the network printer attached is turned off, the printer will not be available. Remember, for this configuration to work, the workstation must be powered on.

Configuring Network Server Printers

Network users can also print to printers that are connected directly to a server. As with the network workstation printer configuration, the user's print jobs are redirected to print queues, which are then serviced by print servers. The server must run the NPRINTER.NLM program so that it can recognize the attached printer. Figure 12.4 illustrates this configuration.

FIGURE 12.4

Network server printing

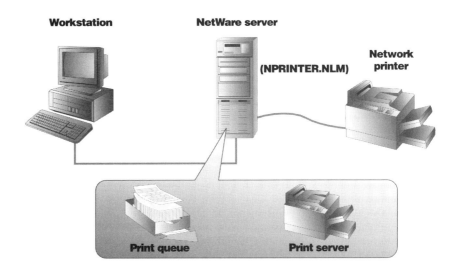

For this configuration, you need to consider the physical location of the server, because the printer is connected directly to the server, and the printer cable can extend for only a limited distance. This would not be the best choice if the server is located away from the users, as may be the case when you keep the server in a locked room. You want your users to be able to access the printer easily, not have to do a lot of walking to retrieve their printouts.

Another consideration is the effect on the server's performance. Connecting a printer to a server will slow the performance of the server, because it must also handle the printing load. The printer will demand CPU interrupts to process the print jobs. Therefore, this configuration is not recommended when the printer will be used heavily.

Configuring Network-Direct Printers, Remote Printer Mode

A network-direct printing configuration is set up by connecting a printer directly to the network. The connectivity to the network is provided by a hardware printer device. The hardware device is connected to a printer and then to the network, or it is installed in a slot in the printer. The device stores the NPRINTER code inside the printer itself. The NPRINTER program resides in the firmware or flash-memory of the printer device.

In the remote printer mode, the printer device functions similar to a workstation running NetWare 4's NPRINTER.EXE or NetWare 3.1*x*'s RPRINTER.EXE. Devices configured for remote printer mode are controlled by a NetWare print server.

The printer device connects to the NetWare print server and waits to receive the print jobs passed to it. The server must run the print server program. This configuration is illustrated in Figure 12.5.

FIGURE 12.5

Network-direct printing, remote printer mode

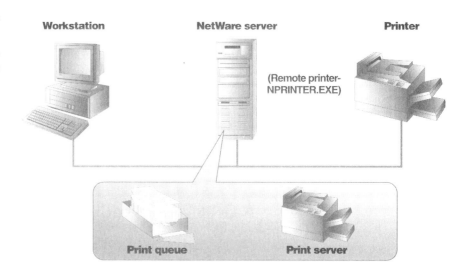

Using this configuration, the printing can be distributed across the network, with the printers placed next to the network users who use them.

NetWare 4 and NetWare 3 use the same communication protocol between the print server and network-direct devices running in remote printer mode. This means that your existing network-direct devices can attach to and receive print jobs from a NetWare 4 print server.

Some printers require the print server to be running in order to be configured. Generally, this is not a problem, because the print server is already running and servicing other printers. The new assignments made to the print server will take effect immediately. There is no need to recycle (take down the print server and then bring it back up).

Some network-direct devices need to be configured with a 16-printer configuration (introduced for the NetWare 3 print servers). If you are using devices with this limit, reserve printer connections 0 through 15 for the devices. Since there is no way to support these connections automatically, you must manually guarantee these connections by selectively booting each printer.

The remaining slots (16 through 255) can be used for network workstation printers (printers attached to workstations running NPRINTER.EXE). You can also attach other "smart" devices in newer printers to the remaining slots.

Some of the utilities provided to configure network-direct printer devices can be operated only with explicit Supervisor rights (they do not recognize Supervisor-equivalence). This means that you will need to log in as Supervisor in bindery mode rather than as Admin in NDS. You must have a read/write replica stored in that server. See Appendix D for more information about setting up network-direct printing in remote printer mode.

Configuring Network-Direct Printers, Queue Server Mode

A network-direct printer, queue server mode configuration is similar to a network-direct printer, remote printer mode, in that it connects the printer directly to the network, using a hardware printer device. However, in queue server mode, the printer acts like a special-purpose print server for the printer.

In queue server mode, the hardware print server accesses the print queue directly using NCP (NetWare Core Protocol) calls.

The queue server must log in to the network or server to service an individual print queue. The queue servers are created and displayed as NDS print servers. Figure 12.6 illustrates this configuration.

FIGURE 12.6

Network-direct printing, queue server mode

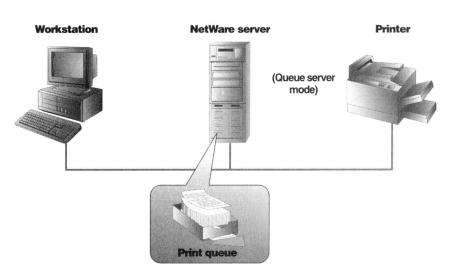

The queue server setup is a popular printing configuration. In many cases, it offers a fast, effective, low-cost method for printing. The printing can be well-distributed across the network, with the printers placed next to the network users. Usually, this mode will place the least load on a NetWare server.

You will need to plan for this configuration carefully, because the queue servers need to log in to the network or server where the print queue resides. The login will take one of the server's licensed connections, leaving fewer connections for the network users. See Appendix D for details on setting up for network-direct printing in queue server mode.

If you are using print devices that are not NDS-aware, you need to consider the following points:

- The queue servers will need to log in using Bindery Services.

- These print devices will not be able to read the print server configuration files from NDS.

Logging in using Bindery Services forces the NDS object definitions for the queues, printers, and print servers to be created in the same server context. (Remember, NetWare 4.11 supports up to 16 bindery contexts.) That bindery context then must be selected as the NetWare 4 server's bindery context so that the queue server can connect. Any additional print queues serviced by the network-direct printer must be created in one of the 16 bindery contexts.

Because most network-direct print devices are not NDS-aware, you must create the print server information in bindery mode. To do this, switch to the bindery mode in PCONSOLE (press F6) before creating the Print Server object. This will enable the queue server to read the print server configuration files.

Many network-direct print devices assume that the group EVERYONE (created by default in NetWare 3) exists in NetWare 4. You may need to create this group in the context where the printer is defined so that the device will be able to communicate with the network.

Creating Print Configuration and Definition Files

YOU CAN CREATE print configuration files to automate the printing setup for network users. These files can specify the printer, banner page, form feeds, time outs, and other printing options. The print configuration file can be stored for individual users or for the container objects (OUs). The container is easier to manage because all the users created in the OU will get the same printer configuration files. You can use the Windows-based NWAdmin utility or the DOS-based PRINTCON utility to create print configuration files.

You can also create specific printer definitions to format users' print jobs. These are necessary only if the application does not format the print job. NetWare provides 58 different print drivers for the most common industry printers. You can use the NWAdmin or PRINTDEF utility to define printer forms for use in print job configurations.

Setting Up NetWare Printing

YOU CAN SET up NetWare 4 printing easily by using the Quick Setup option in the PCONSOLE utility and then loading the appropriate software. You can also set up printing for a mixed NetWare 4 and NetWare 3 environment.

Using PCONSOLE's Quick Setup for NetWare 4 Printing

The simplest way to set up the NetWare 4 print services, especially if you are starting without any existing print objects, is by following these steps:

1. Load PCONSOLE and select the Quick Setup menu item.

2. Select names for each of the print objects (Print Queue, Print Server, and Printer).

3. Save your configuration.

4. Load the PSERVER.NLM software at the server console, using the new Print Server object's name.

5. Load NPRINTER.EXE at the workstation with the printer, or load NPRINTER.NLM if the printer is attached directly to the server.

That's all there is to it. You have set up network printing.

NetWare 4 and NetWare 3 Mixed Printing Setup

The compatibility between the two NetWare versions is bidirectional, which means that NetWare 3 can share printing services from NetWare 4. NetWare 3 users can capture to NetWare 4 print queues, and NetWare 4 users can capture to NetWare 3 queues.

Users Share NetWare 4 Print Queues

You can create NDS print queues and place them on the NetWare 4 server volumes. NetWare 4 users (using VLMs) will access the print queue and read the configuration information from NDS.

NetWare 3 users (using NETX) will access the print queue and the configuration information through Bindery Services. The NetWare 3 users will only be able to use the print queues in the server's bindery context (or contexts, if you have more than one). They must have a login account in the bindery context. This could be a collective account that many users use for printing services.

The print queue can be serviced by a print server running on either the NetWare 4 or NetWare 3 system. A queue server could also service the print queue.

Users Share NetWare 3 Print Queues

In order for the NetWare 4 users to send print jobs to a print queue on a NetWare 3 server, you must create a logical print queue in the NDS tree that routes the print job to the NetWare 3 bindery print queue. The print queue is physically located on the NetWare 3 server volume.

Use the NWAdmin utility to create this NDS print queue. When you are asked where to place the print queue, enter the NetWare 3 server and volume name. Figure 12.7 shows an example of using the NWAdmin utility to create a print queue on a NetWare 3 server volume.

FIGURE 12.7

Setting up a print queue in NWAdmin and storing it on a NetWare 3 server

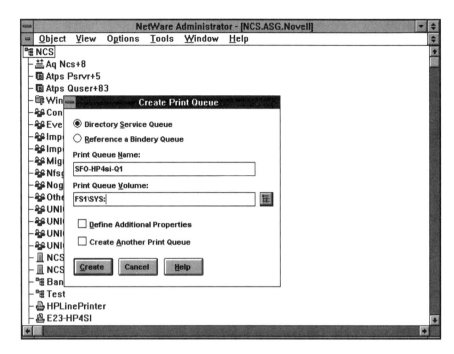

Migrating Printing Information from NetWare 3 to NetWare 4

TWO SETS OF printing information files need special consideration during a migration from NetWare 3 to NetWare 4: the PRINTCON and PRINTDEF databases. These files are named after the DOS utility that administers them.

See Chapter 8 for more information about the Across-the-Wire and In-Place methods of migration.

Migrating Printing with the Across-the-Wire Method

When you use the Across-the-Wire utility, the PRINTCON and PRINTDEF databases are not migrated directly to NDS; they are copied from their respective areas to the same areas on the destination server. You will need to re-create the PRINTCON and PRINTDEF information in NDS after the migration.

The PRINTCON files are copied from the SYS:MAIL\USERID# directory on the source NetWare 3 server to the SYS:MAIL\USERID# on the destination NetWare 4 server. You should make the PRINTCON information an NDS property of either the user or a container object (such as an OU).

The PRINTDEF files are copied from the SYS:PUBLIC directory on the source server to the SYS:PUBLIC directory on the NetWare 4 server. You should move this information into the attribute of a container object in NDS.

Migrating with the In-Place Method

When you use the In-Place method of migration, the PRINTCON and PRINTDEF information is migrated directly into NDS.

After the migration is completed, you will need to run the PUPGRADE.NLM program (from INSTALL or from the server console) to convert the PRINTCON and PRINTDEF databases for NetWare 4. Refer to the *Print Services* manual in the DynaText online documentation supplied on the NetWare 4.1 CD for instructions on using PUPGRADE.NLM.

Using Print Utilities

NETWARE'S PRINT UTILITIES allow you to create NDS print objects, manage print job configurations, and specify printing definitions. In order to create print objects, you must log in as a user that has the Create right at the chosen container.

The new DOS utilities are bimodal, meaning that they support both bindery mode and NDS mode.

The following print utilities are available:

- NWAdmin: A Windows-based utility (with the Windows graphical interface) that allows you to manage NDS print objects. You can browse, create, modify, and grant rights to the print objects.

- PCONSOLE: A DOS utility that allows you to create print objects and to establish the proper assignments between those objects. If you have experience with NetWare 3, this utility will already be familiar to you. PCONSOLE is the only utility that has the Quick Setup option, which creates the print objects and makes the necessary assignments automatically. You can also use this utility to view and manage the print jobs placed in the print queues.

- PRINTCON: This utility allows you to manage the print job configurations for users. You can set the capture, banner, tabs, time out, and other values for print job configurations. The print job configurations are set for either an individual user or container object (such as an OU).

- PRINTDEF: This utility allows you to monitor, create, modify, delete, import, and export specific print definitions. The printer definitions are placed at the NDS container. You can also monitor, modify, and create printer forms to be specified in CAPTURE, NPRINT, or PCONSOLE.

NetWare 4's printing services have been improved to allow more flexibility in your printer setups and to make it easier to use network printing devices. NetWare 4.1 can support up to 256 printers attached to one print server. It also allows users to print in a mixed NetWare 3 and NetWare 4 environment. This means that they can continue to send print jobs through NetWare 3 or NetWare 4 print queues.

During your migration to NetWare 4, make sure that all your users can continue to print by testing the printing features of some of your applications. Follow the recommendations in Appendix D for setting up various printer types.

Understanding
NetWare 4
Utilities

QuickTips: NetWare Utilities

▧ Use the **DSMERGE** utility to merge   **286**

the [Root] of two trees. Currently, the trees must have identical schemas before they can be merged. This means that if you have performed extensions to the schema of one tree, they must be made on the other tree. Also, if you are using different versions of NetWare 4, you may need to adjust the trees to be merged. Having consistent naming standards for both trees will make the merge process much smoother.

▧ Use the **DSREPAIR** utility   **287**

to correct or repair problems in the NDS database, check NDS replica information, and initiate replica synchronization. It is easier to use DSREPAIR instead of DSTRACE for some of the SET DSTRACE = options. The DSRE-PAIR utility can do much of what DSTRACE will do, but with an easier interface and no SET commands. Novell's latest utility, known as NDS Manager, can be used for managing partitions and replicas.

▧ Use **DSTRACE** to monitor   **288**

your servers for errors. Issue the command: SET DSTRACE = ON on your NetWare 4 servers to view synchronization activity. DSTRACE will notify you of errors with NDS. You can then leave DSTRACE running on your server(s) and use RCONSOLE to periodically check the synchronization status of each server. The following are some pointers for using DSTRACE:

- If you see an NDS error appear on a server, check the error code listing in Appendix A of this book for a definition of the error and suggestions for resolving the error. Try to determine the cause of errors before running corrective utilities such as further partitioning operations using DSREPAIR or NDS Manager.

- A large percentage of NDS errors will be communication-related (error -625). Before trying anything else, always check your physical connections—cabling, adapter cards, line cords, WAN links, and so on.

- Never perform any partitioning or repair operations without first checking the status of the partition. Use DSREPAIR or DSTRACE to check the status of synchronization for each replica on each server within the partition. You must see the message "OK" (DSREPAIR) or "ALL PROCESSED = YES" (DSTRACE) before proceeding with partitioning operations.

Use the INSTALL utility to install   289

or upgrade to NetWare 4 on your server, to add more licenses, and to remove NDS. You can also use INSTALL to edit your AUTOEXEC.NCF and other NCF files.

Use the TIMESYNC.NLM utility to   290
manage time synchronization

across your NetWare 4 network. Never unload TIMESYNC, which is loaded automatically, because this will cause problems with time synchronization and the time stamping of NDS events. Issue the command SET TIMESYNC DEBUG = 7 on your server to see time synchronization information. Enter SET TIMESYNC DEBUG = OFF to remove the Debug screen. You can also use DSREPAIR to monitor time synchronization on your network.

Use the NetSync utility to synchronize   290
NetWare binderies

in a mixed NetWare 4 and NetWare 3.1x network. This utility synchronizes changes to bindery objects made using NWAdmin. NetSync also allows for a gradual migration if you are using NetWare Name Service (NNS) software in a NetWare 3 environment.

Familiarize yourself with the key   291
workstation utilities

which include the following:

- NWAdmin, a Windows-based utility used to manage NDS objects and their properties in the tree. Partition Manager, a utility for managing partitions and replicas, is a part of NWAdmin.

- NDS Manager which is a Windows and Windows 95-based utility that allows you to manage the partitions in your NDS tree and diagnose problems.

UIMPORT, which is used to create, delete, and update user objects and their properties.

ETWARE'S UTILITIES HAVE consistently improved with each version. Version 4.11 brings the latest in enhancements to allow you greater flexibility in your NDS tree design and maintenance. NetWare utilities are either run from a NetWare 4 server console (server utilities) or from a workstation (workstation utilities). This chapter reviews the key NetWare server and workstation utilities you can use to set up and manage your NetWare 4 network.

This chapter focuses on the functions of the utilities, to give you an idea of which utility to use for your task. For step-by-step details on how to use all the NetWare utilities, see Novell's Guide to IntranetWare Networks *(Novell Press) or your NetWare documentation.*

New Utilities in NetWare 4

IGURES 13.1 AND 13.2 show a listing of all the utilities and NLM programs in NetWare 4. The new utilities are highlighted in bold italics.

All of these utilities can be run from NetWare 4 servers. With the exception of the DOMAIN.NLM program, all of the utilities can also be run from NetWare 4 servers for OS/2. Workstation utilities for NetWare 4 are generally stored on a NetWare 4 file system and run from a DOS, a Microsoft Windows, or an OS/2 workstation.

Server utilities		NLMs	
ABORT REMIRROR	NAME	*AFP*	MATHLIB
ADD NAME SPACE	OFF	*AFPCON*	MATHLIBC
BIND	PROTOCOL	*ATCON*	MONITOR
BROADCAST	REGISTER MEMORY	*ATCONFIG*	*NPRINTER*
CLEAR STATION	*REINITIALIZE SYSTEM*	*ATPS*	*NUTNWSNUT*
CLS	*REMIRROR PARTITION*	*ATPSCON*	PING
CONFIG	REMOVE DOS	*ATXRP*	*PINSTALL*
DISABLE LOGIN	RESET ROUTER	*BRGSON*	PSERVER
DISABLE TTS	RESTART SERVER	*CDROM*	*PUPGRADE*
DISMOUNT	*SCAN FOR NEW DEVICES*	CLIB	REMOTE
DISPLAY NETWORKS	SEARCH	*CONLOG*	ROUTE
DISPLAY SERVERS	SCEURE CONSOLE	*DOMAIN*	*RPL*
DOWN	SEND	*DSMERGE*	RS232
ENABLE LOGIN	SET	*DSREPAIR*	RSPX
ENABLE TTS	SET TIME	EDIT	*RTDM*
EXIT	SET TIMEZONE	*FILTCFG*	*SBACKUP*
INITIALIZE SYSTEM	SPEED	*HFSCD*	*SCHDELAY*
LANGUAGE	TIME	*HFSCDCON*	*SERVMAN*
LIST DEVICES	TRACK OFF	*INETCFG*	SPXCONFG
LOAD	TRACK ON	*INSTALL*	SPXS
MAGAZINE [parameter]	UNBIND	*IPXCON*	STREAMS
MEDIA [parameter]	UNLOAD	*IPXPING*	*TCPCON*
MEMORY	UPS STATUS	IPXS	*TIMESYNC*
MEMORY MAP	UPS TIME	*KEYS*	TU
MIRROR STATUS	VERSION		*TPING*
MODULES	VOLUMES		UPS
MOUNT			VREPAIR

Graphical
Windows
NetWare Administrator
NetWare User Tools

Text		
Command line		**Menu**
DOS	**OS/2**	**DOS**
ATOTAL	ATOTAL	*AUDITCON*
CAPTURE	CAPTURE	COLORPAL
CX	*CX*	*FILER*
FLAG	FLAG	*NETADMIN*
LOGIN	LOGIN	*NETUSER*
LOGOUT	LOGOUT	*NPRINTER*
MAP	MAP	*PARTMGR*
NCOPY	NCOPY	PCONSOLE
NCUPDATE	*NCUPDATE*	PRINTCON
NDIR	*NDIR*	PRINTDEF
NLIST	*NLIST*	
NMENU	*NPATH*	
NPATH	NPRINT	
NPRINT	*NPRINTER*	
NPRINTER	NVER	
NVER	*NWXTRACT*	
NWXTRACT	PSC	
PSC	PURGE	
PURGE	*RIGHTS*	
RCONSOLE	*SEND*	
RENDIR	SETPASS	
RIGHTS	SETTTS	
SEND	SYSTIME	
SETPASS	*UIMPORT*	
SETTTS	WHOAMI	
SYSTIME		
UIMPORT		
WHOAMI		
WSUPDATE		
WSUPGRD		

New Server Utilities

Server utilities allow you to change the server's parameters, monitor the load on the server, and control the server's allocation of resources. Table 13.1 gives a brief description of each of the new NetWare 4 server utilities.

TABLE 13.1

New NetWare 4 Server Utilities

NETWARE 4 SERVER UTILITY	FUNCTION
ABORT REMIRROR	Stops the remirroring of a logical disk partition.
INITIALIZE SYSTEM	Enables multiprotocol router configuration by executing all commands in the system NETINFO.CFG file. This utility is executed from the AUTOEXEC.NCF file.
LANGUAGE	Sets the server utilities or NLM programs to use specific language message files.
LIST DEVICES	Displays device information for the server.
MAGAZINE [*parameter*]	Confirms whether magazine requests ("Magazine Inserted" and "Magazine Removed") from the server have been satisfied.
MEDIA [*parameter*]	Confirms whether media requests ("Media Inserted" and "Media Removed") from the server have been satisfied.
MIRROR STATUS	Displays all mirrored logical disk partitions and the status of each.
REINITIALIZE SYSTEM	Enables multiprotocol router configuration changes made since the last time the commands in the NETINFO.CFG file were executed. If any new commands are in the NETINFO.CFG file, they are executed.
REMIRROR PARTITION	Starts the remirroring of a logical disk partition.
SCAN FOR NEW DEVICES	Checks for disk hardware that has been added since the server was last booted.

New and Updated NLM Programs

The NLM programs included with NetWare 4 link disk drivers, LAN drivers, name space modules, applications, and so on with the server's operating system. They also allow you to install NetWare 4, perform upgrades, manage time synchronization, and edit server configuration files. Table 13.2 lists the NLMs new to NetWare 4.

	NETWARE 4 NLM	FUNCTION
TABLE 13.2 New NetWare 4 NLM Program	AFP	Provides full, native-mode support for AppleTalk Filing Protocol (AFP), so that any Macintosh user can access files and applications on a NetWare server volume as if they were stored on a local drive, and can share files and applications with non-Macintosh users.
	AFPCON	Enables you to configure the AFP module on your server.
	ATCON	Allows you to monitor the activity of AppleTalk network segments.
	ATCONFIG	Enables you to configure NetWare for Macintosh after the installation is complete.
	ATPS	Provides full, native-mode support for the AppleTalk Print Services (ATPS) protocols. ATPS enables all NetWare users to send print jobs to NetWare queues serviced by AppleTalk printers, and it allows Macintosh users to send jobs to NetWare print queues serviced by printers other than AppleTalk printers.
	ATPSCON	Enables you to configure the ATPS module so that authorized users have access to the AppleTalk Print Services that are appropriate for their needs.
	ATXRP	Works with PSERVER to send a print job to an AppleTalk network printer from a NetWare print queue.
	BRGCON	Allows you to view bridge configuration information for a NetWare Server for OS/2 bridge.

NETWARE 4 NLM	FUNCTION
CDROM	Allows the server to use a CD-ROM disk as a read-only volume.
CONLOG	Allows you to capture console messages generated by modules loaded during system initialization and to write the messages to the default file SYS:/ETC/CONSOLE.LOG (or another file of your specification).
DOMAIN	Creates memory domains used to protect server memory. DOMAIN.NLM does not work on a NetWare Server for OS/2.
DSMERGE	Allows you to rename and merge NDS trees.
DSREPAIR	Allows you to maintain and repair the NDS database on the server where this utility is run.
FILTCFG	Allows you to set up and customize filters for IPX, TCP/IP, and AppleTalk protocols.
HFSCD	Provides support for Apple's HFS format for CD-ROM so that Macintosh users can access files and applications on a CD-ROM drive that is compatible with Macintosh and is attached to the server.
HFSCDCON	Enables you to configure the HFSCD module.
INETCFG.NLM	Allows you to set up and customize your internetworking configuration for IPX, IP, and AppleTalk network protocols. It simplifies the process of configuring LANs to work with network and routing protocols supported by NetWare 4.1.
INSTALL/DSMAINT	DSMAINT utility allows you to back up NDS data files and use them during a restore. DSMAINT is now part of the INSTALL.NLM utility for NetWare 4.11.
IPXCON	Allows you to monitor and troubleshoot IPX routers and network segments throughout your IPX internetwork.

	NETWARE 4 NLM	FUNCTION
TABLE 13.2 New NetWare 4 NLM Program (continued)	IPXPING	Allows you to send an IPX ping request packet to an IPX server or workstation on your internetwork to determine whether a node is reachable.
	KEYB	Allows you to set your server's keyboard to a particular nationality or language.
	NETSYNC3	Loaded on NetWare 3.x servers to make them part of a NetSync managed network.
	NETSYNC4	Loaded on the NetWare 4.x server that will manage up to 12 NetWare 3.x servers in the NetSync environment.
	NPRINTER	Allows a printer attached to any server to be a network printer.
	NUT	Allows you to use the NetWare 3.11 NLMs that require NUT's library of routines and functions.
	NWSNUT	As an NLM utility user interface, provides a library of routines used by certain NLM programs, such as MONITOR and SERVMAN.
	PING	A menu utility that informs you when an IP node on your network is reachable. PING sends an Internet Control Message Protocol (ICMP) echo request packet to an IP node and notifies you when it receives a reply.
	PUPGRADE	Upgrades NetWare 3.1x print objects, print job configurations, and printer definitions to NetWare 4.
	REMAPID	Loaded on NetWare 3.x servers to handle passwords correctly in a NetSync environment.
	RPL	Enables remote booting of IBM PC-compatible diskless workstations that have network boards installed.
	RTDM	For Real Time Data Migration, enables data migration at the server console.
	SCHDELAY	Allows you to prioritize and schedule server processes to use less of the server's CPU. Also allows you to slow processes down when the server is very busy.

TABLE 13.2	NETWARE 4 NLM	FUNCTION
New NetWare 4 NLM Program (continued)	SERVMAN	Allows you to change time synchronization parameters in .NCF files, set parameters for IPX/SPX packets, and do other miscellaneous functions.
	TCPCON	Allows you to monitor activity in the TCP/IP network segments of your internetwork.
	TIMESYNC	Controls time synchronization on servers running NDS.
	TPING	A command line utility that informs you when an IP node on your internetwork is reachable. TPING sends an ICMP echo request packet to an IP node and notifies you when it receives a reply.

Consolidated and Replaced NetWare 3 Utilities

Table 13.3 lists the utilities that Novell has consolidated or replaced from prior versions of NetWare. Although you may have become comfortable with the NetWare 3 utilities, you will find that the NetWare 4 utilities are streamlined and more efficient.

TABLE 13.3	NETWARE 3.11 UTILITIES	NETWARE 4 UTILITIES
NetWare 4 Replacements for NetWare 3 Utilities	**Server-Based**	
	BINDFIX, BINDREST	DSREPAIR
	FCONSOLE	MONITOR
	NBACKUP	SBACKUP
	RCONSOLE, ACONSOLE	RCONSOLE
	Workstation-Based	
	ALLOW, GRANT, REMOVE, REVOKE, RIGHTS, TLIST	RIGHTS
	ATTACH, LOGIN	LOGIN

TABLE 13.3	NETWARE 3.11 UTILITIES	NETWARE 4 UTILITIES
NetWare 4 Replacements for NetWare 3 Utilities (continued)	CASTON, CASTOFF, SEND	SEND
	CHKDIR, CHKVOL, NDIR, LISTDIR	NDIR
	DSPACE, SECURITY, SYSCON, USERDEF	NETADMIN
	FILER, SALVAGE, PURGE, VOLINFO	FILER
	FLAG, FLAGDIR, SMODE	FLAG
	MAKEUSER	UIMPORT
	SESSION	NETUSER
	SLIST, USERLIST	NLIST

Graphical Utilities

Two graphical utilities you can run with Microsoft Windows are NWAdmin (NetWare Administrator) and NWUser (NetWare User Tools). NWUser can also be run under OS/2.

NDS Manager — A 32-bit graphical utility that can be run as a stand-alone or as part of the NWAdmin utility under the tools option. This utility is used to create, manage, and diagnose problems with partitions and replicas.

NWAdmin (MS Windows only) — A graphical utility that allows you to manage your NDS tree by creating, moving, deleting, and renaming objects. This utility includes the Partition Manager for managing your partitions and replicas.

NWUser (MS Windows and OS/2) — A graphical utility that allows users to display and modify or add to their workstation's drive mappings, server attachments, print queues, and so on.

New or Modified Text Utilities

Table 13.4 lists the new or modified text utilities used in both NetWare 3 and NetWare 4 environments. These utilities run on DOS or OS/2 systems.

TABLE 13.4 New or Modified NetWare 4 Text Utilities	**NETWARE 4 TEXT UTILITY**	**FUNCTION**
	AUDITCON	Allows independent audits to be performed on NDS events as well as file and server level events. The auditor is set up initially by an Admin user and then can become independent through changing a password.
	CX	Allows you to change your position, or context, in the NDS tree.
	NCUPTDATE	Allows you to update a NET.CFG file with a new name context after a container object has been moved or renamed.
	NETADMIN	A menu-driven utility that allows you to create objects and manage the tree. This utility has many of the same features as the Windows-based NWAdmin.
	NETUSER	Replaces SESSION (NetWare 3) and enables you to perform basic NetWare tasks. You can set up print jobs, manage drive mappings, access network attachments, and send messages to other users. NETUSER is also listed as a user tool because it can be installed on the workstation as well as on the server.
	NLIST	Allows you to view information about objects in the NDS tree, including users, groups, volumes, servers, and queues, as well as files and directories.
	NMENU	Allows you to create a working menu environment for your users. This version requires less memory than previous versions of NMENU.
	NPATH	Helps you to determine locations of files and other related information.

	NETWARE 4 TEXT UTILITY	FUNCTION
TABLE 13.4 New or Modified NetWare 4 Text Utilities (continued)	NPRINTER	Allows a printer attached to any server to be a network printer. This utility can be installed on a workstation or a server.
	PARTMGR	Allows you to partition your NDS database and manage those partitions and replicas.
	UIMPORT	Allows you to import data from an existing database into the NDS database, such as when you are updating user object information.
	WSUPGRADE	Allows you to update workstation files from the server by comparing the data and time of the source and destination files.

Key Utilities That You Should Understand

NETWARE 4 PROVIDES a large number of utilities. Some of these you may never use, and others you will run quite often. The following sections describe the server and workstation utilities that you are most likely to find useful. If you are not already familiar with any of these utilities, you should gain some experience with them, so you will know which utility to use for a particular task and how to use that utility.

Key Server Utilities

The server utilities you should focus on understanding initially are:

- DSMERGE
- DSREPAIR
- DSTRACE (SET commands)
- INSTALL
- TIMESYNC

These utilities are described in the following sections.

DSMERGE

You can use the DSMERGE utility for the following tasks:

- Merge the roots of two separate NDS trees.

- Rename a tree.

- View name and time synchronization information.

The primary purpose of DSMERGE is to merge the [Root] of two NDS trees into a single tree. The tree you are merging is referred to as the *local* or *source* tree. The other tree is called the *target* tree, which remains unchanged. After the merge is complete, the tree name is the target tree name.

The following conditions must be met to successfully use DSMERGE to merge trees:

- No leaf objects or Alias objects can exist at the [Root] object of the source tree.

- Identical tree names cannot exist on the trees being merged.

- The [Root] master of both trees must be running NetWare 4.1.

- All servers that contain a replica of the [Root] object for both trees must be up.

- The schema for both trees must be identical before merging. This means that if you have performed extensions to the schema of one tree, they must be made on the other tree. Identical schema may not be required in later versions of NetWare.

- All servers on both trees should be synchronized to within two seconds of each other. To make this process easier, place the servers from both trees on the same time source.

- The server that performs the DSMERGE operation must contain the master copy of the source tree's [Root] partition.

The DSMERGE utility is also used to rename an NDS tree. You will need to perform this operation first if you are going to merge two trees with identical names.

You can also use DSMERGE to contact each server in the local tree to verify the version, status, and tree name. It also lets you see time synchronization information about time sources and their status.

DSREPAIR

You can use the DSREPAIR utility for the following tasks:

- Correct or repair problems in the NDS database.

- Check NDS replica information and designate a replica as a master.

- Initiate replica synchronization and view the results.

The DSREPAIR utility has been improved for NetWare 4.1. It now has easy-to-navigate screens in the familiar Novell C-Worthy format. The utility is used on an individual server basis. You can access a server via the RCON-SOLE utility and initiate and operate the utility remotely.

Try to determine the cause of errors before running any corrective utilities such as DSRE-PAIR. A large percentage of NDS errors will be communication-related (error 625). You should always check your physical connections first. These connections include cabling, adapter cards, line cords, WAN links, and so on.

This utility provides the following features:

- Unattended full repair: This feature automatically performs repair operations on the NDS database, without operator assistance.

- Time synchronization: Like the DSMERGE utility, DSREPAIR allows you to monitor time synchronization on your network. This feature is included because monitoring and correcting time synchronization are necessary before performing any repair operation. A replica of the [Root] partition must be on the server running DSREPAIR in order to contact all servers in the tree.

Keep in mind that gathering time synchronization information from the [Root] down can be a lengthy process. You may want to view time synchronization information from a server without a [Root] partition.

- Replica synchronization: This feature shows you the status of any replica contained in the NDS tree. You can easily check the state of any replica in your tree.

- View/edit repair log file: You can track all the operations of the DSREPAIR utility to a file stored on your server. The default log file is SYS:SYSTEM\DSREPAIR.LOG.

- Advanced options: These options give you greater flexibility in repairing your NDS tree. The advanced menu options include the following:

  Repair local NDS database

  Repair all known network addresses

  View, verify, and edit remote server ID list

  Repair replicas, replica lists (rings), and server objects

  Synchronize security equivalence attributes for tree

  Global update schema

  View local partition information

  View and edit log

  Copy compressed NDS database files to disk

  Log file and login configuration

  Create a database dump file

DSTRACE

You can use the DSTRACE utility for the following tasks:

- Monitor the status of NDS synchronization processes

- View errors that occur during NDS synchronization

DSTRACE is a group of SET options used on your NetWare 4 servers for monitoring and controlling NDS. DSTRACE will display NDS errors that occur on your network. The NetWare 4.1 version adds color to the display to highlight key events that occur during synchronization. The trace will display

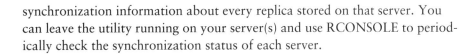

synchronization information about every replica stored on that server. You can leave the utility running on your server(s) and use RCONSOLE to periodically check the synchronization status of each server.

In some cases, it is preferable to use the DSREPAIR utility instead of SET DSTRACE commands. DSREPAIR can do much of what DSTRACE can, and its interface is easier to use.

If the DSTRACE screen displays any NDS errors, you will see a system message displayed on the Directory Services screen, as shown in Figure 13.3. Refer to Appendix A for a listing of these errors, their definitions, and recommendations for handling them.

FIGURE 13.3

DSTRACE screen with an error message

```
(95/01/03 07:50:07)
SYNC: Start sync of partition <[Root]> state:[0] type:[1]
 SYNC: Start outbound sync with (3) [010000C8]<CSI1.SYS_LAB.NCS>
  SYNC: sending updates to server <CN=CSI1>
 SYNC: update to server <CN=CSI1> successfully completed
SYNC: End sync of partition <[Root]> All processed = YES.

(95/01/03 08:17:17)
SYNC: Start sync of partition <[Root]> state:[0] type:[1]
 SYNC: Start outbound sync with (3) [010000C8]<CSI1.SYS_LAB.NCS>
  SYNC: sending updates to server <CN=CSI1>
 SYNC: update to server <CN=CSI1> successfully completed
SYNC: End sync of partition <[Root]> All processed = YES.

(95/01/03 08:20:07)
SYNC: Start sync of partition <NCS> state:[0] type:[3]
SYNC: End sync of partition <NCS> All processed = YES.

(95/01/03 08:20:07)
SYNC: Start sync of partition <[Root]> state:[0] type:[1]
 SYNC: Start outbound sync with (3) [010000C8]<CSI1.SYS_LAB.NCS>
  SYNC: sending updates to server <CN=CSI1>
 SYNC: update to server <CN=CSI1> successfully completed
SYNC: End sync of partition <[Root]> All processed = YES.
```

The NDS TRACE TO FILE parameter allows you to capture trace information to a file for later review or for technical support assistance.

The DSTRACE utility has a number of SET parameters that you can use for troubleshooting. See Appendix A for a listing of SET DSTRACE commands.

INSTALL

The INSTALL.NLM utility is used to install or upgrade to NetWare 4 on your server, to add licenses, and to remove NDS. The INSTALL utility also allows you to modify your NetWare server configuration and perform some server maintenance. The INSTALL.NLM utility is also used for running DSMAINT which will back up NDS data files for later retrieval.

The INSTALL.EXE utility (the workstation-based utility) provides two migration options when you are migrating from NetWare 3: Across-the-Wire (AMU) and In-Place. The Across-the-Wire migration option in this utility is for doing what is called a same-server AMU; it is not for use with two servers (NetWare 3 to NetWare 4). If you have separate hardware and you are doing an Across-the-Wire migration, use the MIGRATE.EXE utility on a workstation. See Chapter 8 for more information.

TIMESYNC

The TIMESYNC.NLM program is loaded automatically by NDS when your server is booted. This NLM is used for managing your time synchronization across your NetWare 4 network.

Never unload the TIMESYNC.NLM, because this will cause problems with time synchronization and the time stamping of NDS events. You will need to reboot a server to load this NLM again.

To see time synchronization status and traffic, you can use the following commands at the server console:

```
SET TIMESYNC DEBUG = 7
```

Displays time synchronization on your server console.

```
SET TIMESYNC DEBUG = OFF
```

Turns the Debug screen off.

NetSync

You can use NetSync to synchronize NetWare binderies in a mixed NetWare 4 and 3.1x network. This utility aids in administration of mixed network environments by synchronizing bindery object changes made with NetWare 4's NWAdmin.

With the NetSync NLMs loaded, you can automatically synchronize updates to user and group objects made on a NetWare 4 server to a maximum of 12 NetWare 3.1x servers.

The use of NetSync also allows for a gradual migration if you are using NetWare Name Service (NNS) software in a NetWare 3 environment.

Key Workstation Utilities

The workstation utilities you will want to get to know are:

- NWAdmin (NetWare Administrator)

- NDS Manager

- UIMPORT

NWAdmin (NetWare Administrator)

The NWAdmin utility is used at a client workstation to manage NDS objects and their properties in the tree. With this utility, you can view, create, move, delete, and assign rights to objects in the tree (according to your level of administrative rights). Most individuals using NWAdmin will be administrators with managed rights over container objects. Usually, users will use this utility only if they need to change their user login script or some other user property.

To restrict access to the NWAdmin utility, place the utility in a subdirectory other than PUBLIC. Then you can give the administrators who need to use the utility access to that other subdirectory. Depending on your level of security you may be placing your network at greater security risk by allowing anyone on the network to access the NWAdmin utility.

The latest NWAdmin utility requires that you use the latest VLM Requester or the Client 32 for DOS/Windows or Client 32 for Windows 95 for operation. Make sure that you have loaded the latest client software, or the NWAdmin utility may not load or function properly.

An option under the NWAdmin utility is NDS Manager (a snap-in utility), which allows you to manage your partitions. The DOS-based utility for managing partitions is PARTMGR. The Windows-based Partition Manager may still be used as well.

NDS Manager

NDS Manager is a Windows-based utility that allows you to manage the partitions on your NDS tree. Keep in mind that if a user has Supervisor rights to a container object, that user can manage partitions. The Windows-based utility for managing partitions and replicas is the NDS Manager, which can be part of the NWAdmin utility as a snap-in application or can be run as a stand-alone application.

UIMPORT

The UIMPORT utility is used at a client workstation to create, delete, and update user objects and their properties. It imports user information from an existing database into the NDS database.

This chapter has provided an overview of the NetWare 4 server and workstation utilities. You will do most of your network management using the NWAdmin and DSREPAIR utilities. But keep in mind that the use of DSREPAIR should be closely controlled, to ensure that repair operations are performed only when they are necessary.

Administering
NetWare 4
Security

QuickTips: NDS Security

- Login security, which is handled automatically by the client and NDS authentication services on the NetWare 4 server.

- Password security, which depends on the password protection practiced at your site. Take measures to safeguard your passwords. Change the password for the Admin user after you implement NetWare 4. You should never delete the Admin user, but you can rename this user.

- The bindery Supervisor, a user created on every NetWare 4 server, has the same password you initially assign to the Admin user, and this password will not change if you change the Admin user password.

- Physical server security, which is achieved by securing your server in a locked room.

to NetWare 4 security. Rights terminology and rules are the same for NetWare 4 as they were in NetWare 3. NetWare 4 extends security by adding access controls to all objects and properties in your tree. Keep in mind that objects can receive object and property rights to other objects. Objects can also receive rights to the file system. The file system can also have attributes assigned to it to further secure your network.

to control access to objects and information.

- Object rights are rights granted to an object to provide access to another object. NDS objects can receive Supervisor, Browse, Create, Delete, and Rename rights.

■ Property rights affect how a user can access information about an object. NetWare 4 includes Supervisor, Compare, Read, Write, and Add/Delete Self property rights.

If you grant an object Supervisor rights to another object, the object has all property rights to the object as well. When you grant an object Supervisor rights to a server object, the object also receives Supervisor rights to the file system. If you grant Supervisor property rights to another object, that object does not receive any of the object rights.

Be careful about assigning Write rights to an object's ACL   304

because granting an object the Write right to an ACL is as powerful as granting the object Supervisor rights. NetWare 4 uses the ACL (Access Control List) to store NDS trustee information. The ACL is similar to the DET in the file systems for both NetWare 3 and NetWare 4.

Use security equivalence to control user access   310

keeping in mind that users are security equivalent to rights assigned to any objects in their distinguished name. For example, if the user's distinguished name is Carl.Tele.Sales.WWW, and you assign rights to any of the container objects (Tele, Sales, or WWW), user Carl will automatically receive those rights, because he is security equivalent to any object in his name.

Use the IRF to control inheritance   316

of rights. You can set up subadministrators by creating an OR (Organizational Role) object that has Supervisor rights granted at the [Root] object, or other container. Place an IRF (Inherited Rights Filter) on the OR so that the OR cannot even be seen in your tree. Place your administrators as occupants in the OR.

ANY SECURITY MECHANISMS are available in NetWare 4. Our focus in this chapter is on NetWare Directory Services (NDS) security which includes the object and property rights, and some of file system security. You will learn how each of the security mechanisms works and how you can use them to manage and protect your NetWare 4 network.

We do not cover the more broad aspects of creating a trusted environment based on the many U.S. Department of Defense (DOD) publications and security classifications. For more information about security classification requirements, see Novell's Application Notes, "An Introduction to Novell's Open Security Architecture" (August 1994) and "Building and Auditing a Trusted Network Environment with NetWare 4" (April 1994).

Areas of NDS Security

DS SECURITY IS broken down into two areas: object and property rights, and file system security. Both areas of NetWare 4 security work together to provide a flexible and effective method for controlling access to your network.

Login Security

Login security is your first line of defense in providing a secure network. This level of security is handled automatically by the client (workstation) and NDS authentication services on the NetWare 4 server.

During the authentication service, the client's password is not broadcast across the network. Therefore, it is not possible for someone to capture a password packet on the network.

For its authentication services, Novell uses the RSA encryption technology during the login process. RSA is a public key encryption method, which uses relatively long keys, and can authenticate the sender as well as encrypting the message.

Another feature, known as *Packet Signature*, is also available. Packet Signature requires each packet to have a valid signature in order to be executed by the server. Packet signing makes it difficult for someone to forge NCP (NetWare Core Protocol) packets and send them on to the server for processing.

Password Security

NetWare 4 security is only as good as the password protection practiced at your site. If someone knows your password, he or she can access your account to the extent of your rights.

Take some precautions to safeguard your passwords:

- Require passwords for all users without exception.

- Require periodic changes of passwords for mobile users dialing into your network or users who work at home. Consider forcing periodic passwords for all users (although this will not make you a very popular administrator).

- Require a minimum password length of at least five to eight characters.

- Protect your Admin password (see Chapter 2 for more information).

- Occasionally publish a security bulletin that reminds your users to protect their passwords by choosing passwords that will be extremely difficult to guess (avoid family names, for example), by never divulging their password to anyone, and so on.

Physical Security of Your Servers

Take precautions, if possible, to physically secure your server in a locked room. If someone can access your server, your security precautions are void.

The server can be used by any savvy hacker, and worse, it could be stolen from the premises. You must determine the importance of the data on your servers and what steps you will take to secure their physical environment.

Security in NetWare 3 and NetWare 4

IF YOU HAVE a good understanding of NetWare 3 file system security, you will find it easy to master NetWare 4 security. The rules for file system security are identical in both versions of NetWare. NetWare 4 extends security to the NDS environment by adding access controls to all objects and properties in your tree. The NDS security rules use the same terminology as in NetWare 3 versions.

Terms such as *trustee assignments*, *inherited rights*, *security equivalence*, and *effective rights* are the same in both NetWare 3 and NetWare 4, and they follow the same rules.

Using the same terms in both versions is both a benefit and a source of confusion for many people. You benefit because you do not need to learn any new terms. But you must keep a clear distinction between object and property rights, and file system rights.

The NetWare 4 and NetWare 3 security features are similar. See Table 14.1 for a quick comparison of the security features in both versions. The list following the table reviews the similarities and differences in more detail.

TABLE 14.1 Security Features in NetWare 3 and NetWare 4	**NETWARE 3**	**NETWARE 4**
	Bindery	NetWare Directory Services (NDS)
	File and directory rights; file attributes	File and directory rights; file attributes; object rights; property rights
	User, queue, print server, profile, and group objects	User, queue, print server, group, organizational unit, organizational role, ncp server, volume, directory map, profile, and many more objects
	Supervisor user	Admin user

TABLE 14.1	NETWARE 3	NETWARE 4
Security Features in NetWare 3 and NetWare 4 (continued)	Group Everyone	[Root] object or O=Organization
	Guest user	[Public] trustee user
	Operator	Organizational role occupant
	IRM (Inherited Rights Mask)	IRF (Inherited Rights Filter)
	DET (Data Entry Table)	DET, ACL (Access Control List)

- NetWare 3 has the bindery for system control; NetWare 4 has NDS.

- NetWare 3 has file and directory rights and file attributes. NetWare 4 adds object rights and property rights.

- In NetWare 3, there are objects for users, queues, print servers, profiles, and groups. NetWare 4 adds many objects (for a total of 32 objects), such as Organizational Unit, Organizational Role, Server, Volume, and Directory Map objects. NetWare 4 also has many more attributes associated with each object than are available for NetWare 3 objects.

- NetWare 3 uses an Inherited Rights Mask (IRM) to control rights. NetWare 4 uses an Inherited Rights Filter (IRF) instead, which performs the same function as the IRM. The IRF term more accurately describes the operation of filtering out certain types of rights for that object. It is indeed an inclusive filter and not a mask.

- In NetWare 3, the Supervisor user has all rights to the system. In NetWare 4, this is the Admin user, who initially has all rights to the NDS tree and to the server's file system. Admin is not a reserved name, so you can change this to another user name. A bindery Supervisor is also created on every NetWare 4 server, but this Supervisor is only accessible if the bindery context is set.

- When you install NetWare 3, the user Guest account is automatically created. In NetWare 4, the [Public] trustee may be somewhat similar to Guest. However, the [Public] trustee allows users to see the NDS tree before logging in to a server. [Public] receives the Browse right by default when NDS is first installed.

- The group Everyone is also automatically created when you install Net-Ware 3, the users Guest and Everyone are automatically created. In NetWare 4, there is no group automatically created, however, the object [Root] or the O=Organization will content all the users in the tree. Each user in the tree is security equivalent to both [Root] and O=Organization. This name allows you to make one assignment which affects all the users in the tree.

- NetWare 3 has operator users to handle specific tasks, such as print queue operators. In addition to queue operators, NetWare 4 provides Organizational Role (OR) objects. ORs give you much more control and flexibility to create different types of operators, such as subtree administrators for NDS and administrators for the file system of various servers in your network.

- Both NetWare 3 and NetWare 4 use Directory Entry Tables (DETs) to store file system trustees. Additionally, NetWare 4 uses the Access Control List (ACL) to store NDS trustee information.

What Are Object Rights?

O BJECT RIGHTS ARE rights granted to an object to gain access to another object. This may be a new concept if you are upgrading from NetWare 3. In NetWare 3, you granted objects (users) rights to the file system. The NetWare 3 Supervisor was really the only object that was granted rights to create other objects and assign rights to them. NDS objects can receive the following rights:

- **Supervisor:** Grants full privileges to the object and has complete access to all the object's property rights.

- **Browse:** Allows you to see the object in the tree.

- **Create:** Allows you to create objects below this object. This applies to container objects only.

- **Delete:** Allows you to delete an object from the tree.

- **Rename:** Allows you to rename an object.

What Are Property Rights?

ROPERTY RIGHTS AFFECT how a user can access information about an object. You can have access to certain properties (attributes) or all the properties of a particular object. This type of access can be received by granting you (as a user object) various rights at the property level. NetWare 4 includes the following property rights:

- **Supervisor:** Grants all other rights at the property level of an object. Note that Supervisor rights at the property level do not grant you Supervisor rights at the object level. Only the reverse is true.

- **Compare:** Tests for a value match and returns a true or false. Compare is a subset of the Read right. If you have Read rights, you automatically have Compare rights at the property level.

- **Read:** Returns a value (the contents) of a property. Read implies the Compare right.

- **Write:** Allows you to modify, add, change, or delete a property value. Write implies the Add/Delete Self right.

- **Add/Delete Self:** Allows you to add or remove yourself as a value of a property. This right is included in the Write right; if you have the Write right to a property, you also have the ability to perform Add/Delete Self operations. This right is used only for properties where your user object can be listed as a value, such as group membership lists or mailing lists.

The NWAdmin utility allows you to selectively assign property rights to particular objects or to assign all property rights through the [All Properties] option. For example, if you assign the Write right to [All Properties] of an object, you are granting Write rights to every property in the object. Selectively assigned property rights override those assigned through the NWAdmin utility's [All Properties] option.

Initially, a user object receives the Read property right to the [All Properties] category. This means that users can read the values of all their own user object's properties.

Understanding the Relationship between Object and File Rights

U NDERSTANDING THE RELATIONSHIP between objects and files is the key to understanding NetWare 4 security. Keep in mind that objects can receive object and property rights to other objects. Objects can also receive rights to the file system. The file system can also have attributes assigned to it. Figure 14.1 shows the relationship between objects, properties, and files.

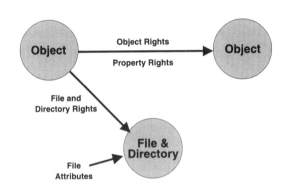

File Attributes

File attributes have been added to the file system to give more functionality to NetWare 4, The attributes in NetWare 4 are listed in Table 14.2.

	ATTRIBUTE	ABBREVIATION	DEFINITION
TABLE 14.2 NetWare 4 File Attributes	Compress	Co	Status attribute that indicates the file is compressed.
	Can't Compress	Cc	Status attribute that indicates the file cannot be compressed because of limited space savings.

	ATTRIBUTE	ABBREVIATION	DEFINITION
TABLE 14.2 NetWare 4 File Attributes (continued)	Don't Compress	Dc	Added to a directory, the Dc attribute keeps all files within the directory from being compressed. This attribute can also be added to a specific file.
	Immediate Compress	Ic	Added to a directory or file, the Ic attribute alerts the file system to compress a file as soon as the operating system can handle the action.
	Migrated	M	This status attribute indicates that the file has been migrated.
	Don't Migrate	Dm	Added to a directory, the Dm attribute will not allow files within the directory to be migrated to secondary storage. This attribute can also be added to a specific file.

The Access Control List (ACL)

Each object has an Access Control List (ACL). The ACL is a multi-valued property of each object in the NDS tree. The ACL contains three entries:

- Trustee name

- Type of access (object, property, and [All Properties])

- Actual rights being assigned

Figure 14.2 illustrates the rights stored in an ACL.

FIGURE 14.2

Rights stored in
user Jeff's ACL

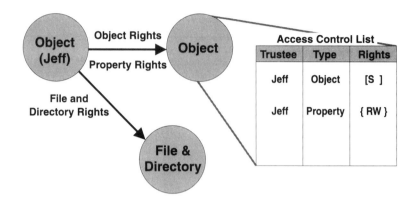

The ACL is similar to the DET in the file systems for both NetWare 3 and NetWare 4. The DET is the mechanism used to store trustee information for the file system.

The ACL is very powerful, and its access should be closely controlled for every object on your network. Because the ACL is a property of an object, it can be modified if someone has Write rights to the object's ACL property. This means that if someone possesses this right, they can reassign rights to that object, delete it, or rename it.

The NWAdmin utility allows you to selectively assign property rights to selected objects, or to assign rights to all the properties by using the [All Properties] option. For example, if you assign the Write right to the [All Properties] category of an object, you are granting the Write property right to every property including the Access Control List (ACL). See the warning.

The selectively assigned property rights override those assigned through the NWAdmin utility [All Properties] option.

Remember, the ACL is a property. A user with the Write right to the ACL has complete control over that object and can assign any rights. By default, users do not receive Write rights to even their own user object ACL. Novell utilities do not freely grant this privilege. However, anyone logging in to the network as Admin or equivalent can grant a user object the Write right to any object's ACL, thus creating a possible breach in your security.

Implementing NetWare 4 Security

W ITH THE DEFINITIONS and groundwork in place, we will proceed with our discussion of NetWare 4's security mechanisms and how to implement them in your environment. Rights are assigned and flow in the order shown in the pyramid in Figure 14.3. This pyramid (part of the QuickPath Process) is ordered in the most logical fashion for understanding NetWare 4 security.

FIGURE 14.3

The pyramid of NDS security concepts

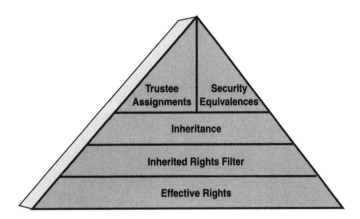

For our discussion, let's assume that World Wide Widgets has given us, as network administrators, the following assignments:

1. Install a new file server under the new OU:Tele (the Organizational Unit for the telemarketing division).

2. On this new server, install word processing software and a new client-tracking database to manage our customers.

3. Designate an individual to manage the NDS objects in OU=Tele.

4. Designate another person to be the file system administrator only in OU=Tele.

Our scenario is shown in Figure 14.4.

FIGURE 14.4

New department requirements for our example

- **Install new file server under OU=Tele**
- **Word processor software and client-tracking database**
- **Someone else to manage the OU=Tele**
- **Someone else to be in charge of the applications and database**

Using Trustee Assignments

A trustee assignment is the rights granted to an object for a specific file, directory, object, or property. A *trustee assignment* is a direct, explicit assignment of rights.

During installation of NetWare 4, certain explicit assignments are automatically made for you. Trustee assignments are granted for various NDS objects, servers, and users. Trustee assignments are stored in the ACL property of every object.

Default Trustee Assignments for Users

For example, the Admin user receives an explicit assignment of Supervisor at the [Root] object, as shown in Figure 14.5. This assignment is known as a trustee assignment because Admin is made a trustee of the [Root] object. [Public] is a trustee and receives an explicit trustee assignment of Browse for the [Root] object. This allows users to browse the entire tree before logging in.

Some companies may consider the Browse assignment for the [Public] trustee as a security breach. You can limit the view of your tree by revoking Browse rights to the [Public] trustee. An alternative is to assign the [Root] object Browse rights, so that after a user has logged in to a server, that user can browse the objects in the tree.

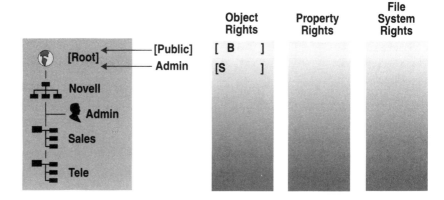

FIGURE 14.5

The default trustee assignments made when you initially install NetWare 4

Default Trustee Assignment for Servers

The NetWare 4 installation utility also makes trustee assignments at the file-system level. The following are the default file system assignments:

- The Admin user is granted Supervisor rights to the server's object. Supervisor privileges granted to a server object also grant Supervisor rights to the NetWare file system. (This is the only instance in NetWare 4 security where object rights overlap with file system rights.)

- [Public] receives the {Read} property right to the server object's network address property.

- OU=Tele (the Organizational Unit in our example) receives Read and File Scan rights to the server's PUBLIC directory. These rights are granted so that all users inside OU=Tele can execute files and utilities located within that OU object.

- The [Root] object receives the {Read} property right to the volume object attributes Host_Server name and Host_Volume name.

- [Public] receives {Read} rights to a NetWare 4.1 server's messaging service, if present.

Figure 14.6 shows how these trustee assignments are made for a server object.

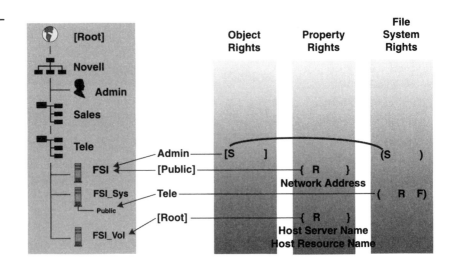

Default Trustee Assignment for Users

Network users also receive some default trustee assignments. These assignments greatly reduce the amount of work required to set up user accounts and their access.

Using the user object named Jeff as an example, the following access is automatically granted during creation of a user:

- A user object Jeff is created.

- Object Jeff receives the {Read} right to the [All Properties] category. This allows Jeff to read all the properties of his object.

- Object Jeff is granted Read and Write rights to his object's Login Script and Print Job Configuration properties. This allows user Jeff to read and modify his login script or print job configuration.

- The [Root] object receives the {Read} property right to user object Jeff's Network Address and Group Membership properties.

- The [Root] object receives Browse rights to user object Jeff and the {Read} property right to object Jeff's Default Server property.

These assignments are illustrated in Figure 14.7.

FIGURE 14.7

Rights assignments made when a user object is created

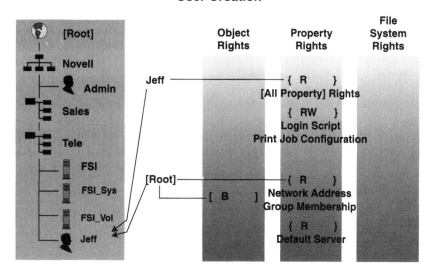

User Creation

Rules Governing Trustee Assignments

When you are setting up trustee assignments, remember that these assignments flow down the tree. When an assignment is made at any level in the tree to an OU, this assignment flows down the tree unless blocked by an IRF.

An explicit trustee assignment at a lower level replaces all previous trustee assignments. As shown in the example in Figure 14.8, user Jeff has been granted explicit Create and Rename rights beginning at the [Root] object. This trustee assignment flows down until blocked by an IRF or reassigned by another explicit assignment. In our example, we are reassigning the object Jeff the Browse right at the OU=Tele. This explicit assignment has replaced all other higher assignments at the OU=Tele level in the tree. Therefore, Jeff has only Browse rights to OU=Tele.

Creating Adminstrators through Trustee Assignments

In the example we're using in this chapter, we've been given the assignments of creating two subadministrators: an NDS administrator to manage the NDS objects in your new telemarketing division Organizational Unit (OU=Tele),

FIGURE 14.8

How explicit trustee assignments flow down and can be reassigned at a lower level in the tree

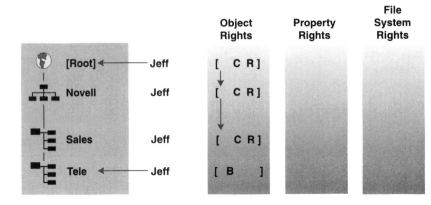

and a file system administrator for the server, named FS1 in this example, in OU=Tele.

Figure 14.9 shows an example of how we could create these subadministrators by giving these users explicit trustee assignments. In this example, we grant user Blair explicit Supervisor rights at the OU=Tele level. Blair would also receive Supervisor rights to the file server FS1 under OU=Tele. This is an implied right received through security equivalence. Next, we grant Carl explicit Supervisor rights to the server FS1. This would allow Carl to be a file system supervisor.

Although you can create subadministrators through trustee assignments, using OR objects and security equivalence usually provides a better way to do this. You can also use an Inherited Rights Filter (IRF) to separate administrative tasks. These methods are discussed later in this chapter.

Using Security Equivalence

Security equivalence means that an object is made equivalent in rights to another object's rights. The following are some examples of how security equivalence can be used to control user access:

- In conjunction with OR objects to create subadministrators

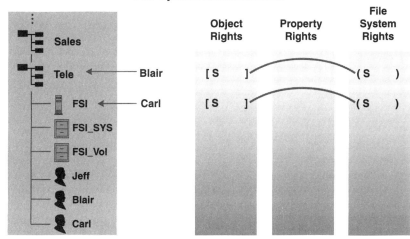

FIGURE 14.9

Explicit trustee assignments to create an OU administrator and a separate file system administrator

■ In conjunction with Group objects to specify rights for members of a group

■ In conjunction with Directory Map objects to map directories for a group of users

Much of the access received by users in a NetWare 4 environment is handled through security equivalence.

Creating Administrators through Security Equivalence

In the section about understanding trustee assignments, we explained one way to create subadministrators. We described how we could create an NDS administrator and a file system administrator for OU=Tele by giving these users explicit trustee assignments. An easier and safer way to create these administrators is through the use of OR objects. You can use an OR object to define a role and assign it rights. This way, you avoid assigning particular users explicit trustee assignments, which are more difficult to monitor and audit.

Figure 14.10 illustrates how we can create OR objects for an NDS administrator and a file system administrator, and give them Supervisor rights through security equivalence.

FIGURE 14.10

Creating OR objects for an NDS administrator and a file system administrator. Blair and Carl receive their Supervisor rights through security equivalence.

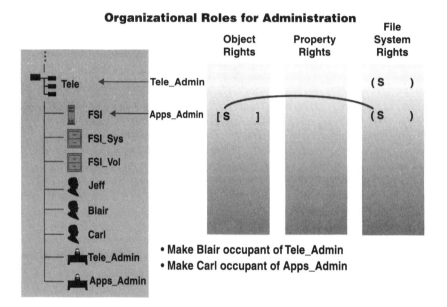

Here are the steps in this example:

1. Create a Tele_Admin role and an Apps_Admin role inside OU=Tele.

2. Grant explicit Supervisor rights to Tele_Admin at OU=Tele.

3. Grant Supervisor rights to Apps_Admin at FS1.

4. Make the users occupants of their respective roles.

In the Figure 4.10, users Blair and Carl receive their Supervisor rights because they are security equivalent to the OR object as long as they are occupants of that role. Once removed from the role, they no longer have a security equivalency to that role.

Implied Security Equivalence

Every object is security equivalent in rights to all container objects that are part of its fully distinguished name. This security is known as *implied security equivalence*.

As you can see in Figure 14.10 (in the previous section), user Carl is security equivalent to all objects contained in his name: Carl.Tele.Sales.WWW. Therefore, if you assign rights to any of the container objects (Tele, Sales, or WWW), Carl will automatically receive those rights, because he is security equivalent to any object in his name.

Because of this design, you can make broad rights assignments at high levels in the tree, and those rights can apply to a whole group or even an entire company. For example, you could place a mail server under OU=Sales to provide all the users in the sales department access to that server.

Another way you could use implied security equivalence is to assign rights to applications stored on a superserver. Place the superserver object one level higher than the OU objects in the tree that needed access to it. The rights you grant to the superserver's OU will be received by each subordinate OU and the users in each OU.

Using Security Equivalence with Groups

Security equivalence is also a handy way to take care of rights for groups of users. Remember our assignments at the beginning of our discussion of implementing security? One of our tasks is to set up word processing in our new telemarketing division (OU=Tele). We can create a word processing group, assign rights to the newly created group, and then add members to the group. The rights of the users in the group are security equivalent to those given to the Group object.

Figure 14.11 illustrates an example of using this method with a Group object named WP_Group. After creating WP_Group, we can assign it Read and File Scan rights to the FS1_SYS\APPS\WP directory.

Using Security Equivalence to Map Directories

Security equivalence can also be used for mapping directory paths for users. Another one of our assignments for this chapter's example is to give the users in the new telemarketing division access to our new client-tracking database. To accomplish this, we could create a Directory Map object that points to our client-tracking software, and then create a Group object for the telemarketing division. Assign the necessary file rights to the group, and the mapping will work.

An alternative is to make each user security equivalent to the Directory Map object, which has the assigned file rights. The users would receive the file rights through their security equivalence to the Directory Map object.

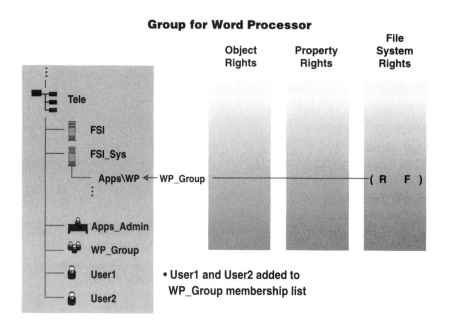

FIGURE 14.11

Users 1 and 2 are added to the WP_Group membership list. Each user receives the rights granted to the WP_Group through security equivalence.

A Directory Map object contains the volume and path that you specify. If you ever need to install a newer version of software, all you need to change is the pointer in your Directory Map object. See Chapter 2 for more information about Directory Map objects.

Rules Governing Security Equivalence

The following are the rules that govern security equivalence:

- Security equivalent rights flow down. If you receive security equivalence assignment at a higher level in the tree, these rights flow down independently of any other trustee assignments. In other words, an explicit trustee assignment does not affect rights received through security equivalence; they are independent of each other.

- Every object is security equivalent in rights to all container objects that are part of its fully distinguished name. This is known as *implied security equivalence*.

- Every object is security equivalent to the [Root] object. This is part of an object's fully distinguished name, although it is implied (not written).

- Every object is security equivalent to [Public], which allows users to browse the tree before logging on to a server (when the default Browse right assignment is in effect).

- Security equivalence is not transitive which means that the rights will only pass to one other object and stop. For example, if the object A is security equivalent to object B (A= B) and object B is security equivalent to object C (B= C), then object A is *not* security equivalent to object C (A != C). Object A is not security equivalent to object C because security equivalence is not transitive.

Generally, you should avoid the use of [Public] for granting rights. Remember, each user is security equivalent to the [Public] trustee, and [Public] has been granted Browse rights at the [Root] object. See the section about default trustee assignments for users, earlier in this chapter, for more information about the [Public] trustee.

Understanding Inherited Rights

Inheritance is the method by which rights to objects and files flow down to subordinate levels of the tree. The rights you receive at lower levels without assignment are known as *inherited rights*. Inheritance works the same way in the file system.

Do not confuse security equivalence and inheritance; they are not the same. Security equivalence applies when an object is made equivalent to another object's explicit trustee assignments. Inherited rights are rights assigned higher in the tree that flow down to an object at a lower level in the tree, without specific assignment.

Earlier in the chapter, we showed how user Jeff can be given Create and Rename rights at the [Root] object. We illustrated (in Figure 14.8) how the Create and Rename right assignments flow down the tree unless otherwise blocked. At the second and third OU levels of the tree, user Jeff inherits the Create and Rename rights from the level above.

The following rights can be inherited:

- Object rights

- File and directory rights

- [All Properties] category rights (made through the [All Properties] option in the NWAdmin utility)

Individual selected property rights are not inherited. For this reason, it is somewhat difficult to create a very specific type of administrator. For example, if you wanted to create a password administrator who only has the power to reset users' passwords, you would need to assign the password administrator (or OR object) explicit properties for each user in the OU object. This becomes a problem if you have hundreds of users in your OU.

You can use the [All Properties] option, which is inherited, but you will be assigning rights to the administrative role for all the properties of the user object. Again, one of the properties of any object is the ACL, which you need to carefully control.

One way to create specialized administrators is to use Novell's AppWare Appbuilder tool with the NDS ALM (Application Loadable Module). You can quickly create a small application to do the busywork of assigning selected property rights for an administrative role to all users in an OU.

Inherited rights flow down independently of other rights assignments. Figure 14.12 shows how explicit rights assignments flow down independently of security equivalent rights. In the example, user Jeff has different rights at different levels in the tree.

Understanding Inherited Rights Filters

NetWare 4 uses the Inherited Rights Filter (IRF) to control the inheritance of rights. The IRF can be applied to any object, and it is an inclusive filter. This means that the rights that are included in the filter are the rights that object will receive, if granted from other sources. For example, an IRF of Browse placed on an OU object allows only users in that OU (or any OU in the tree) to Browse that OU object.

FIGURE 14.12

The explicit assignment of Supervisor flows down the tree independently of the Browse right, which was received because user Jeff is security equivalent to the [Public] trustee.

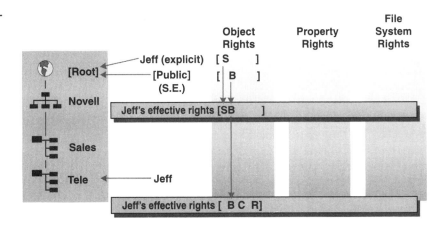

		Object Rights	Property Rights	File System Rights
Jeff (explicit)	[Root]	[S]		
[Public] (S.E.)		[B]		
Jeff's effective rights [SB]				
Jeff	Tele			
Jeff's effective rights [B C R]				

If you are placing an IRF on an OU object, the NWAdmin utility will require you to make an explicit trustee assignment of Supervisor to some other object, so that access to the OU is not permanently lost.

Securing Administrator Roles with an IRF

One way to use an IRF is to separate administration of particular objects. Remember the NDS and file system administrators for OU=Tele that we've been using in our examples in this chapter? An IRF can help make those roles more secure. Earlier, we created an OR object called Tele_Admin to administer NDS security for this role. We granted Tele_Admin Supervisor rights at OU=Tele. Because of this step, Tele_Admin also has Supervisor rights over any object created in the OU=Tele. One of the objects created is the file server object FS1. Having Supervisor rights to a server object means that you also have Supervisor rights to the file system for that server.

Because we have designated a separate file system administrator (with the OR object Apps_Admin), we need to use an IRF to block access to manage the file system to everyone but the Apps_Admin. You will need to carefully follow these steps in the order shown:

1. Grant the Apps_Admin OR Supervisor rights to the server object FS1.

2. Place an IRF on the server object FS1 of Browse rights only. This filter will allow users to have only Browse rights at the server object FS1. Only the Apps_Admin role has been granted explicit Supervisor rights to object FS1.

3. Place an IRF of Browse only on the OR Apps_Admin. Be sure to assign your Admin user (or subtree administrator) explicit Supervisor rights to the OR object so that somebody can continue to manage this OR. The IRF on the OR restricts the occupants of the Apps_Admin role from adding or deleting any of its occupants. This step presumes that the Tele_Admin or some other administrator determines who manages the FS1 file system.

By taking these steps, you will separate file system responsibilities from NDS responsibilities. This is only one example of how IRFs can be used in your company. Keep in mind that an IRF applies only to an object or properties, and it is the last step in the determination of rights.

Rules Governing IRFs

The following rules govern IRFs:

- The IRF cannot grant rights; it only revokes previously assigned rights.

- You can enable an IRF for every object, property, directory, and file.

- Supervisor object and property rights can be revoked by an IRF.

- Supervisor file and directory rights cannot be revoked by an IRF. This feature is identical to the NetWare 3 Supervisor rights.

Understanding Effective Rights

The final step in our security pyramid is the calculation of effective rights. *Effective rights* are what an object can actually do after all other security factors are calculated against the object.

Effective rights can vary for a user object at different levels in the tree. As shown in Figure 14.13, Jeff's effective rights are calculated at different levels in the tree. When you use Novell's NWAdmin Utility, your effective rights will be displayed for the particular context you are in. If you move up or down the tree, your effective rights will be different.

FIGURE 14.13

Effective rights are calculated for each level in the tree. When you refer to an object's effective rights, you need to understand the context of that object in the tree.

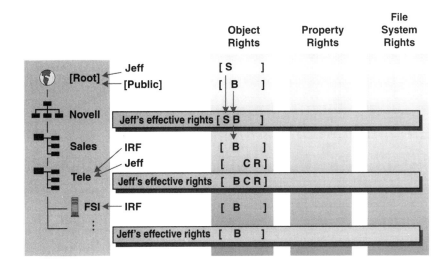

The scenarios for enabling NDS security are enormous. Fortunately, many of the basic user, server, and NDS assignments are made automatically. Your task as a network administrator is to create the specialized roles and assign rights to these roles. You will also create directory maps and groups that need special rights assignments for your users.

Monitoring and Maintaining NetWare 4

QuickTips: Managing NetWare 4

■ Use the NetWare 4 utilities to monitor 324

and maintain NDS. Leave all NetWare 4 servers on at all times. Each Net-Ware 4 server that contains replicas is part of a replica list and consequently is part of a group of servers that interact with each other.

- If a server is down for more than a few hours, use a partition utility (Partition Manager in NWAdmin or PARTMGR.EXE) to remove any master replicas that exist on the server. Verify through DSREPAIR or DSTRACE that other servers are not trying to synchronize to the server before you bring it down.

- Use DPING to discover the NetWare 4 servers on your network. Keep in mind that DPING does not work over a router. You must be on the other side of the router to discover other NetWare 4 servers. (DPING is available from NetWire.)

■ Monitor time synchronization by using 325

DSREPAIR or the TIME command on the server console to make sure that the server's time is synchronized to the network time on all other servers. If you must change the time, down the server and then change the time on the workstation by using the DOS TIME command. You can then reboot the server by powering down and back on again.

■ Monitor the disk space available on the 331
SYS volume

so that the SYS volume does not run out of disk space. If the SYS volume becomes full, TTS shuts down. Be sure to set the minimum disk space alerts on your NetWare 4 server, so you are warned of a potential problem. Save space by placing print queues and user files on a volume other than SYS.

■ Before you perform any partition or replica 332
operations,

verify through DSREPAIR or DSTRACE that all replica synchronization processes have successfully completed. Here are some tips for performing partition and replica operations:

- Perform partition join operations at off-peak hours so that the operations do not compete for bandwidth and crowd network traffic.

- Avoid using the Rebuild Replica option during busy network times because it can generate a large amount of network traffic. This option should only be used for persistent -659 time synchronization errors.

Before renaming the server or changing   333
the internal IPX address,

check the synchronization state of the server. Also be sure that the server contains a replica of the partition in which the server object is contained. Use extreme caution when changing a server's internal IPX address. Duplicate internal IPX addresses cause erratic problems with NDS synchronization.

If a hardware failure of the SYS   337
volume occurs,

you may need to reinstall NetWare 4.11 on the new hardware. First, use the DSMAINT utility to preserve your server references without deleting the NDS object that represents the server. If the downed server held any master replicas, use DSREPAIR to designate a read/write or a read-only replica on another server as the new master replica. Then reinstall NetWare 4.11 on the new hardware. You can reuse the same server name context. Finally, restore the NDS objects and file system directories and files. Additionally, you can use a new utility from Novell known as DSMAINT to temporarily back up NDS's hidden files while you replace SYS volume hardware. Keep in mind that this utility is designed for planned hardware outages, where you want to add additional space to your SYS volume.

If users are having workstation problems,   342

check to see if many clients are experiencing the same problem. If only a single workstation has problems, first check that the hardware adapter is connected properly and look for other hardware problems. You can also check the client's NET.CFG file for any problems. Make sure that the workstation has the latest client software. Log in as another user to determine if the user account is experiencing problems. Log in with the /B option for a bindery connection to see if the problem is with an NDS connection.

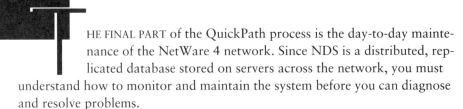

HE FINAL PART of the QuickPath process is the day-to-day maintenance of the NetWare 4 network. Since NDS is a distributed, replicated database stored on servers across the network, you must understand how to monitor and maintain the system before you can diagnose and resolve problems.

This chapter provides guidelines for monitoring and maintaining NDS. Follow the suggestions here and your network should be a stable and dependable one.

Using NetWare 4 Tools

AINTAINING NDS REQUIRES that you know how to monitor the NDS activity. Only by doing that can you keep the system running well and recognize potential problems. In order to recognize problems, you need to be familiar with a few NDS internal mechanisms. You should also know how to use the NDS tools, particularly the DSREPAIR utility and the DSTRACE command.

Refer to the Novell online documentation for 4.11 or your NetWare manuals for more details on using the maintenance utilities.

Monitoring NDS with **DSREPAIR**

DSREPAIR is an NLM-based utility for monitoring the status of the NDS database and repairing problems on the server. DSREPAIR checks the replica status for all replicas in a partition and validates the objects, properties, and values in the NDS database.

You should always log the output of DSREPAIR to a log file and check the log file after the repair to see if the objects in the replicas have been affected.

Tracing NDS Problems with **DSTRACE**

DSTRACE is a SET command supported by all versions of NetWare 4. DSTRACE provides the administrator with trace information about the NDS synchronization process. When DSTRACE is enabled, an NDS information screen is created. This screen displays trace information on the server console. DSTRACE is similar to Novell's Track On, which is used on NetWare 3 servers for monitoring server communications.

You can monitor the DSTRACE information to see how well the synchronization process is going. You can watch each replica of a partition contact each of the other replicas in its list.

Refer to Appendix A for a listing of the DSTRACE commands and their functions.

Viewing a Server's Database with **DSVIEW**

The DSVIEW.NLM utility was originally used by NDS development engineers to view a single-server NDS database and its records. The fields in the records are displayed in a raw format, without much explanation. The utility can be useful for determining the physical size of an NDS database on a server. You can do more with DSVIEW if you have a lot of experience with NDS structure and schema.

Because DSVIEW.NLM is not intended for administrators, it does not ship on the NetWare 4 CD-ROM. DSVIEW.NLM is only available on NetWire, where it can be found in Library 14.

Checking Servers with **DPING**

You can use the DPING utility to discover the NetWare 4 servers on your network. You can run DPING.EXE from any workstation to display the NetWare 4 server names.

DPING does not ship with NetWare 4.11, but you can get it from NetWire.

Keep in mind that DPING does not work over a router. You must be on the other side of the router to discover other NetWare 4 servers.

Monitoring NDS

MONITORING NDS INVOLVES monitoring the synchronization state of replicas, monitoring time synchronization, and monitoring the disk space on the SYS volume. All three tasks are explained here. Leave all NetWare 4 servers ON at all times. Each NetWare 4 server will be part of a replica list and consequently is part of a group of servers that interact with each other.

Determining the Synchronization State of a Replica

Since NDS is replicated across many servers in the network, it is important to monitor the synchronization state of each replica. The replicas of a partition may contain different information during various times, but they are always moving toward consistency. For example, you should check the state of the replicas before performing any partition operations. Also, if you are planning to down the server for an extended period of time, you should first check the synchronization state of the replicas stored on the server.

You can easily determine the state of all replicas stored on the server by using either the DSREPAIR or DSTRACE utility. Both methods are described in the following sections.

Using **DSREPAIR** to Check Replica Synchronization

Follow these steps to use DSREPAIR to check the synchronization state of a replica:

I. Load DSREPAIR.NLM at the system console or through RCON-SOLE.NLM. You see the main DSREPAIR menu shown in Figure 15.1.

2. From the DSREPAIR menu, select Advanced options menu.

FIGURE 15.1

The NetWare 4.11
DSREPAIR menu

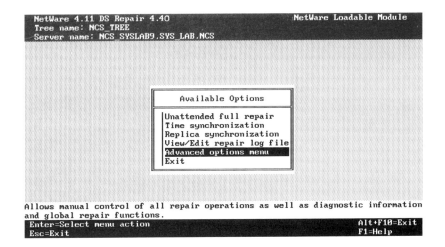

```
NetWare 4.11 DS Repair 4.40                    NetWare Loadable Module
Tree name: NCS_TREE
Server name: NCS_SYSLAB9.SYS_LAB.NCS


                        ┌──────────────────────────────┐
                        │      Available Options        │
                        ├──────────────────────────────┤
                        │Unattended full repair         │
                        │Time synchronization           │
                        │Replica synchronization        │
                        │View/Edit repair log file      │
                        │Advanced options menu          │
                        │Exit                           │
                        └──────────────────────────────┘



Allows manual control of all repair operations as well as diagnostic information
and global repair functions.
  Enter=Select menu action                                   Alt+F10=Exit
  Esc=Exit                                                      F1=Help
```

3. From the Advanced Options menu, select Replica and partition operations, as shown in Figure 15.2.

4. Check the information on the screen to see the synchronization state. In the example shown in Figure 15.3, the state of the replica is shown as ON. This replica is available for use.

Using **DSTRACE** to Check the Replica State

The second method for determining the state of replicas is to use the DSTRACE screen. To start the DSTRACE screen, type the following from the server console:

```
SET DSTRACE = ON
```

FIGURE 15.2

DSREPAIR's Replica and partition operations option allows you to change and/or repair replicas and partitions.

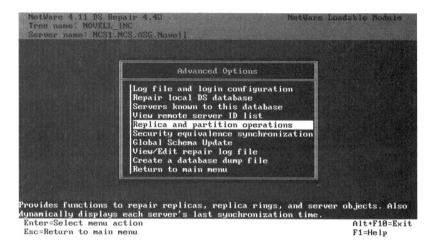

FIGURE 15.3

Partition and replica information is displayed. Notice that the state of the replica is ON, which means that it is available for use.

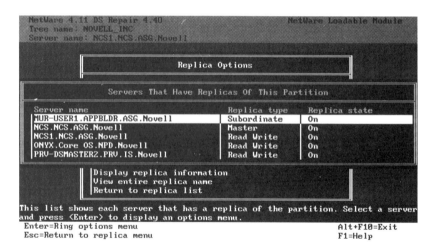

An example of a DSTRACE screen is shown in Figure 15.4.

You can also use the synchronization check feature of DSREPAIR to gather the same information and determine the state of your replicas.

Switch from the console screen to the DSTRACE screen. Check for the following message for each replica:

```
SYNC: End sync of partition <name>. All processed = YES
```

FIGURE 15.4

The DSTRACE screen displays synchronization information as it is occurring on that server.

```
SYNC: update to server <CN=PRV-DSMASTER2> successfully completed
SYNC: Start outbound sync with (5) [01000907]<MUR-USER1.APPBLDR.ASG.Novell>
 SYNC: sending updates to server <CN=MUR-USER1>
SYNC: update to server <CN=MUR-USER1> successfully completed
SYNC: Start outbound sync with (2) [010000A0]<NCS.NCS.ASG.Novell>
 SYNC: sending updates to server <CN=NCS>
SYNC: update to server <CN=NCS> successfully completed
SYNC: End sync of partition                    All processed = YES.

(94/12/19 14:10:05)
SYNC: Start sync of partition                    state:[0] type:[1]
SYNC: Start outbound sync with (1) [01000867]<ONYX.Core OS.NPD.Novell>
 SYNC: sending updates to server <CN=ONYX>
SYNC: update to server <CN=ONYX> successfully completed
SYNC: Start outbound sync with (6) [89000A05]<PRV-DSMASTER2.PRV.IS.Novell>
 SYNC: sending updates to server <CN=PRV-DSMASTER2>
SYNC: update to server <CN=PRV-DSMASTER2> successfully completed
SYNC: Start outbound sync with (5) [01000907]<MUR-USER1.APPBLDR.ASG.Novell>
 SYNC: sending updates to server <CN=MUR-USER1>
SYNC: update to server <CN=MUR-USER1> successfully completed
SYNC: Start outbound sync with (2) [010000A0]<NCS.NCS.ASG.Novell>
 SYNC: sending updates to server <CN=NCS>
SYNC: update to server <CN=NCS> successfully completed
SYNC: End sync of partition                    All processed = YES.
```

If you see the following message, the replica is not synchronized:

```
All processed = NO
```

You may need to wait a short time for the replica to synchronize. How much time depends on the number of objects in the partition and the number of replicas on the server. If the replica fails to synchronize, an NDS error condition may need correcting.

To remove the DSTRACE information screen, type the following at the server console:

```
SET DSTRACE = OFF
```

We recommend leaving DSTRACE running on all your NetWare 4 servers.

Monitoring Time Synchronization

As discussed in Chapter 6, you can use the TIME command from the server console to make sure that the server's time is synchronized to the network time on all other servers. If the time is synchronized, you see this message:

```
TIME IS SYNCHRONIZED TO THE NETWORK
```

You can also use DSREPAIR to check the status of time synchronization.

Do not use the TIME command on each server console to change the time on that server. Changing time on a server with the TIME command can cause problems with NDS synchronization.

If you want to feed the time (time of day) into the network, you should do that from the Reference or Single Reference time servers, not at an individual NetWare 4 server. If you must change the time, first down the server and then change the time on the server hardware by using the DOS TIME command. You can then reboot the server.

Before installing or rebooting a NetWare 4 server, always check your hardware time to make sure it is close to your local network's time. This makes convergence easier for the server when it becomes part of the NetWare 4 network.

If the server had previously synchronized its time to the network, but you see this message when you enter the TIME command,

```
TIME NOT SYNCHRONIZED TO THE NETWORK
```

several things may have happened to keep the time from being synchronized:

- The server cannot communicate with the other time servers because WAN links are not functioning.

- The time synchronization uses SAP to communicate, and the SAP value 26Bh is now being filtered by a router.

- The time synchronization is using the Single Reference (default) configuration and that server is not operational.

- The time synchronization is using the time provider group configuration. The Reference and Primary time server cannot talk to each other.

- You have configured only one Primary time server with a Reference time server, and one of these is not functioning.

If the time parameters are after the server name/address parameters in the AUTOEXEC.NCF file, your NDS time-stamps can be issued before the time zone is set. This can result in the NDS time being set backward.

In order to receive diagnostic information about time synchronization, type the following at the server console:

```
SET TIMESYNC DEBUG = 7
```

This tells TIMESYNC.NLM to display its messages on the server console. To turn the TIMESYNC information off, enter

```
SET TIMESYNC DEBUG = 0
```

See Chapter 6 for more information about NetWare time synchronization and time servers.

Monitoring the Disk Space on the SYS Volume

Never let the SYS volume run out of disk space. NDS is stored in a hidden directory on the SYS volume. It tracks all the writes to the database by using TTS (Transaction Tracking System), which provides server fault tolerance. If the SYS volume becomes full, TTS shuts down, and writes to the NDS database are no longer possible when that happens.

To prevent TTS from shutting down, you can take the following steps:

1. Set the minimum disk space alerts on your NetWare 4 server, so you are warned of a potential problem. You can set alerts through the NWAdmin utility.

2. Place your print queues on a volume other than SYS to preserve space.

3. Place user files on other volumes, or set the volume space limits for each user.

4. Periodically check the available disk space remaining on your SYS volume.

Maintaining NDS

M
AINTAINING NDS CAN involve performing partition and replica operations, renaming a server, changing the IPX address, removing a server, reinstalling a server, and performing backup and restore operations. These tasks are discussed in the following sections.

Performing Partition and Replica Operations

As discussed in Chapters 5 and 13, three NetWare 4 utilities perform partition and replica operations: NWAdmin (Partition Manager in the Tools option), DOS PARTMGR.EXE, and the newest NDSManager. Figure 15.5 shows an example of creating a new partition with the Partition Manager.

FIGURE 15.5

You can use NetAdmin's Partition Manager to create new partitions.

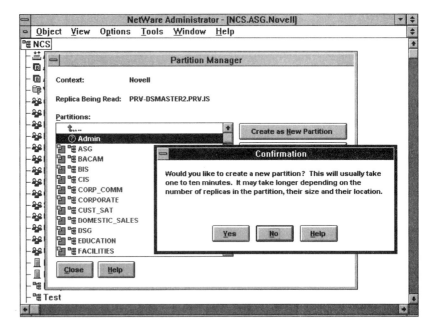

When you use a partition utility, it tells NDS to perform the partition or replica task and return control immediately to your workstation. Because NDS accepts the task, you can keep working and you don't have to wait for the NDS operation to complete (the NDS operation can take several minutes or several hours, depending on the request). A common mistake is to think that the task is complete when control is returned to the workstation.

See Chapter 5 for information about specific partition and replica operations and our recommendations for managing these operations.

Renaming a Server or Changing the IPX Address

Before renaming the server or changing the internal IPX address, always check the synchronization state of the server. Also, to make the process a little more efficient, you can have the server contain a replica of the partition in which the server object is contained (although NetWare 4.11 handles this operation very well).

To change the server name or address, follow these steps:

1. Edit the AUTOEXEC.NCF file to change the name or address.

2. DOWN the server.

3. Reboot the server.

4. SET DSTRACE=ON.

5. SET DSTRACE=+LIMBER.

6. SET DSTRACE=*l.

7. Switch to the DSTRACE screen and check for the following two messages:

   ```
   Limber: start connectivity check
   Limber: end connectivity check
   ```

   These messages indicate that the server name or IPX address change has been initiated (although the change is not yet complete).

The same steps are necessary if you want to move the server object from one part of the tree to another. You are simply changing the server name context in the tree, which is actually changing the name of the server.

Because this operation can be intensive to the server and replicas involved, we recommend making server name or address changes when the network is less active. For example, a good time to execute the function is before leaving for the evening or weekend, which leaves plenty of time for the name or address to be updated.

Removing a Server from the NDS Tree

You can remove a functioning server from an NDS tree by using INSTALL.NLM. As part of removing NDS from a server, a mapping of names to object IDs is created for every object on the server. The references are stored in a file that can later be used to reinstall the server. This way, trustee rights are not lost when the server is reinstalled.

If you are going to remove NDS from a server and you want to preserve the trustee assignments for the file system, you should run a full NDS backup first. See "Backup and Restore Operations for NDS" later in this chapter for more information. You can also use Novell's DSMAINT or INSTALL utilities to preserve server references.

Before running INSTALL.NLM, you can use NETADMIN or NWAdmin to remove the volume objects that represent the volumes on the target server. The 4.11 Install utility will also do this for you. Use PARTMGR.EXE or Partition Manager to remove all the replicas from the target server. Then select the Remove Directory Services from This Server option in INSTALL.NLM to remove NDS from the server.

INSTALL.NLM checks to make sure that it is safe to remove NDS from the server. To do that, it verifies that all replicas on the server have a state of ON and that all servers in the replica list have a status of UP. No downed servers or links to servers in the replica list should exist. If it isn't safe to remove NDS, INSTALL.NLM does not proceed with the operation.

INSTALL.NLM also prompts you to change the replica type of any master replica that exists on the target server.

The process automatically deletes the server object and all volume objects associated with that server.

Removing a functioning server from the NDS tree is not a good troubleshooting technique. In most cases, it is not necessary, especially when you do not fully understand the problem you are having.

Reinstalling a Server into the NDS Tree

If you want to reinstall a server that you removed from the NDS tree (one that still contains all its volumes and NetWare system files), follow these steps:

1. Boot the server and load INSTALL.NLM at the server console.

2. While in INSTALL.NLM, move through the maintenance menus until you can select to install NDS on the server. You are required to log in as an administrator with sufficient rights to place the server in the desired context in the tree. You can place the reinstalled server in any context you wish, even if it is different from the one you used before.

3. Place a read/write replica on the server, if needed. The Bindery Services feature requires a read/write replica in order to set the server's bindery context. Set the server's bindery context in SERVMAN.NLM in the NDS menu in NetWare 4.11 or in the Miscellaneous menu in NetWare 4.02.

Backup and Restore Operations for NDS

NDS uses a distributed, replicated name service to store the network resource objects. This means that you can easily restore any lost NDS data by means of the active replicas. If one replica becomes unavailable, a second replica services the user without interruption.

This discussion refers to NDS backup and restore procedures. You must also back up your file system data properly and frequently.

However, the replication backup mechanism does not provide sufficient protection in a single-server NetWare 4 installation. Nor does it provide sufficient protection if there are no replicas (or replicas are damaged). Furthermore, replication does not protect the NDS against the loss of an object or its accidental or deliberate deletion.

To protect your system from a catastrophic data loss of NDS, you must keep a properly maintained backup of NDS and server data. Having a backup of the NDS tree structure provides one more level of fault tolerance.

Having a backup of NDS can also be helpful in case of administrative errors. For example, suppose an administrator accidentally deletes an object or some values in an object's attributes. Having a backup allows the administrator to restore an object and its lost information.

The first prerequisite to having a good backup strategy is to acquire an NDS-compatible tape backup unit. Novell Labs provides a certification testing service to the manufacturers of tape backup hardware devices. The tape backup solution needs to support Novell's Storage Management System (SMS). SMS provides a Target Service Agent (TSA) designed to back up and restore NDS (TSA_NDS).

If the backup solution you choose has been tested and approved by Novell Labs, you can obtain test bulletins through Novell's Fax-Back system. The Fax-Back system can be reached at (800)414-LABS.

You can back up the NDS tree from any location. The SMS TSA_NDS.NLM allows you to back up or restore individual objects or groups of objects, such as Organizational Units (container OUs). Therefore, you can back up and restore select portions of a tree.

A major difference between NDS and the bindery in earlier versions of NetWare is the way in which the systems are backed up and restored. Since the object IDs are different across servers for the same user, the SMS TSA_NDS support module uses the object's distinguished name to back up and restore the trustee rights from the file system, although the file system in NetWare 4.11 still uses IDs stored in the Directory Entry Table for rights assignments. The bindery uses the objects' IDs. Because SMS uses object names, the user's trustee assignments are preserved, even if the user is deleted and re-created (a new object ID is assigned).

In order to back up NDS, at least one server in the tree must have the SMS TSA_NDS loaded. This server is used to start the backup operation for the rest of the tree. The backup and restore operation is not server-centric, but it can be completed from one server. The backup procedure may also allow you to select the entire tree, a specific container, or an individual object. When the tree is being backed up, the information for the partitions is not backed up—you cannot select just one partition and its information for the backup. The objects are restored to a single replica and then synchronized.

If you need to restore NDS from tape, NetWare 4.11 allows you to selectively restore the NDS information (NetWare 4.02 does not allow this). If an object does not exist in the tree (the object was deleted), new object IDs are assigned on the servers during the restore operation. If an object already exists in the tree, the object IDs are maintained and not overwritten.

Diagnosing NetWare 4 Problems

THE PROBLEMS YOU may need to resolve for your network fall in two categories: hardware failure of the SYS volume and TTS errors. The following sections provide some guidelines for diagnosing and repairing these problems.

Resolving Hardware Failure of the SYS Volume

If a hardware failure occurs on a NetWare 4.11 server that contains the SYS volume and the device is not repairable, you should perform the following steps:

1. Use the Install restore feature to preserve the server object. The file created by the File Server Target Service Agent (FSTSA) will have the name SERVDATA.NDS.

2. If the downed server held master replicas, use DSREPAIR to designate a read/write or a read-only replica on another server as the new master replica.

3. Reinstall NetWare 4 on the new hardware. The same server name context can be reused.

4. Restore the objects by using a tape backup or the partition management utilities to copy replicas of the partitions previously located on the downed server.

5. Restore file system directories and files from a previous tape backup. Backup software that backs up the trustees of the files and directories using the names of the objects (not object IDs) can restore the trustees of the file system.

Resolving TTS Errors

An out-of-memory condition can cause TTS to fail and start an infinite loop. The only solution to this problem is to power the server off.

If the SYS volume becomes full and TTS shuts down, NDS closes its files to any writes because it uses TTS for tracking the transactions. If this condition occurs (if a -621 transactions disabled error is reported), you should log in as a user that has been given explicit (not equivalent) Supervisor rights in NDS, free some disk space on the SYS volume by deleting some files, and then restart TTS.

Repair Strategies

The following information is intended to help you determine the cause of NDS problems. Troubleshooting is considered somewhat of an art form, but you can follow these basic procedures when you have an NDS error or related problem:

- Check the physical network environment first. Most network problems are caused by cabling, wiring, adapter cards, or infrastructure problems. Check and recheck the connections between servers and other network devices.

- Determine if the servers can see each other by typing the command DISPLAY SERVERS at the NetWare 4 server console. If you cannot see another server that you know exists, you likely have a physical communication problem. Determine if the server is powered on and if it is connected to the network.

- Check all wide-area connections, including bridges, routers, T1 connections, and so on. Make certain that you are not filtering SAP type 26Bh (time sync packets) or 278h on your routers. Also check for RIP filters that may have been enabled.

- Determine whether time is synchronized on all NetWare 4 servers. Time may not be synchronized if an error occurred during communication with another NetWare 4 server. You may also have misconfigured a time synchronization parameter. As discussed in Chapter 5, your time provider group should be kept fairly small so that you can quickly view the configuration of your time provider servers if errors occur.

- For further diagnostics, use the SET TIMESYNC DEBUG = 7 command to display detailed time information. As you are monitoring a server, you see the name of the server and its offset calculation. The offset calculation is the UTC time plus or minus the offset for your time zone. Each time server also displays its polling weight in the synchronization process. The following weights are assigned:

SERVER	POLLING WEIGHT
Reference Server	16
Primary Server	1
Server with communication failure	0

An example of the TIMESYNC Debug screen is shown in Figure 15.6.

Do not proceed with other repair operations until time is synchronized on your network. You can make things worse by proceeding without time synchronization.

Checking Error Conditions

NDS error codes give you an indication of what has caused an NDS error. Appendix A lists the NDS error codes and suggests corrective actions. This section describes the two most common error conditions.

The -625 Error

The most common error you will encounter is the -625 communications error. It occurs when a NetWare 4 server cannot send packets to another server.

This error can be caused by something as simple as a network cable not being securely attached to a server or as complex as a changed internal IPX

FIGURE 15.6

The TIMESYNC Debug screen can be very useful for determining the cause of time synchronization problems.

```
Server Type = 2
myPollDelay 750

TIMESYNC: Polled server PRV-DSMASTER
        Weight = 16, offset.h = 00000000  offset.l = 001C27C7

Uniform Adjustment Requested:  +0.001C27C7
Server Type = 2
Adjustment smaller than Correction Floor was ignored.
myPollDelay 900

TIMESYNC: Polled server PRV-DSMASTER
        Weight = 16, offset.h = 00000000  offset.l = 0E0F98DD

Uniform Adjustment Requested:  +0.0E0F98DD
Server Type = 2
myPollDelay 675

TIMESYNC: Polled server PRV-DSMASTER
        Weight = 16, offset.h = 00000000  offset.l = 001A81A1

Uniform Adjustment Requested:  +0.001A81A1
Server Type = 2
Adjustment smaller than Correction Floor was ignored.
myPollDelay 750
```

address. Check your physical connections first. Use the DISPLAY SERVERS command to verify the existence of the server in question. Perhaps the server has been shut off.

The -659 Error

If time is not configured properly, you see a -659 time synchronization error. This error occurs because a partition that needs updating has a time that is newer than the current network time. If your time provider group is not configured properly or someone has set time backward on a server, you see this error.

A configuration error on a server can cause problems throughout the entire network. Allow only network administrators to access the server console.

If you encounter a time synchronization error because the time was set incorrectly at a server, you can rebuild the replica based on the master replica's time. If the master replica's time has been set incorrectly, you can designate another replica as the master and then rebuild. Or you can reset the time on the current master replica and then rebuild the replica. Use DSREPAIR's

Rebuild Replica to rebuild replicas. Keep in mind that the rebuild operation is bandwidth-intensive.

Resolving Client Problems

OU MAY NEED to resolve NDS client-related problems on occasion. These problems usually arise when executing the client utilities or when workstations are performing slowly.

Executing Client Utilities

If you are experiencing problems executing client utilities, consider the following measures:

- Determine which server is processing the user's NDS requests by using the WHOAMI command.

- See if many clients are experiencing the same problem or if the problem is isolated at a single workstation. If it is a single workstation, first check the hardware adapter for proper connection and/or errors.

- Check the client's NET.CFG file for any problems, such as the preferred server setting to a server over a WAN link. You should be able to change the user's preferred server setting to a closer server. Also check the user's context setting. A user's context resides in a particular partition. If the partition is not local to the user, the request will be sent to a server that contains the user's partition. Also, check the user's default server attribute to determine if it has been set to a server that is not close to the user.

- If many users have a problem, check the versions of the utilities. For example, outdated DLL files may need to be upgraded to run the 4.11 utilities. This would require you to upgrade the workstation to the Client 1.20 version.

Investigating Slow Workstation Performance

Users may complain of slow performance on their workstations. You can check the following points to determine the cause:

- Are all users experiencing the problem or are users at a single workstation experiencing it? Again, a single workstation is much easier to resolve, because in most cases it is an infrastructure problem.

- Does the workstation have the latest VLM client software?

- Check the user's NET.CFG configuration for possible problems, such as the load order of the VLMs. Performance can vary depending on the load order of BIND.VLM and NDS.VLM.

- Take a network trace (using Novell's LANalyzer or a similar product) to and from the workstation to determine if any packet-level or NDS errors are occurring on the network.

- Try logging in as another user to determine if the user account is experiencing problems.

- Try logging in with the /B option for a bindery connection to see if the problem is with an NDS connection.

- Determine what changes (if any) have been made to the workstation or user's account prior to the problem. (Most users deny making changes to their systems!)

DSREPAIR and DSTRACE are key tools for monitoring a network. Although diagnosing problems can be difficult, the tools and procedures discussed in this chapter can greatly reduce the time needed to resolve problems with NDS.

This book has explained the QuickPath Process for understanding and implementing NetWare 4 in any network environment, be it a single-server environment or a large enterprise operation. You should now have a strong foundation on which to build a successful and powerful NetWare 4 network that expands as your needs change. The appendices that follow provide details that you may find useful for your particular NetWare 4 installation.

Appendixes

Troubleshooting NDS

his appendix offers information that can be useful for trouble-shooting NDS problems. It includes a listing of error codes and their meanings, as well as a discussion of the DSTRACE commands.

Deciphering the NDS Error Codes

Following is a list of the NDS error codes, what they mean, and any actions you can take to correct the error. Use this list as a reference when troubleshooting NDS-related problems on your network.

Error -601 (Hex: FFFFFDA7)

No such entry. The object name entered could not be found in the context specified. This error may occur because the workstation's context is incorrect for the object being sought, the name was mistyped, or leading dots or trailing dots were used incorrectly.

Check the context specified for the object name entered. If the command-line input was the object name, check the workstation's context. Make sure that it points to the correct level of the NDS tree for the object name specified. If the input includes the object's full or partial context, make sure that the leading and trailing dots are specified appropriately and the types are correct.

Error -602 (Hex: FFFFFDA6)

No such value. The requested attribute value could not be found.

Use NLIST to determine if the value exists for the specified attribute. If this error occurs during the login or authentication process, it usually means that either the user's or the server's public keys could not be located. Regenerate the user's key pair by changing the password.

If this error occurs during the synchronization process between servers, it is usually because one of the public keys cannot be located or the replica lists of one of the servers contains inconsistent results. This error may be a temporary condition that exists due to the loosely consistent nature of NDS. Another possible reason for the error is that the server's net address is missing.

Error -603 (Hex: FFFFFDA5)

No such attribute. The requested attribute (property) could not be found. In NDS, if an attribute does not contain a value, the attribute does not exist for the specific object.

Make sure that the attribute being requested is a valid NDS attribute (check the spelling and syntax). Use NLIST to determine if the attribute exists for the specified object. For example, NLIST *user=username*/d will show all attributes and their values for the specified user name. (Remember, you need Read attribute rights to an object to see all of the attributes associated with that object.)

Error -604 (Hex: FFFFFDA4)

No such class. An object class that does not exist in the NDS is being referenced by a utility. Object class in NDS is similar to object type in the bindery. For example, object type 1 in the bindery is a user object; in NDS, the object class is User. The class indicates the kind of object to be created.

NetWare 4 utilities access only Novell's base schema, which must be present for NDS to operate. Determine which utility is being used to create the object. The utilities that ship with NetWare 4 display only valid object classes.

This error also may indicate that the schema has not been synchronized. Use DSREPAIR's Schema Repair option.

Error -605 (Hex: FFFFFDA3)

No such partition. A partition with the specified name does not exist. An NDS partition is named by the [Root] object of the specified partition. The first partition in the Directory is [Root], which is the top of the NDS tree.

Make sure that the partition name requested is valid and is a valid object name.

Error -606 (Hex: FFFFFDA2)

Entry already exists. An attempt was made to add an object at the same level as a pre-existing object of the same name but not necessarily the same class.

Specify a different name for the object being added or rename the existing object.

Error -607 (Hex: FFFFFDA1)

Not effective class. The class being used to create the specified object cannot be used when creating an object. The two types of object classes in NDS are effective and noneffective. All effective classes (Users, for example) can be used when creating objects. Noneffective classes are used as "superclasses" to define information associated with various effective classes.

The standard Novell utilities that ship with NetWare 4 allow only effective classes to be used when creating objects. (The class being used to create the specified object is referred to as the *base class* of the object.)

Determine which utility is being used to create the object. This utility is not following the rules of the specified object.

Error -608 (Hex: FFFFFDA0)

Illegal attribute. An attempt was made to add an attribute that is illegal to an object. You cannot add the specified attribute to the specified object. The NDS schema determines which attributes can be inherited by an object class. (Refer to the NDS schema documentation for more information.)

Error -609 (Hex: FFFFFD9F)

Missing mandatory. One or more of the mandatory attributes for the object being created is missing. You must input the required information when creating the object.

Each object class in NDS has a set of mandatory attributes (attributes that must contain a value before the object can be created). For example, a User object in NDS is required to have a Common Name (CN) and a Surname. Without these attributes, the object will not be created. An attribute exists only if there is a value specified for the given attribute.

Error -610 (Hex: FFFFFD9E)

Illegal DS name. Illegal Directory names are those that are too long (more than 256 characters) or contain illegal character combinations. A backslash (\) can only be followed by a period (.), equal sign (=), plus sign (+), or another backslash.

Error -611 (Hex: FFFFFD9D)

Illegal containment. The containment rules of NDS specify where an object class may appear in relation to other objects in the NDS tree. For example, the object class Country can only be created at the top of the tree. The object class User can only be created under Organization and Organizational Unit objects. The schema enforces the containment rules for NDS. You must go to the appropriate container to create the object.

Error -612 (Hex: FFFFFD9C)

Object specified cannot have multiple values. The specified attribute is single-valued. All attributes are either single- or multiple-valued. An example of a single-value attribute is a Profile attribute. A multiple-value attribute is the Group Membership attribute.

Supply only one value (piece of information) for this attribute (information category in the utility).

Error -613 (Hex: FFFFFD9B)

Syntax violation. An attribute value being added to an object is incorrect. This error is most often encountered when that value is the name of another object that does not exist.

Verify that the object name being added as a value is correct or wait until the object has synchronized.

Error -614 (Hex: FFFFFD9A)

Duplicate value. An attempt was made to add a duplicate value to the specified attribute. Enter a different value.

Error -615 (Hex: FFFFFD99)

Attribute already exists. An attempt was made to add an attribute that already exists.

Error -616 (Hex: FFFFFD98)

Maximum entries exist. The maximum entries (objects) exist in the NDS tree. The maximum number of objects that can be created in NDS is FFFFFF (three bytes of FF), which is 16,777,220 decimal.

   For the current version of NDS, you have reached the maximum number of objects that can be created. To continue, delete objects that are no longer needed.

Error -617 (Hex: FFFFFD97)

Database format. The database format is invalid. Use the DSREPAIR utility's Repair Schema option.

Error -618 (Hex: FFFFFD96)

Inconsistent database. The server has detected an inconsistent database. Run DSREPAIR.

Error -619 (Hex: FFFFFD95)

Invalid comparison. An attempt was made to compare two attributes that are not comparable or to use an invalid compare syntax.

Error -621 (Hex: FFFFFD93)

Transactions disabled. The Transaction Tracking Service (TTS) has been disabled for the server on which the NDS operation is taking place. When TTS is disabled, NDS operations that require modifying the database on that server are disabled as well.

   At the console prompt of the file server, type **ENABLE TTS**. If TTS was disabled because the SYS volume is full, log in to the server and delete unnecessary files from the SYS volume, and then type ENABLE TTS at the console.

Error -622 (Hex: FFFFFD92)

Invalid transport. The type of transport passed in to the server is not supported by the server.

Error -623 (Hex: FFFFFD91)

Syntax invalid in name. The syntax for the name provided is invalid.

Error -624 (Hex: FFFFFD90)

Replica already exists. A replica of the specified partition already exists on the server.

Select a different server. (A maximum of seven or eight replicas for a partition is recommended.)

Error -625 (Hex: FFFFFD8F)

Communication failure. The server is unable to communicate across the network. The server reports a -625 error for 30 minutes after it detects a "down" state.

This is the most common error in NDS. It can occur for the following reasons:

- There is a temporary (or permanent) LAN or WAN failure.

- The destination server is down.

- The destination server has a different IPX internal net address than the replica list indicates.

- Multiple servers have the same IPX internal net address.

- The IPX timeout value is too low.

Check cabling and LAN communications. Check the server names and network addresses.

Error -626 (Hex: FFFFFD8E)

All referrals failed. The object could not be found. It is possible that the object exists, but the server could not communicate with the server holding a copy of the object.

This error message is common when partition management is requested and events cannot occur because a server is inaccessible. This may be a temporary condition during partition functions. The error can occur when links are down.

Error -629 (Hex:FFFFFD8B)

Entry is not leaf. The object being deleted or modified is not a leaf object. A container object that does not contain any objects is considered a leaf object, and therefore can be deleted. You cannot delete a container object that contains an object of any class. A container object that is a partition root cannot be deleted, even if it doesn't contain any objects.

Delete all objects under the container object that is being deleted or modified. If the object is a partition root, merge the partition with the parent partition and then delete the object.

Error -630 (Hex: FFFFFD8A)

Different tree. An attempt was made to access a server from a different tree.

Error -631 (Hex: FFFFFD89)

Illegal replica type. A replica needed to perform this function was not found.

Typically, you receive this error when you attempt to set your bindery context at the server console and the server does not have a read/write replica of the container you are attempting to reference in the bindery context. Use Partition Manager to add a replica that includes the bindery context to that server.

Error -632 (Hex: FFFFFD88)

System failure. Unexpected results have occurred. For example, the client requested that NDS return a network address attribute, and NDS actually returned a public key attribute.

This condition may be temporary. The client usually returns errors in the -301 to -399 range, but both the client and server return this error during the authentication process.

Error -633 (Hex: FFFFFD87)

Invalid entry for [Root]. An invalid entry for the [Root] object was made. This can be caused by restoring or moving an object that is flagged as a partition root but whose base class is not a container, or by trying to split an object whose base class is not a container.

Error -634 (Hex: FFFFFD86)

No referrals. The server has no objects that match the request and has no referrals on which to search for the object. This appears on a trace screen of servers without replicas.

Error -635 (Hex: FFFFFD85)

Remote failure. To complete some operations, a server needs to contact another server. If this is not possible (because a link is down, for example), this error is returned.

Error -636 (Hex: FFFFFD84)

Unreachable server. No action required.

Error -637 (Hex: FFFFFD83)

Previous move in progress. Once an object has been moved from one context in NDS to another, NDS does not allow that object to be moved again until all replicas of that object have been updated. The length of time this takes varies depending on the size of the replica, the number of replicas, and the condition of the communication links between all the servers holding the replicas.

You must leave the object in its current context until it can be moved again, which may be several minutes.

Error -641 (Hex: FFFFFD7F)

Invalid request. The server did not understand the request. For example, an action sent by a client could be incorrect.

Error -642 (Hex: FFFFFD7E)

Invalid iteration. An iteration handle sent by a client is invalid.

Error -643 (Hex: FFFFFD7D)

Schema is not removable. An attempt was made to delete an NDS structure or configuration.

Error -644 (Hex: FFFFFD7C)

Schema is in use. An attempt was made to delete an NDS attribute or class that is in use.

Error -645 (Hex: FFFFFD7B)

Class already exists. The object class being created already exists as a class in the schema of NDS (see Error -604).

This error should only occur in a utility that updated the schema of NDS. NetWare 4 does not include a utility to modify the schema. Determine which utility is causing the error.

Error -646 (Hex: FFFFFD7A)

Bad naming attributes. Invalid naming attributes were used.

Error -647 (Hex: FFFFFD79)

Not [Root] partition. An attempt was made to execute a function that is required on the [Root] partition. The client attempted to perform the function somewhere besides the [Root] partition.

Error -648 (Hex: FFFFFD78)

Insufficient stack. The server stack was not large enough.

Error -649 (Hex: FFFFFD77)

Insufficient buffer. The client did not allocate a large enough buffer for the request. See "Resolving Server Memory Problems" in Novell's *Supervising the Network*.

Error -650 (Hex: FFFFFD76)

Ambiguous containment. An attempt was made to create an NDS definition for a class that contained an ambiguous containment rule.

Error -651 (Hex: FFFFFD75)

Ambiguous naming. An attempt was made to create an NDS definition for a class that contained an ambiguous containment rule.

Error -652 (Hex: FFFFFD74)

Duplicate mandatory. An attempt was made to create an NDS definition for a class that contained a duplicate mandatory rule.

Error -653 (Hex: FFFFFD73)

Duplicate optional. An attempt was made to create an NDS definition for a class that contained a duplicate optional rule.

Error -654 (Hex: FFFFFD72)

Partition busy. Another partition operation is currently taking place. For example, if a request has previously been issued to split a partition, a second request for a split (even at another point in the same partition) results in this error.

Wait for the previous partition operation to synchronize completely.

Error -656 (Hex: FFFFFD70)

Crucial replica. This can be caused by trying to add a replica to the server where the master replica exists or trying to perform illegal operations on the master replica.

You can take one of the following actions:

- Remove the master replica from a server.

- Change the replica type of the master (by requesting that another server hold the master replica).

- Request that the master replica receive all updates.

Error -657 (Hex: FFFFFD6F)

Schema sync in progress. The function could not be completed because NDS synchronization of the schema is in progress. Wait a few minutes and try again.

Error -658 (Hex: FFFFFD6E)

Synchronization in progress. The function could not be completed because replica synchronization is in progress. Wait a few minutes and try again.

Error -659 (Hex: FFFFFD6D)

Time not synchronized. NDS uses time-stamps to determine the order of events that take place in NDS. Modification operations require the issuance of time-stamps. If a replica on a server has issued a time-stamp and the time on that server is set back, no further modification operations may take place until the time on the server moves past the last modification time on the partition. This applies only to operations that modify, not those that just read information.

Use Partition Manager's Rebuild Replicas option to reset the time-stamps to the current time, and then wait for the replicas to synchronize. You may need to do this on a partition-by-partition basis.

Error -660 (Hex: FFFFFD6C)

Record in use. The requested record is already in use.

Error -661 (Hex: FFFFFD6B)

DS volume not mounted. The NDS volume is not mounted.

Error -662 (Hex: FFFFFD6A)

DS volume IO failure. An I/O failure occurred on the NDS volume.

Error -663 (Hex: FFFFFD69)

DS locked. The Directory database is locked on the server. It may be necessary to run DSREPAIR on the server.

Error -664 (Hex: FFFFFD68)

Old epoch. An epoch is a partition. This error occurs when the partition's Partition Creation Time attribute has not been updated with the new, correct time.

Error -665 (Hex: FFFFFD67)

New epoch. Same as error -664.

Error -666 (Hex: FFFFFD66)

Incompatible DS version. Once the master replica exists on a NetWare 4.11 server, no further replica operations that involve earlier version NetWare servers can be performed on this partition.

For example, you cannot add a replica to a NetWare 4.02 server once a NetWare 4.11 server holds the master replica. Also, you cannot split a partition if the master replica is on a NetWare 4.11 server and there are earlier version servers in the replica list.

Error -667 (Hex: FFFFFD65)

[Partition] root. The object being manipulated is the root of an NDS partition. This error appears most often when you are attempting to delete a container object that is a [Partition] root.

Use the partition management tools to merge this partition into the parent partition.

Error -668 (Hex: FFFFFD64)

Entry not container. An illegal function was attempted on a leaf object.

Error -669 (Hex: FFFFFD63)

Failed authentication. The NDS database is locked on the server. An invalid password was sent. Authentication failed.

Error -671 (Hex: FFFFFD61)

No such parent. A parent was specified that does not exist.

Error -672 (Hex: FFFFFD60)

No access. The client does not have sufficient rights to perform the requested operation.

Error -673 (Hex: FFFFFD5F)

Replica not on. The replica is being created on a server. Until all the object information has been received on that server, the replica is "off" (not available for use by NDS clients). You must wait until the replica is created on the other server.

Error -678 (Hex: FFFFFD5A)

Duplicate ACL. An ACL for the object already exists.

Error -679 (Hex: FFFFFD59)

Partition already exists. An attempt was made to create a partition that already exists.

Error -680 (Hex: FFFFFD58)

An attempt was made to use a reference that is not a subordinate reference.

Error -681 (Hex: FFFFFD57)

Alias of an alias. An attempt was made to use an alias of an alias.

Error -682 (Hex: FFFFFD56)

Auditing failed. The auditing function failed.

Error -683 (Hex: FFFFFD55)

Invalid API version. An invalid application API is being used. You need to update your software.

Error -684 (Hex: FFFFFD54)

Secure NCP violation. An attempt was made to forge an NCP packet on a server using packet signing.

Error -686 (Hex: FFFFFD52)

Not leaf partition. A subtree can be moved only if it is a leaf partition.

Error -687 (Hex: FFFFFD51)

Cannot abort. This error occurs when you are trying to abort one of the following partition operations:

- Changing the replica type when the state of the replica does not show that the replica type is changing or that the change is not in the initial state.

- Splitting a partition when the state of the replica does not show that the partition is splitting or that the split is not in the initial state.

- Joining partitions when the state of the parent partition does not show that the partition is in the initial join state with the partition in the request.

- Moving a subtree when the move has proceeded past the initial move subtree state.

Error -698 (Hex: FFFFFD46)

Replica in synchronization. A server is currently in the process or receiving an incoming synchronization from another server in the replica list.

Error -699 (Hex: FFFFFD45)

Unknown. An unrecoverable error has occurred and the operation cannot be completed.

Error -701 (Hex: FFFFFD43)

Synchronization disabled. Synchronization has been disabled at the server.

Error -709 (Hex: FFFFFD3B)

Insufficient sockets. A DS client makes an invalid request and receives an invalid response.

Error -715 (Hex: FFFFFD35)

A checksum error has occurred.

Error -716 (Hex: FFFFFD34)

An error was received because checksumming is not supported.

Error -717 (Hex: FFFFFD33)

CRC error. A cyclical redundancy check has failed on a packet received during this operation.

Using the DSTRACE Commands

The DSTRACE SET commands offer many options for NDS trouble-shooting. To use the utility's commands, type the following at the NetWare 4 server console:

SET DSTRACE=+<command>

For example, to display all debugging information, type

SET DSTRACE=+ALL

To remove the display from the screen, type the same command again.

Table A.1 lists the DSTRACE commands. Note that some commands must be preceded by an asterisk (*) command instead of a plus sign (+).

T A B L E A . I DSTRACE Command Parameters	**C O M M A N D**	**F U N C T I O N**
	+ALL	Displays all debugging information.
	+AUDIT	Displays auditing information.
	+AUTHEN	Displays information about NDS authentication as it is happening.
	+BACK, +BACKLINK, *or* +BLINK	Displays back-link information.
	+COLL *or* +COLLISION	Displays NDS time-stamp collisions.
	+DEBUG	Displays predefined debugging level information.
	+DSA *or* +DSAGENT	Shows requests to the server agent.
	+E, +ERR, *or* +ERRORS	Displays NDS errors.
	+EMU	Displays bindery emulator information.
	+ERRET	Displays NDS errors.
	+I *or* +INSPECTOR	Verifies entry and entry references on local server. Requires large amounts of processing time.

COMMAND	FUNCTION
+J or +JANITOR	Displays removal of deleted entries.
+LIMBER	Shows verification and initialization of server name/address/replica tree connectivity.
+MISC	Displays miscellaneous related debugging information.
NODEBUG	Turns off debug information.
OFF	Turns off debug information.
ON	Turns on DSTRACE (minimum debugging level).
+PART	Displays partition information, such as debug statements.
+RECMAN	Displays hashing/iteration state handling.
+RN or +RES	Displays name resolution information.
+S or +SYNC	Displays synchronization process.
+SAP	Displays SAP information that is received on that server.
+SCHEMA	Shows schema synchronization.
+STREAMS	Displays processing of streams.
+TV or +TIMEVECTOR	Displays synchronization time-stamp information.
+VC or +VCLIENT	Displays virtual client activity between synchronizing servers.
*B	Starts the back-link process.
*F	Begins the process to remove deleted entries and attributes from files.
*H	Heartbeat, starts synchronization process immediately.

	COMMAND	FUNCTION
TABLE A.1 DSTRACE Command Parameters (continued)	*L	Starts Limber Up process, which verifies and initializes the server name and server address (if necessary), and displays connectivity of replicas.
	*R	Resets DSTRACEDBG file to 0 length.
	*S	Schedules Skulker.
	*U	Sets the state of all servers on the local server's replica list to Up so that this server can try to contact other servers without waiting the default time.
	*X#	Sets the number of IPX retries before getting a -625 error (default 3, range 1–500).

Always start debugging with the following three commands, in the order shown:

```
SET DSTRACE =+VC
SET DSTRACE =*H
SET DSTRACE =*U
```

The +VC command displays virtual client activity between the servers that are synchronizing. The *H command starts the synchronization process immediately. The *U command resets the 625 flag in NDS so that the replicas attempt to contact the server experiencing the -625 error immediately.

Following are some examples of DSTRACE commands you can use for troubleshooting:

COMMAND	WHAT IT DOES
SET DSTRACE=ON	Initializes DSTRACE on your console
SET DSTRACE=INIT+MISC	Displays messages about initialization and miscellaneous functions
SET DSTRACE=+J	Adds any trace messages about the janitor process
SET DSTRACE=SCHEMA	Displays messages about the schema process. Note that this does not add to the current displays, but replaces the current DSTRACE display with only schema messages.

Client Options
for Tuning VLM
Workstations

B

HIS APPENDIX COVERS memory parameters, NET.CFG variables, and login variables for the DOS/Windows client. This information is useful when you are tuning a workstation for memory or performance optimization.

VLM Memory Requirements

HE VLMS AND their memory requirements are listed in Chapter 10 of this book (Table 10.1). Figure B.1 shows a VLM memory dump.

The following terms are used in describing VLM and memory usage:

- *GSize*, which is the total memory size of the global segment (+ 6–8KB). You will notice the VLM GSize shows zero. The VLM actually requires 4.8KB of conventional memory.

- *TSeg*, which is the address of the transient swap block for executing the VLMs.

- *TSize*, which is the memory size of each VLM and its cumulative total (see the bottom of the memory dump shown in Figure B.1). This block can be in extended memory. Below the total memory is the maximum memory, which designates the largest VLM loaded. This largest block of memory is known as the *transient swap block*.

FIGURE B.1

A VLM screen dump

The VLM.EXE file v1.20 is currently loaded
VLM transient switch count   :1975
VLM call count   :8626
VLM current ID   :0040h
VLM memory type   :XMS
VLM modules loaded count   :12
VLM block ID (0 if CON)   :0001h
VLM transient block   :D8F4h
VLM global seg (0 if CON)   :CDD3h
VLM async queue (h, t, s)   :0000:0000, 104D:0030, 0
VLM busy queue (h, t, s)   :0000:0000, 104D:003C, 0
VLM re-entrance level   :1
VLM full map count   :1973

VLM diagnostic information   Address   Memory Sizes (decimal)

NAME	ID	Flag	Func	Maps	Call	TSeg	GSeg	Low	High	TSize	GSize	SSize
VLM	0001	A000	0005	0000	071B	104D	0B20	FFFF	0000	5376	0	0
CONN	0010	B000	0011	0000	0B93	CDD3	CE9E	FFFF	FFFF	3248	384	6704
IPXNCP	0021	B000	000B	0000	0042	CEB6	CFED	FFFF	FFFF	4976	2912	2032
TRAN	0020	E000	000B	0001	01D4	CEB6	CFED	FFFF	FFFF	311	182	2032
NDS	0032	A000	0010	0086	00B3	D8F4	D0A3	0000	0000	6112	896	992
BIND	0031	A000	0010	002F	0013	D8F4	D0DB	17E0	0000	3008	448	720
PNW	0033	A000	0010	0028	0026	D8F4	D0F7	23A0	0000	5680	2528	1376
NWP	0030	A000	0011	005F	0098	D8F4	D195	39D0	0000	3040	1840	1248
FIO	0041	A000	000B	0038	00ED	D8F4	D208	45B0	0000	7104	17376	0
GENER	0043	A000	000A	00A8	00A7	D8F4	D646	6170	0000	1760	720	1536
REDIR	0040	A000	0009	0306	07A0	D8F4	D673	6850	0000	10256	2688	1328
PRINT	0042	A000	000F	003E	0062	D8F4	D71B	9060	0000	3952	3440	1520
NETX	0050	A000	0007	0256	01D1	D8F4	D7F2	9FD0	0000	10064	4112	2224
Total							64576	37344				
Maximum										10256	17376	6704

The following are some general rules for determining memory usage with the VLMs:

- VLM/d shows a detailed VLM diagnostic screen.

- MSDOS MEM/d shows a detailed memory summary.

- MSDOS MEM/m:*<module>* shows the memory usage for the given *<module>*.

- VLM/d *VLM memory type* (CON, XMS, EMS) shows the memory location of the transient swap block for the loaded VLMs.

- The transient block known as the VLM TSize in VLM/d is the portion that may be swapped in and out of XMS/EMS memory.

- The Total TSize memory is loaded in the memory type listed in the VLM memory type category under VLM/d.

- The maximum listed under TSize in VLM/d is the worst-case swap from XMS/EMS to conventional memory. This becomes the transient swap block that will be located either in conventional or UMB memory.

- VLM shows 0 GSize memory, however, it takes about 4.8KB of conventional memory (or UMB memory if loaded high, as with LH VLM).

- VLM/d Address LOW: FFFF means the VLM is loaded in conventional memory.

- The GSize listed under VLM/d is the global memory requirement for each VLM. This GSize consists of interrupt handler ESR (Event Scheduled Routines), buffers passed as pointers, and asynchronous events, which *must* be loaded in conventional or UMB (upper memory block) memory at all times. The GSize cannot be located in XMS/EMS memory.

- The GSize memory must be allocated in one block. If insufficient UMBs are present to hold the entire GSize memory (GSize Total in VLM/d), the total listed under GSize will be located in conventional memory.

- If you are using XMS/EMS memory, add 6–8KB to the GSize total for VLM memory management overhead.

- If you are using *only* conventional memory (HIMEM.SYS), or an equivalent driver is not loaded, subtract 2–4KB not needed from the GSize total for VLM memory management.

- If the user has loaded *both* HIMEM.SYS and EMM386.EXE, but is not using the DOS=UMB parameter, the VLMs will allocate their own UMB through the memory manager, rather than through DOS. The GSize Total in VLM/d will load into UMBs, but MS DOS MEM will not show any UMB usage, because it is not in control of the UMB area. This makes it appear as if VLM.EXE is taking only 4.8KB of conventional memory, and no UMB memory. However, the GSize total is located in the UMB area.

Login Script Variables

ABLE B.1 LISTS the login script variables that can be used to enhance your login scripts. You must precede each of these commands with a WRITE command. Note that some of the variables do not have underscores in them. This is not a typographical error.

	VARIABLE	PURPOSE
TABLE B.1 Login Script Variables	%ACCESS_SERVER	Shows whether the access server is functional (TRUE=functional, FALSE=not functional).
	%ACCOUNT_BALANCE	Displays account balance information (if the accounting feature is being used).
	%ALLOW UNLIMITED CREDIT	Displays whether unlimited credit has been assigned for that user: Y or N.
	%CN	Displays the common name of the user who logs in to the network.
	%DESCRIPTION	Displays any value contained in the Description field for that user.
	%EMAIL ADDRESS	Displays the e-mail address of the user who has logged in.
	%ERROR_LEVEL	Displays an error number (0 = no errors).
	%FILE_SERVER	Displays the name of the file server stored in your NET.CFG preferred server statement.
	%FULL_NAME	Displays the user's unique user name. It is the value of the FULL_NAME property for both NDS and bindery-based NetWare. Spaces are replaced with underscores.
	%GROUP MEMBERSHIP	Displays the Group object if the user is a member of any group.
	%HOME DIRECTORY	Displays the home directory property set for the user who has logged in.

TABLE B.I

Login Script Variables
(continued)

VARIABLE	PURPOSE
%L	Displays the Locality.
%LANGUAGE	Displays the current language being used by the user.
%LAST_NAME	Displays the user's last name (surname) in NDS or full login name in bindery-based NetWare.
%LOGIN_CONTEXT	Displays the context for the user as found in NDS. This is the context where the user exists.
%LOGIN_NAME	Displays the user's unique login name (long names are truncated to eight characters).
%MACHINE	Displays the machine type of that workstation (IBM_PC, etc.).
%NETWORK	Displays the physical network address.
%OS	Displays the type of operating system on the workstation (MSDOS, OS2, etc.).
%OS_VERSION	Displays the operating system version on the workstation (3.30, etc.).
%PASSWORD ALLOW CHANGE	Shows the value of this user property: Y or N.
%PASSWORD_EXPIRES	Displays the number of days before the user password will expire.
%PASSWORD MINIMUM LENGTH	Displays the minimum password length setting.
%PASSWORD REQUIRED	Displays the value of the password required: Y or N.
%PASSWORD UNIQUE REQUIRED	Displays the property value of the unique password required: Y or N.
%POSTAL CODE	Displays the value of the user's postal code, if any.
%POSTAL OFFICE BOX	Displays the user's postal office box value, if any.

VARIABLE	PURPOSE
%PROFILE	Displays the name of the Profile object (if the user has a profile).
%P_STATION	Displays the workstation's node number (12-digit hexadecimal).
%REQUESTER_CONTEXT	Displays the context that is found in the workstation's NET.CFG file at the time of login.
%REQUESTER_VERSION	Displays the version of the VLM requester.
%SECURITY EQUALS	Displays security equivalence assignments made for that user.
%SHELL_VERSION, SHELL_TYPE	Displays the version of the workstation's DOS shell (1.02, etc.). Supports NetWare 2 and 3 shells and NetWare 4 Requester for DOS.
%STATION	Displays the workstation address for that user.
%SURNAME	Displays the user's surname property value, if any.
%TELEPHONE NUMBER	Shows the user's phone entered in his phone number property.
%TITLE	Displays a title for the user if one has been entered as a user property.
%USER_ID	Displays the number assigned to each user.

Any DOS environment variable can be used in a login script. Enclose the variable in angle brackets, as in <PATH>. To use a DOS environment variable in MAP, COMSPEC, and FIRE PHASERS commands, add a percent sign (%) in front of the variable, as in:

```
MAP S16:=%<PATH>
```

You can also use attribute (property) values of NDS objects as variables. Use the attribute values just as you do any other identifier variable. If the attribute value includes a space, enclose the name in quotation marks. To use an attribute name with a space, within a WRITE statement, you must place it at the end of the quoted string, as in:

```
WRITE "Given name=%GIVEN_NAME" IF "%MESSAGE SERVER"=
    "MS1" THEN MAP INS S16:=MS1\SYS:EMAIL
```

For a list of object attributes, refer to Novell's *Utilities Reference*, Appendix A, "NDS and Bindery Objects and Properties." Not all attributes are supported as login script variables.

To update users' NET.CFG files, you can run a batch file from the login script. In your login script, use an INCLUDE statement that calls a batch file to make the changes. For example, if a context for a container of users has changed, you can call a batch file from the login script to perform a search and replace the users' NET.CFG Context parameter.

NET.CFG Variables and Parameters

THE PARAMETERS LISTED in this section are new to the VLM version 1.20.

```
Load Low REDIR = Off/On
```

Default: Off. Improves small I/O performance. There is an increase of conventional memory usage in exchange for the increased performance. By loading REDIR low, additional conventional memory is used.

```
Load Low FIO = Off/On
```

Default: Off. Provides additional tuning, favoring performance over size. By loading FIO low, additional conventional memory is used.

```
Load Low NETX = Off/On
```

Default: Off. Provides additional tuning, favoring performance over size. By loading NETX low, additional conventional memory is used.

```
Force First Network Drive = Off/On
```

Default: Off. When turned on, this parameter will force the reestablishment of the first network drive when logging out from any other network drive. Note that the connection to the first network drive will be based on the connection of the drive from which the logout was performed.

```
LIP Start Size = 0 (576-65535 bytes)
```

0 = Off. Provided for networks that operate across multiple hop routes, with one segment of the connection that has smaller packet sizes than the local routes, but larger than the minimum packet size of 576 bytes. This improved algorithm improves performance while dramatically improving throughput.

```
Confirm Critical Error Action = On/Off
```

Default = On. Used to turn off the critical action pop-up dialog box in Microsoft Windows. This dialog box appears prior to tearing down a lost connection while in Microsoft Windows, to let the user choose to attempt a retry (and possibly auto-reconnect of connection) of the last request. This parameter is provided to ensure a critical error message is provided in the Microsoft Windows environment.

Many applications turn off the Microsoft Windows critical error-handling mechanism, forcing an automatic failure/cancel. This prevents the user from attempting to retry the connection before it is torn down.

```
Read Only Compatibility = Off/On
```

Default: Off. This is not a new parameter, but its default setting is new. It was set to On with the last major release of the product. This caused problems with too many applications, so the parameter has been set to Off by default.

Other New Features in the VLM 1.20 Client

T
HE FOLLOWING ARE other new client features:

■ **Node addressing:** If the node address is set to -1, the client will not require the presence of a NetWare 4 server to complete loading. This capability has been provided to allow the mobile networking products to work. This feature works in conjunction with the new IPXODI.COM, which provides the ability to set the node address to the -1 value.

■ **LIP negotiation:** The LIP negotiation algorithm has been changed to improve negotiation speed and decrease throughput. Previously, groups of three packets were used in the negotiation of the maximal LIP size. Two states have been defined to reduce the number of packets sent across the network. The redesign allows faster negotiation of LIP with far less packets going across the wire.

■ **Link handling:** A hook into the INT 24 handler has been provided to enable link handling of mobile products. This permits mobile products to tear down dormant connections, then reestablish them without causing critical network errors.

■ **NUL device support:** The NUL device support has been implemented in the version 1.20 VLMs. This enables command-line commands such as "If exists *NetWare path*\NUL(."

■ **VLM optimization:** The VLMs have been optimized to work cleanly with multiple redirectors. Some of the specific redirectors tested include those from 3COM, Novell NFS Client, and DEC Pathworks.

■ **Sideband error reporting:** A sideband network error reporting mechanism has been implemented to ensure network errors are not translated into DOS errors (where appropriate).

■ **Auto-retry:** The auto-retry character has been language-enabled. This permits the auto-retry feature to work in other languages in which an *R* does not signify retry. Support has been added to enable the auto-retry feature under Microsoft Windows.

■ **Internal notify code:** The internal notify code has been optimized to the load time performance of the VLMs, and to improve performance during login.

VLM Limitations

There are several limitations to the version 1.20 VLMs due to architectural factors. These limitations are being addressed in the design of the next release of the VLMs.

■ Maximum path length is 67 bytes. Previously, this was a 128-byte path length limitation. Due to the redirector implementation of the version 1.20 VLMs, this path length cannot be enhanced. This is due to the limitations of DOS. In many cases, path length limitations can be overcome by using a map root into the NDS tree.

■ Full command-line device redirection, where a NetWare path is used (such as F:\..\APPS) cannot be provided because of limitations imposed by DOS. The NUL device support is the only device that has been implemented.

■ The VLMs do not match the performance of NETX in the area of transaction speed. NETX can perform about 12 transactions per second; the VLMs can perform about 11 transactions per second. The difference in performance for the VLMs is due to the transition through DOS for each request/reply. The testing results are based upon an application designed to perform small record transactions. The VLMs meet and exceed the performance of NETX in mid- and large-sized reads and writes.

■ The VLMs are not able to operate in the private nor the global DOS sessions of NT and OS/2. These DOS environments do not provide the back-end Interrupt 2F support upon which the version 1.20 VLMs are built.

■ Some DOS device support may be slightly different from local DOS behavior. For example, if an application opened device F:\USER\JIM\PRN for printing, the requester would pass the request on to DOS, and DOS would fail the request since it's on a network path. A PTF (program temporary fix) version of GENERAL.VLM works around this problem, but the complete solution will be in the architecture of the version 2.00 client.

- Auto-reconnect will not work with packet signing enabled on an NDS connection (4.*x* server)

- Auto-reconnect will not work with 3.*x* servers if the LOGIN.EXE isn't a 4.*x* version of LOGIN.

- The default login drive is always mapped to root. For example, if your first network drive is F, after loading the VLM, your F drive will look like a root to SYS:LOGIN. (F:> instead of F:\LOGIN).

- If a print job is deleted while in an ADDING state, the client will terminate the capture since it received a file IO error. This is the same behavior as NETX, except NETX prints a message indicating the failure, and may also display a "disk full" message. The message is not displayed in VLMs. This will be remedied in the future.

- The DOS Requester (VLM) relies more on the DOS environment PATH variable for its search drive information than did the old NETX SHELL. For this reason, handling of the PATH needs to be watched closer than with the SHELL.

- The DEC Pathworks product can use the standard or enhanced Microsoft Redirector in parallel with the VLMs. The Microsoft Redirector has a file problem with file execution on read-only executables. This problem can be avoided by setting the file attributes to read/write.

These issues are addressed in a limited module update available on NetWire.

Major VLM Fixes

The major problems fixed in the version 1.20 VLMs are listed in this section. Generally, these are problems that Novell received a large number of complaints about, or identified as high visibility with a high impact upon the customer.

- Packet Burst code was cleaned up for special-case scenarios where fragments could be lost. Problems that could present themselves in WAN environments were also fixed.

- The end of job (EOJ) code was fixed to work properly under all conditions.

- Task ID problems were fixed to ensure that proper task IDs are used for the VLMs, and to ensure proper interaction with other tasks.

- The COMSPEC code was fixed to handle command processors other than COMMAND.COM.

Other Miscellaneous VLM Fixes

The following are other VLM fixes in the latest version.

- Corrected the behavior of the TEMP drive and TEMP directory handle support (Interrupt 21 E2).

- Modified the Qualify code paths to ensure proper operation and to improve performance.

- Fixed code associated with the NET.CFG parameter Search Mode to ensure proper operation.

- Fixed auto-reconnect code path to support simultaneous auto-reconnect for multiple connections.

- Corrected cache buffer segment overflow scenario. Was typically manifested using large token ring packets where the CACHE BUFFERS NET.CFG parameter needed to be backed off to fit within the memory available to cache.

- Added IPX signature string next to the Interrupt 7A vector address to emulate NETX behavior.

- Improved NETX and DOS return code compatibility.

- Corrected errors with multiple record-lock attempts involving three or more stations.

- Corrected problems with use of multiple redirectors, including MSCDEX.

- Fixed to allow for NUL device redirection and directory detection on a network drive.

- READ ONLY COMPATIBILITY now defaults to OFF to match that of NETX.

- Fixed many anomalies with batch files involving LOGIN.EXE (certain caveats apply).

- Improved network path parsing to act more like that of DOS.

- Corrected problems in the packet-timing algorithm to better support slow WAN links.

- Corrected packet signature problems to work over WANs while packet bursting.

- Corrected negotiation issues to enforced check summing and packet signatures at the client when requested.

- Disabled short-lived socket support under Microsoft Windows, per the Microsoft Windows Software Developer's Kit (SDK).

- Fixed support to properly handle broadcasts when VLMs are loaded in multiple virtual machines (VMs) under Microsoft Windows.

- Corrected Interrupt 24 error string problem, where garbage was displayed in certain circumstances.

- Eliminated invalid message formatting from use of an incorrect message file, through implementation of message file version control.

- Fixed the problem with renaming files across servers so that it is now properly detected and the correct error is reported.

- Fixed the old library function GetPrimaryID() call. This could cause problems with specific login and logout sequences.

- Corrected handling of improperly formatted or invalid file name information on qualify remote file name calls.

- Corrected issue in the Set Task Mode call to ensure that the bit is set and in the correct segment in memory. Also corrected the Get Task Mode call for the same problem.

Helpful Hints for Tuning Workstations

FOR FASTER PERFORMANCE in XMS memory, consider loading REDIR.VLM low with the new NET.CFG parameter. The workstation's performance will be about the same as it would be if you loaded the entire VLMs in conventional memory, but with much less memory cost. Don't overlook the ability to reduce the memory footprint by the following:

- Exclude PRINT.VLM if no printing is desired.

- Lower the number of network printers if LPT1 is the only captured port.

- Reduce the number of connections if the client is on a small network.

- Exclude SECURITY.VLM if packet signing is not required.

- Exclude those modules that are not part of your network, such as BIND.VLM for bindery servers, NDS.VLM for NDS services, and PNW.VLM for Personal NetWare services.

See Chapter 10 for more information about which VLMs are optional and which are required.

One of the best ways to improve memory utilization is to know which applications are using the UMB area and how it's being used. VLMs will try and maximize the use of the UMB, but it will be unsuccessful if other TSRs have already used or fragmented the memory. If some TSRs can be loaded after the VLMs, this may allow the VLMs to maximize the memory use of the UMB area. A VLM needs more memory at load time than it does after it has been loaded. This is another good reason to load those TSRs that use the UMB area after VLMs load.

For more information about memory utilization and optimization for the DOS Requester, see the Novell Application Notes, May and June 1994 issues.

Future VLM Enhancements

HE VLMS WILL continue to be developed as the 16-bit NetWare Client for DOS and MS Windows. The product will be designed for optimal performance and footprint on the 80286 platform with 1MB of real memory.

The next generation VLMs will also provide NDS support for the private and global DOS sessions of OS/2 and NT. The VLMs should also work in 16-bit DOS emulation environments on other platforms where lower-level network connectivity can be accessed.

The two major goals for the version 2.00 VLMs will be to run as fast or faster than NETX.EXE in all cases, and to do so in a smaller conventional memory footprint. The performance goals will be realized through major modifications to current implementations of various algorithms and low-level services in the client.

The VLMs will continue to be enhanced and maintained for at least five more years. This coincides with the continued life expectancy of the 80286 platform in the market. After this time, the client may continue to be maintained in support of 80286 platforms on other continents. The client of choice in the continental United States will be the NetWare 32-bit Client.

Migrating Other Operating Systems to NetWare 4.11

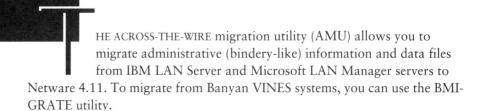

THE ACROSS-THE-WIRE migration utility (AMU) allows you to migrate administrative (bindery-like) information and data files from IBM LAN Server and Microsoft LAN Manager servers to Netware 4.11. To migrate from Banyan VINES systems, you can use the BMI-GRATE utility.

Migrating from LAN Server or LAN Manager

THE NETWORK ORGANIZATION used by LAN Server 1.2 or 1.3 and LAN Manager is different than that of Netware 4.11. Rather than dealing with individual servers, as you do in NetWare, you deal with a collection of servers called a *domain*. The AMU obtains domain information from the file server designated as the *domain controller*. Thus, only information that has been shared with the whole domain can be accessed; information (other than data files) specific to individual servers is not migrated.

To migrate from these network operating systems, you must be logged on to the domain as a user with administrative privileges.

Prepare for migration as described in Chapter 8 of this book. Then run the migration utility (MIGRATE.EXE) following the general procedure outlined in Chapter 11. The following sections discuss details that pertain to LAN Server and LAN Manager migration.

Information Migrated from **LAN Server and LAN Manager**

The types of information migrated from a domain include data file (including directory structure and data files) and DOS attributes for files and directories.

Files are copied from domain file servers one drive at a time. Once you select a drive on a domain server, all files on that drive are copied to the destination server.

Only DOS information is copied. If the drive contains files or directories that have OS/2 extended attributes, those attributes are not copied to the destination server.

If you choose to migrate data files, you will need to specify which domain drives to migrate, as well as a volume and, optionally, a directory on the destination server where you want each domain drive to be copied.

Note that the AMU does not overwrite any existing files on the destination server. When copying a file from the source server to the destination server, if a file with the same name already exists in the destination directory, a message is written to the report file stating that the file was not copied.

The following information is read from each user account:

- The user comment

- Whether or not the account is active

- Whether or not the user has administrative privileges

- Whether or not a password is required

- Whether or not the user is allowed to change his or her password

- The maximum password age

- The minimum password length

- Login time restrictions

- The account expiration date (if any)

If a user account has administrative privileges, this will be translated into Supervisor-equivalence on the destination server.

Unlike LAN Server, LAN Manager allows user names to contain spaces. While creating users on the destination NetWare server, the AMU converts spaces to underscores in each user name.

The information read for each migrated group includes the group comment and the group members. Access control profiles include access permissions for both files and directories. Table C.1 summarizes how the access permissions are translated.

TABLE C.1 Access Privileges in LAN Server and NetWare	**LAN SERVER ACCESS PERMISSIONS**	**NETWARE TRUSTEE RIGHTS**
	Read	Read (includes File Scan)
	Write	Write (includes File Scan)
	Create	Create (includes File Scan)
	Delete	Erase (includes File Scan)
	Attributes	Modify (includes File Scan)
	Execute	File Scan (the Execute Only attribute is not affected)
	Permissions	Access Control (includes File Scan)
	None	None

Print queues include the comment associated with the print queue. For a print queue to be read from the source domain, it must be a shared resource. Print queues that are not shared are not migrated from the domain.

When you are migrating print queues from LAN Server, you may need to consider how the migration utility names print queues. LAN Server allows resource sharing through both netnames and aliases. With LAN Server, the AMU uses the alias rather than the netname. If you want to migrate a printer queue from the LAN Server domain that is shared via a netname, you should create an alias and assign it to that printer queue before performing the migration. The alias name is the name that will be used when creating the print queue on the destination NetWare server.

Interoperability Issues in Migrating from LAN Server or LAN Manager

The AMU works best when it can access both the source and destination servers at the same time. If both of these servers are running NetWare this is a simple requirement to fulfill. All you need to do is make sure your workstation has either the NetWare shell or redirector loaded, and you can establish the connections to the source and destination file servers from within the AMU.

However, if your source server is not running NetWare, you'll need to load additional software to allow the workstation to communicate interoperably between the source and destination network operating systems. For a discussion of how to set up your workstation in an interoperable environment, see "ODINSUP Configurations for DOS Workstations" later in this appendix.

Two other interoperability issues concern the VLM client software:

- Be sure to use version 1.2 of the NetWare VLM client software. If you use an earlier version of the NetWare VLM client software in conjunction with the LAN Server client software, applications may lose track of which requester owns a given file handle. As a result, the AMU will not be able to copy data files from the source server; it will report that it is using an invalid file handle.

- You need to enable read-only compatibility. By default, read-only compatibility is turned off in earlier versions of the VLM software. If read-only compatibility is turned off when you use the VLM client software with the LAN Server client requester, files on a NetWare server that are flagged read-only (such as in the PUBLIC and LOGIN directories) cannot be loaded and run on the client. To turn on read-only compatibility, add the following statement to the NetWare DOS Requester section in your NET.CFG file:

  ```
  READ ONLY COMPATIBILITY=ON
  ```

- Be sure to unload and then reload the VLM software so the new value takes effect.

Issues in the AMU's Use of Bindery Services

The AMU uses Bindery Services to access Netware 4.11 servers; it does not have direct access to NDS. If the destination server is a Netware 4.11 server running NDS, Bindery Services must be enabled and the bindery context must be set up properly. All objects created by the AMU will be created in the bindery context that is in force when the migration takes place. If the bindery context for the server is changed after the migration, the users created in the old context by the AMU will be able to log in through NDS but not through Bindery Services.

You can use this to your advantage if you want to migrate several servers to different locations in NDS and you aren't worried about providing access to those locations through Bindery Services. Before migrating each server, change the bindery context of the destination server to the desired container in NDS. (In order to change the bindery context for a Netware 4.11 server to a container in NDS, a replica of the partition in which that container resides must reside on the server.) Then, when you run the AMU, all the objects migrated to the destination server will reside in that container. After migrating all the servers, change the bindery context back to the location in the NDS that you want Bindery Services clients to be able to access. The bindery context can be changed at the Netware 4.11 server's console or via a remote console connection.

When you change the bindery context to a different container, the password for the bindery Supervisor user does not change.

Because the AMU uses Bindery Services, naming conflicts can arise where they did not exist before. In NDS, each name in a given context must be unique; two objects of different types cannot have the same name. Be sure to rename objects as necessary before migrating.

Reviewing the Migration Report File

After you run the AMU (MIGRATE.EXE), review the results and make any necessary adjustments. The AMU keeps track of all operations performed on both the source and destination servers by writing them to a report file. Be sure to examine the contents of the report file and note any operations that could not be completed.

You can view report files by selecting the View Migration Reports option on the Select a Migration Action menu. These files are automatically given consecutive numbers, such as MIG000.RPT, MIG001.RPT, and so on.

Importing User Login Scripts from LAN Server or LAN Manager

Because it does not have direct access to NDS, the AMU cannot create a Login Script property in NDS for the users that it creates, even though each login script is written to the user's mail directory on the destination file server. To help overcome this limitation, the AMU creates two files on the destination server, UIMPORT.CTL and UIMPORT.DAT, which can be used in conjunction with the UIMPORT utility to import the DOS login scripts into NDS. If any of the migrated users have DOS login scripts, the UIMPORT.CTL and UIMPORT.DAT files are created and stored in the SYS:SYSTEM directory on the destination server.

To import the user login scripts from the file system to NDS, follow these steps:

1. Exit the AMU.

2. Make sure you have an NDS connection to the Netware 4.11 destination server and that you have rights to modify objects in the container in which the AMU created the users. The easiest way to do this is to log in to NDS as user Admin. Be sure your context is set to the same container as the destination server's bindery context.

3. Change to the SYS:SYSTEM directory on the destination server. You will need to have Read and File Scan rights in this directory.

4. Make sure you have a search drive mapped to the SYS:PUBLIC directory on a Netware 4.11 server.

5. Run the UIMPORT utility, providing the names of the control and data files as parameters, such as:

```
G:\SYSTEM> UIMPORT UIMPORT.CTL UIMPORT.DAT
```

The UIMPORT program will create the NDS Login Script property for each migrated user named in the UIMPORT.DAT file and copy the contents of the login script from the user's mail directory into that property.

ODINSUP Configurations for DOS Workstations

NOVELL'S OPEN DATA-LINK INTERFACE (ODI) specification supports the Network Device Interface Specification (NDIS) developed by IBM and Microsoft. ODI's modular architecture allows you to use NDIS protocol stacks along with IPX and other Novell-supported protocols.

A module called ODINSUP.COM allows NDIS protocol stacks to run unmodified over the ODI Link Support Layer and talk to an ODI LAN driver. This means that LAN Server network transports can be run over a common data-link (driver) specification.

This section details configurations for running NetWare with a LAN Server-specific environment.

The information presented here is adapted from the ODINSUP.DOC file that accompanies the ODINSUP.COM module. These files are available on CompuServe's NetWire forum as part of the DOS client software package included in the DOSUP6.ZIP file in the NOVFILES Library. For more information about ODI, read the ODIINFO.DOC file included in this .ZIP file, as well as the NetWare ODI Shell *for DOS manual.*

Installing and Configuring ODINSUP

The following is a summary of the procedure for installing and configuring ODINSUP and related modules:

1. At the workstation, all NDIS MAC (Medium Access Control) drivers should be replaced with their corresponding ODI LAN drivers.

2. Install ODINSUP.COM. Installing the ODINSUP module itself is simply a matter of loading it into memory. On a DOS machine, this is accomplished by loading ODINSUP.COM either at the command line or in a batch file (usually AUTOEXEC.BAT).

The NDIS PROTMAN device driver must be loaded before the ODINSUP module is loaded. You need to load ODINSUP only once; it can handle multiple ODI LAN drivers from the same module image in memory.

3. Configure ODINSUP via the NET.CFG file. You configure ODINSUP by adding statements to various sections of the workstation's NET.CFG, AUTOEXEC.BAT, and PROTOCOL.INI files, as outlined in the next sections.

Editing the NET.CFG File

NET.CFG is a configuration file that contains section headings and options that deviate from the established defaults of the regular NetWare workstation boot process. You can use any DOS text editor to create and modify the file.

Frame Types

Currently, ODINSUP supports only Ethernet and Token Ring compatible ODI LAN drivers. ODINSUP requires that the underlying LAN drivers have a number of frame types enabled:

- For Ethernet ODI LAN drivers, the ETHERNET_802.2, ETHERNET_SNAP, and ETHERNET_II frames types must be enabled.

- For Token Ring ODI LAN drivers, the TOKEN-RING, and TOKEN-RING_SNAP frames types must be enabled.

You enable frame types by specifying the keyword frame followed by the frame type name under the appropriate ODI LAN driver's section header. For example, the following lines illustrate how to enable frame types for the NE1000 driver:

```
LINK DRIVER NE1000
    FRAME ETHERNET_802.2
    FRAME ETHERNET_SNAP
    FRAME ETHERNET_II
    FRAME ETHERNET_802.3
```

The last line, to enable Ethernet 802.3 frame types, is optional, and is included mainly for backward-compatibility with NetWare version 2.*x*.

Binding a Protocol

If no binding information is present in the NET.CFG file, ODINSUP attempts to locate an Ethernet or Token Ring ODI LAN driver. If it finds one, ODINSUP attempts to bind to it. If this default action of ODINSUP is not desired, you should place binding information in the protocol ODINSUP section of the NET.CFG file to tell ODINSUP which ODI LAN drivers it should bind to. ODINSUP can be bound to a maximum of four ODI LAN drivers.

Bind entries specify the name of the ODI LAN driver and (optionally) the instance number, like this:

```
BIND LANDriverName InstanceNumber
```

The *LANDriverName* is usually the same as the ODI LAN driver's file name, without the extension (for example, NE1000 for NE1000.COM).

The *InstanceNumber* may be necessary in cases where more than one of the same type of network adapter are installed in the machine (two 3C523 adapters, for example). If an instance value is not specified, ODINSUP defaults to the first ODI LAN driver found in memory. In other words, if two 3C523 adapters are present, ODINSUP binds to the first loaded instance of the ODI LAN driver. The lowest possible instance value is 1.

Here are some sample NET.CFG Bind commands showing how to assign instance numbers:

```
PROTOCOL ODINSUP

    BIND NE1000; bind to the first instance of the
        NE1000 ODI LAN DRIVER

    BIND 3C523 2; bind to the second instance of the
        3C523 ODI LAN DRIVER

    BIND TOKEN 1; bind to the first instance of the
        TOKEN ODI LAN DRIVER
```

Editing the **AUTOEXEC.BAT** File

In the AUTOEXEC.BAT file, ODINSUP must be loaded after the LSL.COM module and ODI LAN drivers (such as NE1000.COM or 3C503.COM), and before the NDIS protocols and NETBIND.EXE. Load the ODI protocol stacks (such as IPXODI.COM and TCPIP.EXE) after NETBIND:

```
LSL

3C503

ODINSUP

(load NDIS protocols (if not loaded in CONFIG.SYS)

NETBIND

(load ODI protocols
```

Editing the **PROTOCOL.INI** File

No ODINSUP-specific information is necessary in the NDIS PROTOCOL.INI file. However, the PROTOCOL.INI file is still necessary to tell the NDIS protocols which MAC they should bind to and use. Normally, you can remove all information for NDIS MAC drivers from the PROTOCOL.INI file.

The PROTOCOL.INI file must include a section for each NDIS protocol used. Part of the protocol section is the Bindings=statement, which specifies what NDIS MAC the protocol should bind to. This MAC name should be the name of the ODI LAN driver (NE2, NE1000, TOKEN, and so on).

If the ODI LAN driver's name starts with a number (for instance, 3C503), precede the ODI LAN driver name with the letter *x* (for example, x3C503).

If you want to bind ODINSUP to an adapter instance number other than 1 (as when ODINSUP is bound to the second NE2 ODI LAN driver), append the instance number to the end of the ODI LAN driver name. For example, if ODINSUP is to be bound to the second instance of an NE1000 driver, use NE10002 for the MAC name. Similarly, to bind ODINSUP to the fourth instance of a 3C523 driver, use x3C5234 for the MAC name. The appropriate MAC names are displayed when ODINSUP is loaded.

Here are some sample PROTOCOL.INI commands showing binding instructions:

```
[PROTOCOL_MANAGER]
    DRIVERNAME=PROTMAN$
[ETHERAND]
    DRIVERNAME=DXME0$
    BINDINGS=NE2
    ;BINDINGS=x3C523
    ;BINDINGS=NE22 ;for second instance of NE2 board
```

Check the statements in the PROTOCOL.INI file carefully. If they are incorrect, you may get a message such as:

```
PRO0025E: Failed to bind
```

when you run NETBIND.EXE. This message can be caused by an invalid Bindings= statement in the PROTOCOL.INI file. Make sure the PROTOCOL.INI file resides in the path given in the /I: parameter on the line in CONFIG.SYS that references the PROTMAN driver. Another common mistake is not having removed your NDIS driver from the CONFIG.SYS file.

ODINSUP Memory Usage

Once installed, ODINSUP.COM consumes approximately 4900 bytes of DOS memory. Each additional adapter ODINSUP is bound to will increase memory usage by approximately 2800 bytes.

The size of the installed LSL and ODI LAN driver is usually about the same amount of memory as the corresponding NDIS PROTMAN and NDIS MAC Driver. Using ODINSUP instead of an NDIS MAC driver incurs an additional 4900 bytes of memory usage, but this will vary depending on the LAN driver used.

Routing Issues

NDIS application packets cannot be routed across a Novell router. A Novell router will only route packets for protocols that are loaded on the router. Currently, only IPX and TCP/IP protocols are provided and supported by Novell. Since ODINSUP interfaces to the NDIS protocol being used, the packets on the wire are not necessarily supported on the router. For this reason, you can't communicate with LAN Manager (or any other NDIS service) which is on the other side of a Novell router, even with ODINSUP.

Future revisions of Novell's Multi-Protocol Router may be able to route additional protocols. Check your current version to see if your protocol can be routed.

Node Address Overrides

An optional NDIS MAC capability that allows on-the-fly node address overrides is not supported by ODINSUP because ODI MLIDs do not support this feature. However, ODI MLIDs do support node address overrides from the NET.CFG file. NDIS protocols that want to change the node address will not work with ODINSUP. This should not be a problem, since the user desiring a different node address can simply specify it in the NET.CFG file.

Note that ODINSUP will allow its NDIS node address function to be called. However, it will return an error if the node address given does not match the node address already configured in the ODI MLID driver it is using.

Sample Configuration for IBM LAN Server

This section shows a sample IBM LAN Server and NetWare ODINSUP solution with an NE2000 Ethernet adapter (the version of ODINSUP.COM must be dated 2-27-92 or later).

The **CONFIG.SYS** File

```
DEVICE=C:\PROTMAN.EXE
DEVICE=C:\DXMA0MOD.SYS 001
DEVICE=C:\DXME0MOD.SYS
DEVICE=C:\DXMT0MOD.SYS S=12 C=14 ST=12 O=N
FILES=40
BUFFERS=40
SHELL=C:\COMMAND.COM /E:2000 /P
LASTDRIVE=M
```

The **AUTOEXEC.BAT** File

```
PROMPT $P$G
LSL
NE2000
ODINSUP
NETBIND
NET START
CALL INITFSI.BAT
IPXODI
NETX
N:
```

You must load NETX after NET START and CALL INITFSI.BAT.

The **NET.CFG** File

```
PROTOCOL ODINSUP
    BIND NE2000
```

```
LINK DRIVER NE2000
    INT 5
    PORT 360
    FRAME ETHERNET_802.2
    FRAME ETHERNET_II
    FRAME ETHERNET_SNAP
    FRAME ETHERNET_802.3
    PROTOCOL IPX 0 ETHERNET_802.3
```

The PROTOCOL.INI File

```
[PROTOCOL_MANAGER]
    DRIVERNAME=PROTMAN$

[ETHERNET]
    DRIVERNAME=DXME0$
    BINDINGS=NE2000
```

Migrating from Banyan VINES

TO MIGRATE TO NETWARE 4.11 from Banyan VINES, you use the NCS BMIGRATE utility update. This update operates in a similar manner to the standard MIGRATE utility. However, it only operates using the Across-the-Wire migration method.

With a workstation logged in to both network systems, the BMIGRATE utility will read the required information from the VINES side, store it at the workstation, and then write the information to the NetWare side. The length of time the migration process will take depends on the speed of your workstation and the amount of data you are trying to transfer.

The BMIGRATE utility lets you select specific information from the VINES StreetTalk directory, and the VINES server's data files, so that you can upgrade a server and create a customized destination server. The BMIGRATE utility leaves the source server intact and only copies information to the destination server.

This utility allows you to preserve your user environment (users and their rights assignments) as well as other user account information.

The BMIGRATE utility is a special-release product and has not yet been issued as a regular Novell product. There is no technical support available for this migration product.

Performing a system migration requires time for planning prior to running the utility, time for running the utility, followed up by time for reviewing the migration. You will need to inspect the migration results and perform some system administration clean up by hand. The entire process can take several days, depending on the size of the system.

Preparing to Migrate to VINES

System administrators involved in the migration should be trained in both VINES and NetWare network system administration, including Novell Certified NetWare Engineer (CNE) training or the equivalent knowledge. Administrators should also have read and understood the proper publications for both network architectures. The Novell and Banyan product manuals are available from either company. *Novell Application Notes* are available directly from Novell, by subscription, or by back-issue orders.

The other tasks for preparing for the migration, such as making full system backups, are similar to those for preparing to migrate from earlier versions of NetWare. Make sure your VINES server meets the Netware 4.11 hardware and memory requirements. See Chapters 8 and Chapter 11 for more information about migration preparations.

Hardware Requirements for Migrating to VINES

Three computers are needed to upgrade using the Across-the-Wire method:

- The Banyan VINES server. This is called the *source* server.

- A NetWare server running Netware 4.11. This is called the *destination* server.

- A DOS workstation with NetWare Client for DOS and MS Windows software loaded. This is called the *client workstation*.

BMIGRATE Capabilities

This BMIGRATE utility will migrate the following NetWare NDS items from their respective Banyan StreetTalk counterparts (where available):

- User information

- User name

- Login restrictions

- Password restrictions (except grace logins)

- Login time restrictions

- Network address restrictions

- Directory and file rights

- Group membership

- Security equivalences

- Aliases

- Group information

- Group name

- Directory and file rights

- Group membership

Migrating Users from VINES

Users on the source server are created as new users on the destination server. User login names, user account restrictions (such as account balance, expiration, password, and time restrictions) are copied.

Users with the same user names are merged; that is, their user information (login names, print job configurations, and login scripts) are added together. However, their user account restrictions are not merged; they remain unchanged.

Migrating Groups to VINES

Migration from one Directory-based network to another Directory-based network can take a considerable amount of time. If you are migrating a large Directory tree, this process can take a full day to complete. In some cases, it will be more efficient to migrate a group at a time.

The migration utility will make an effort to resolve all rights issues with the users and groups that it migrates. For example, if you have a user who is a member of a group that is not being migrated, and that user has rights to users, groups, or files in a part of the tree you are migrating, those rights are not migrated to the NDS tree.

An error message is generated in the log file, and you will need to assign those rights manually after the migration is completed.

Having the proper documentation in hand before migrating your Directory structure is one of your best defenses against migration problems. You can be aware of, and in some cases resolve, many of these issues before you even run the migration utility.

Migrating Files to VINES

The second component that is migrated by the migration utility is the file system. BMIGRATE will migrate only Banyan DOS file systems. Macintosh or UNIX file system support is not provided with this utility. Additionally, Banyan VINES network system shared files are not copied to the destination server.

Any file on a source server that has the same name as one that exists on the destination server is not copied to the destination server. An error message appears on the screen during the migration, and this error is also written to the migration report, to let you know that a file by that name already exists on the destination server.

You can overwrite the file if it is older. If you want to keep the file, you can rename it and copy it to the destination server, or you can manually copy it over the other file after the migration is completed.

Migrating Directories to VINES

If a directory is being migrated that has the same name and path as a directory that already exists on the Netware 4.11 server, the files from both directories are merged under the destination directory name.

The source server directory structure and files are migrated and become a part of the new NetWare destination server file system. If necessary, you can modify the organization on the destination server after all the source servers are migrated.

BMIGRATE does not migrate the following items to NetWare NDS from StreetTalk:

- User profiles

- Print services

- Mail services

- Name space files (Macintosh, UNIX, or OS/2)

- Informational attributes, such as mailing address, phone number, and fax number

- Nested groups (lists containing lists)

- Passwords

The migration utility allows you to either assign passwords that are generated randomly for all migrated users or allow users to log in to the new system without a password. Randomly generated passwords are stored in a file called NEW.PWD in SYS:SYSTEM on the Netware 4.11 destination server. They can be accessed only by the Admin user.

The migration utility creates two files in SYS:SYSTEM on the destination server: UIMPORT.CTL and UIMPORT.DAT. These files can be used with the UIMPORT utility to import VINES user profiles into NDS login scripts. UIMPORT allows you to import data from an existing database to the NDS database. See the section "Importing User Login Scripts from LAN Server or LAN Manager," earlier in this appendix, for more information.

Installing New Netware 4.11 Servers for Migration from VINES

Once the Netware 4.11 NDS tree is planned, you should install and configure the new Netware 4.11 servers. Add any configuration information that was not included with the StreetTalk migration, such as additional Admin-level users.

Make sure that the destination servers meet all the storage system requirements for the entire migration. If you are performing the migration in sections, make sure that there is enough disk space to handle the largest storage system migration needs of any particular section.

At this stage, you should plan any applications that will be replaced with the switch to Netware 4.11, such as e-mail and system backup programs. These applications should be installed and tested prior to proceeding with the migration.

Installing Clients for Migration to VINES

You should carefully plan how you will distribute the new NetWare client software to the Banyan VINES clients and meet the needs of booting a workstation with a dual stack.

Also take into account issues regarding those clients that are converted to Netware 4.11 and those that are still running VINES while they wait to be converted. These issues include e-mail and data file redundancy.

Connecting to NetWare and VINES Servers

The critical task of migrating information and system files from the VINES network to the NetWare network typically falls to one workstation. This workstation must be able to connect to both environments at the same time. This workstation will require some specialized configuration.

The following sections discuss some of the memory and client software issues that are important to providing this connection and provide some sample startup files for connecting to both environments.

Memory Management

The memory requirements of the BMIGRATE utility are approximately 480KB of conventional memory. The migration workstation must use some type of upper memory manager to provide upper memory blocks (UMBs) for loading network driver terminate-and-stay-resident (TSR) programs.

The following is a sample CONFIG.SYS file that provides sufficient conventional memory for running the BMIGRATE utility:

```
DEVICE=A:\HIMEM.SYS
DEVICE=A:\EMM386.EXE 4096 /RAM /NOEMS
DEVICE=A:\VINES\PROTMAN.DOS /I:A:\VINES
SHELL=A:\COMMAND.COM A:\ /P /E:1024
```

```
BUFFERS=10
FILES=21
STACKS=9,256
FCBS=1,0
LASTDRIVE=Z
DOS=UMB
DOS=HIGH
```

Both the NetWare and VINES client software must share a single network interface card (NIC) software driver. The migration utility has been tested using Ethernet networks only.

Since NetWare provides support for VINES native client architecture, NDIS, via the ODINSUP program, this can be facilitated using ODINSUP, as discussed earlier in this appendix.

Additionally, in order for the migration workstation to support multiple frame types, you must use a NIC that supports multiple frame types.

Setting Up a Workstation with an NE2000 Ethernet Card

The migration utility was tested using the NE2000 NIC. The following are examples of a batch file to load the network drivers for a migration workstation using an NE2000 Ethernet card, called CLIENT.BAT, a NET.CFG file, and a PROTOCOL.INI file.

The CLIENT.BAT File:

```
LH A:\NWCLIENT\LSL
LH A:\NWCLIENT\NE2000
LH A:\NWCLIENT\ODINSUP
CD \VINES
BAN /NC
NDISBAN
LH NETBIND
ARSWAIT
LH REDIRALL
```

```
CD \
LH A:\NWCLIENT\IPXODI
A:\NWCLIENT\VLM
Z:LOGIN
F:LOGIN .ADMIN.NOVELL
```

The NetWare NET.CFG File:

```
LINK SUPPORT
    MEMPOOL 4096
    BUFFERS 4 1514
    MAX STACKS 8
PROTOCOL ODINSUP
    BIND NE2000
    BUFFERED
LINK DRIVER NE2000
    PORT 300
    INT 3
    FRAME ETHERNET_802.2
    FRAME ETHERNET_II
    FRAME ETHERNET_SNAP
    FRAME ETHERNET_802.3

NETWARE DOS REQUESTER
    CHECKSUM=OFF
    READ ONLY COMPATIBILITY=ON
    LARGE INTERNET PACKETS=OFF
    FIRST NETWORK DRIVE=F
    IPX RETRY COUNT=60
```

The Banyan PROTOCOL.INI File:

```
[PROTOCOL_MANAGER]
DRIVERNAME=PROTMAN$
[NE2000]
DRIVERNAME=NDISBAN.DOS$
BINDINGS=NE2000
```

Setting Up a Workstation with a 3Com Ethernet Card

Using a 3Com Ethernet card is slightly more difficult, because the multiple frame type support is different with the 3Com card. The following are examples of a batch file to load the network drivers for a migration workstation, a NetWare NET.CFG file, and a Banyan PROTOCOL.INI file, using a 3Com 3C509 Ethernet card.

The CLIENT.BAT File:

```
LH A:\NWCLIENT\LSL
LH A:\NWCLIENT\3C5X9
LH A:\NWCLIENT\ODINSUP
CD \VINES
BAN /NC
NDISBAN
LH NETBIND
ARSWAIT
LH REDIRALL
CD \
LH A:\NWCLIENT\IPXODI
A:\NWCLIENT\VLM
Z:LOGIN
F:LOGIN
```

The NetWare NET.CFG File:

```
LINK SUPPORT
    MEMPOOL 4096
    BUFFERS 4 1514
```

```
          MAX STACKS 8
   PROTOCOL ODINSUP
      BIND 3C5X9
      BUFFERED
   LINK DRIVER 3C5X9
      FRAME ETHERNET_802.2
      FRAME ETHERNET_II
      FRAME ETHERNET_SNAP
      FRAME ETHERNET_802.3
   NETWARE DOS REQUESTER
      CHECKSUM=OFF
      READ ONLY COMPATIBILITY=ON
      LARGE INTERNET PACKETS=OFF
      FIRST NETWORK DRIVE=F
      IPX RETRY COUNT=60
```

The Banyan PROTOCOL.INI File:

```
[PROTOCOL MANAGER]
   DRIVERNAME=PROTMAN$
[VINES_XIF]
   DRIVERNAME=NDISBAN$
   ; BINDINGS=ELNK3
   BINDINGS=X3C5X9
; [ELNK3]
   ; DRIVERNAME=ELNK3$
; [X3C5X9]
   ; DRIVERNAME=X3C5X9
```

Running the **BMIGRATE** Utility

The BMIGRATE utility is a variation of the MIGRATE.EXE utility, used to migrate to Netware 4.11 from earlier versions of NetWare. You follow the same basic steps to set up for VINES migration and to run the migration utility. See Chapter 11 for details about running the MIGRATE.EXE utility, which also apply to using the BMIGRATE utility.

LM/NTS/LS Migration Utility

If you are migrating from any of the following versions of operating systems you must use Novell's LM/NTS/LS migration utility also known as Quiet Thunder:

LAN Manager version 2.0 or 2.2

LAN Server version 2.x, 3.x, or 4.0

NT Server version 3.5 or 3.51

Novell Consulting recently produced the LM/NTS/LS utility that enables you to quickly and easily migrate your NT Server, LAN Server, and LAN Manager operating systems to Netware 4.11. This product is produced as part of Novell Consulting's Migration Toolkit and is available with complete documentation from their Web page at www.novell.com on the Consulting Toolkit Web page.

The Novell Consulting Migration Toolkit is offered "as is" and is not a standard Novell tested and approved product. Novell does not warranty this product or any situation arising from its use.

Setting Up Network-Direct Printing Devices

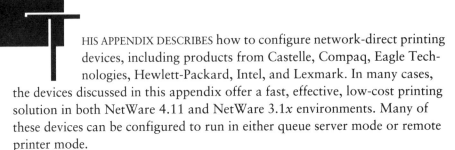

HIS APPENDIX DESCRIBES how to configure network-direct printing devices, including products from Castelle, Compaq, Eagle Technologies, Hewlett-Packard, Intel, and Lexmark. In many cases, the devices discussed in this appendix offer a fast, effective, low-cost printing solution in both NetWare 4.11 and NetWare 3.1*x* environments. Many of these devices can be configured to run in either queue server mode or remote printer mode.

In queue server mode, the hardware print server directly accesses the print queue using NCP (NetWare Core Protocol) calls. Under most circumstances, this mode will place the least load on a NetWare server.

In remote printer mode, the device functions in a way similar to a workstation running NetWare 4.11's NPRINTER.EXE or RPRINTER.EXE in 3.1*x*. Devices configured for remote printer mode are controlled by a NetWare print server.

An Overview of Setting Up Queue Server Mode

N GENERAL, SETTING up a network-direct printing device in queue server mode involves the following steps:

1. Use the printer configuration utility to reinitialize assignments. (This is necessary if the network-attached printer was previously assigned as a print queue server or remote printer.) You may also need to use PCONSOLE to delete any previous assignments.

2. Use PCONSOLE or NETADMIN/NWAdmin to create your printing services.

- Create one or more queues to be serviced by the printer.

- Create a Printer object for the printer, configure the Printer object as Other/Unknown, and assign it the queues previously created.

- Create the Print Server object to service the printer and assign the printer to the print server object.

3. Run the printer configuration software.

- Select the printer to be configured.

- Choose to configure as a queue server.

- Type in the name of the print server.

- Select the file server where the queues are located.

An Overview of Setting Up Remote Printer Mode

I N REMOTE PRINTER mode, the device functions in a way similar to a workstation running NPRINTER.EXE (NetWare 4.11) or RPRINTER.EXE (NetWare 3.1*x*). Devices configured for remote printer mode are controlled by a NetWare print server.

Devices running in this mode under NetWare 4.11 run considerably faster than they did under NetWare 3.1*x*. The increased speed and flexibility offered with NetWare 4.11 makes remote printer mode a very effective way of providing network printing.

In order to run devices in remote printer mode under NetWare 4.11, you must load PSERVER.NLM from the NetWare server console.

The only limitation is that the Print Server object must be defined in the NetWare 4.11 server's bindery context(s). All other print objects—including Print Queues and Printers—can be in any context.

In general, setting up a network-direct print device in remote printer mode involves the following steps:

1. Use the printer configuration utility to reinitialize assignments. (This is necessary if the network-attached printer was previously assigned as a print queue server or remote printer.) You may also need to use PCON-SOLE to delete any previous assignments.

2. Use PCONSOLE or NWAdmin to create your printing services.

   ■ Create one or more queues to be serviced by the printer.

   ■ Create a Printer object for the printer, configure the Printer object as Other/Unknown, and assign it the queues previously created.

   ■ Create the Print Server object to service the printer and assign the printer to the Print Server object. You can use an existing print server for this purpose. Simply assign to it the printer to be serviced.

3. Load or reload the PSERVER NLM at the server console to reinitialize the print server with the new changes.

4. Run the network-attached printer configuration software.

   ■ Select the printer to be configured.

   ■ Choose to configure as a remote printer.

   ■ Select the print server to service this printer.

   ■ Select the printer number.

Setting the Bindery Context

BEFORE YOU PROCEED with any steps to configure a printing device, you should determine the valid bindery context(s) of the server. Type the following at your NetWare 4.11 server console:

```
CONFIG
```

and press Enter. The bindery context appears on the screen. If necessary, change the context by running PCONSOLE and selecting Change Context from the Available Options menu. At the Enter context prompt, enter the desired context, or press the Insert key to browse for a context.

Group EVERYONE must exist in this bindery context. Either set the bindery context to the context that contains group EVERYONE or create the group using NWAdmin at a DOS workstation.

Running PCONSOLE's Quick Setup

A FTER YOU HAVE determined the bindery context of the server you are using, in many cases, you can use PCONSOLE's Quick Setup option to set up your print objects in NDS. Log in to the same server. Depending on the product and configuration, you may need to log in as user Admin (or equivalent) and remain in NDS mode, or log in as user Supervisor in bindery mode. For example, if you used NetWare server SALES, to log in as Admin, type:

```
LOGIN SALES/Admin
```

To log in as Supervisor, you would type:

```
LOGIN SALES/SUPERVISOR /B
```

Then follow these steps to use PCONSOLE's Quick Setup option:

1. Run PCONSOLE. Make sure the current context displayed at the top of the screen is the same as the bindery context you set when you began. If it is not the same, choose Change Context and press the Insert key to browse for that bindery context.

2. Choose Quick Setup. The Print Services Quick Setup screen appears. Change the printer and print queue names (and print server name, if you are creating one) as desired. Follow the information and key lines at the bottom of the screen. Press F1 for context-sensitive information.

3. Choose a volume on the same NetWare server that you have been using. To browse for a volume, highlight the Print queue volume field and press Enter, and then press Insert. Choose a volume with sufficient disk space to temporarily store users' print jobs.

In PCONSOLE, press Insert and browse the tree to select the appropriate items.

4. Configure the printer as type Parallel and Manual Load or Other/Unknown.

5. Press F10 to save your changes. PCONSOLE saves the configuration and automatically assigns the printer to the print queue and the print server to the printer.

6. Note the printer's logical number for use in subsequent steps. Choose Printers from the main menu, highlight the printer you just created, and press Enter. The logical number is displayed in the Printer number field.

7. Press Alt-F10 or Esc to exit PCONSOLE.

For more information about using Quick Setup, see "Quick Path for Setting Up Printing" in Chapter 3 of *Novell's Print Services Manual*.

Castelle Products

THIS SECTION INCLUDES information about installing Castelle's JetPress network boards and LANPress interface boxes. Since JetPress network boards bypass the parallel port, they usually are much faster than LANPress interface boxes. You can set either one to operate as its own print server or as a network (remote) printer serviced by PSERVER.NLM.

Queue Server Mode for a Castelle Print Server

Follow these steps to configure a Castelle print server in queue server mode:

1. Determine the bindery context, as described at the beginning of this appendix.

2. Log in to the same NetWare server as user Admin and run the JPINSTAL program. For example, if you used NetWare server SALES in step 1, you would type:

   ```
   LOGIN SALES/ADMIN
   ```

   and then execute JPINSTAL.

3. In JPINSTAL, answer the preliminary questions. Type **Y** and press Enter; type the serial number of your network board or box and press Enter; and then type **Y** and press Enter.

4. Type **S** and press Enter to select print server mode.

5. Assuming that this is a first-time configuration or that the network board has not been renamed, press Enter to continue.

6. Accept this network board as the master server by typing **Y** and pressing Enter.

7. Use no additional servers. Press Enter to continue.

8. Enter a new print queue name. Existing print queue names will not work. Type a new print queue name and press Enter.

9. Use no additional print queues. Press Enter to continue.

10. Answer the "...PostScript..." query. Novell tested this without a cartridge. Type **N** and press Enter.

11. Answer the "...copy..." query. Novell tested this without a copy. Type **N** and press Enter.

12. Verify and accept the configuration. Type **Y** and press Enter. After a few seconds the DOS prompt should appear. Do not interrupt operation until the prompt appears.

Print jobs can now be submitted to the print queue in either NDS or bindery modes. User Supervisor is the only print queue operator automatically assigned by JPINSTAL.

We recommend that you add user Admin as an operator. Group EVERYONE is the only print queue user assigned automatically. Under NDS, do one of the following:

- Add Organization or Organizational Unit container objects to the print queue user list using NWAdmin or PCONSOLE.

- Use NETADMIN or NWAdmin to assign existing and new NDS users to group EVERYONE.

Remote Printer Mode for a Castelle Print Server

Follow these steps to configure a Castelle print server in remote printer mode:

1. Determine the bindery context (as described at the beginning of the appendix).

2. Log in to the same NetWare server as user Admin, execute PCONSOLE (remain in NDS mode), and use the Quick Setup option (as described at the beginning of this appendix). Configure the printer as type Parallel and Manual Load. Castelle ignores the interrupt setting.

3. After you exit PCONSOLE, load the print server software (PSERVER.NLM) at the NetWare server console. To browse, type:

   ```
   LOAD PSERVER
   ```

   and press Enter twice.

4. Choose the print server you created with Quick Setup in the context you used in step 1. You can also specify the name at the prompt or in the AUTOEXEC.NCF file. For example, to load print server PS_SALES in the Sales context of organization WWW, type the following:

   ```
   LOAD PSERVER .PSSALES.OU=SALES.O=WWW
   ```

   and press Enter.

5. Run JPINSTAL at the DOS workstation where you are logged in as user Admin.

6. Answer the preliminary questions. Type **Y** and press Enter, type the serial number of your network board or box and press Enter, type **Y** and press Enter.

7. Select network (formerly remote) printer mode by typing **R** and pressing Enter.

8. Type the print server name used above and press Enter.

9. Type the logical printer number determined earlier and press Enter.

10. Type the printer name used above and press Enter.

11. Enter the print queue name used above and press Enter. Verify the name by typing **Y** and pressing Enter.

12. Use no additional print queues. Press Enter to continue.

13. Answer the "...PostScript..." query. Novell tested this without a cartridge. Type **N** and press Enter.

14. Verify and accept the configuration. Type **Y** and press Enter. After a few seconds, a message prompts you to restart the print server.

15. Unload the print server and load it again. You can unload PSERVER.NLM by typing:

    ```
    UNLOAD PSERVER
    ```

    and pressing Enter at the server console (the same one you used in step 1). To load the print server again, type:

    ```
    LOAD PSERVER
    ```

    and press Enter.

16. Type **Y** and press Enter at the workstation to complete JPINSTAL.

Print jobs can now be submitted to the print queue in either NDS or bindery mode. PCONSOLE automatically assigned user Admin and the container object as print queue users.

In bindery mode, only user Admin appears as a print queue user. If NetWare 3.1*x* users print to this printer, use NWAdmin to create the group EVERYONE and assign users to it; then use PCONSOLE to assign the group EVERYONE as a print queue user.

Compaq Printer Network Boards

OU CAN CONFIGURE the network board in your Compaq printer to operate as its own print server or as a network printer serviced by PSERVER.NLM.

Queue Server Mode for Compaq Network Boards

Configuring the printer for queue server mode involves making changes in PCONSOLE and running NICPRINT. Follow these steps to make the necessary changes in PCONSOLE:

1. Determine the bindery context (as described at the beginning of the appendix).

2. Log in to the same NetWare server used in step 1 as user Supervisor in bindery mode, execute PCONSOLE, and use the Quick Setup option (as described at the beginning of the appendix). Choose Other/Unknown from the Printer type field.

3. After you exit PCONSOLE, turn on the printer that has the network board installed. If the network board has not been configured yet, the printer will print an information page that includes the physical ID number of the network board.

4. Run NICPRINT. A list of network boards broadcasting on your network appears.

5. Highlight the line with the physical ID number determined in step 4 and press Enter. A list of options appears on your screen.

6. Highlight Configure Printer and press Enter. A list of configuration options appears.

7. Highlight Print Server and press Enter. A configuration screen appears.

8. Highlight the Login Server field and press Enter. A list of NetWare servers appears.

9. Highlight the NetWare server used in step 1 and press Enter.

10. Highlight the Print Server Logical Name field and press Enter.

11. Type the print server name you used in Quick Setup and press Enter.

12. Highlight the Print Server Mode field and press Enter. A cursor appears in the field.

13. Press the right-arrow key to toggle the value to active.

14. Press Esc and choose Yes to save your changes. You may be asked twice to verify saving your changes.

15. When prompted to exit to PCONSOLE, choose No. The list of configuration options appears.

16. Press Esc. The list of options appears.

17. Highlight Network Interface Card (NIC) Management and press Enter. A list of management options appears.

18. Highlight Reset NIC, press Enter, and choose OK. After a few seconds, the list of management options appears again.

19. Press Esc twice; then press F2 to update the status. The status should report "running." Press F2 again if necessary.

20. Press Esc to exit NICPRINT.

Print jobs can now be submitted to the print queue in either NDS or bindery mode. User Supervisor is the only print queue operator automatically assigned by PCONSOLE.

We recommend that you add user Admin as an operator. Group EVERYONE is the only print queue user assigned automatically. Under NDS, do one of the following:

- Add Organization or Organizational Unit container objects to the print queue user list using NWAdmin or PCONSOLE.

- Use NETADMIN or NWAdmin to assign existing and new NDS users to group EVERYONE.

Remote Printer Mode for Compaq Network Boards

Configuring the printer for remote printer mode involves making changes in PCONSOLE and running NICPRINT. Follow these steps to make the necessary changes in PCONSOLE:

1. Determine the bindery context (as described at the beginning of the appendix).

2. Log in to the same NetWare server used in step 1 as user Admin, execute PCONSOLE (remain in NDS mode), and use the Quick Setup option (as described at the beginning of the appendix). Configure the printer as type Parallel and Manual Load. The network board ignores the interrupt setting.

3. After you exit PCONSOLE, at the NetWare server console, load the print server software (PSERVER.NLM). To browse, type:

   ```
   LOAD PSERVER
   ```

   Then press Enter, and press Enter again.

4. Choose the print server you created in Quick Setup in the context used in step 1. You can also specify the name at the prompt or in the AUTOEXEC.NCF file. For example, to load print server PS-SALES in the Sales context of organization WWW, type the following:

   ```
   LOAD PSERVER .PSSALES.OU=SALES.O=WWW
   ```

   and then press Enter.

5. Turn on the printer that has the network board installed. If the network board has not yet been configured, the printer prints an information page that includes the physical ID number of the network board.

6. Log out as user Admin, and then log in as user Supervisor in bindery mode (as described at the beginning of the appendix).

7. Start NICPRINT. A list of network boards broadcasting on your network appears.

8. Highlight the line with the physical ID number determined in step 5 and press Enter. A list of options appears on your screen.

9. Highlight Configure Printer and press Enter. A list of configuration options appears.

10. Highlight Remote Printer and press Enter. A configuration screen appears. (Remember, remote printers are considered network printers in NetWare 4.11.)

11. Highlight the Print Server field and press Enter. A list of print servers broadcasting on the network appears.

12. Highlight the print server used above and press Enter.

13. Highlight the Remote Printer Logical Name field and press Enter.

14. Type the printer name used above and press Enter.

15. Highlight the Remote Printer Mode field and press Enter. A cursor appears in the field.

16. Press the right arrow key to toggle the value to active.

17. Press Esc and choose Yes to save your changes. You may be asked to verify saving your changes twice.

18. When prompted to exit to PCONSOLE, choose No. The list of configuration options appears.

19. Highlight Network Interface Card (NIC) Management and press Enter. A list of management options appears.

20. Highlight Reset NIC, press Enter, and choose OK. After a few seconds, the list of management options appears again.

21. Press Esc twice; then press F2 to update the status. The status should report "running." Press F2 again if necessary.

22. Press Esc to exit NICPRINT.

Print jobs can now be submitted to the print queue in either NDS or bindery mode. PCONSOLE automatically assigned user Admin and the container object as print queue users. In bindery mode, only user Admin will appear as a print queue user.

If NetWare 3.1x users print to this printer, use NetAdmin to create the group EVERYONE and assign users to it, then use PCONSOLE to assign the group EVERYONE as a print queue user.

Eagle Technology Printing Devices

THIS SECTION INCLUDES information about installing Eagle's Extended Systems NetWare-based products to work with NDS. Follow these steps to configure printing:

1. Determine the bindery context (as described at the beginning of the appendix).

2. Log in to the same NetWare server used in step 1, execute PCONSOLE, and use the Quick Setup option (as described at the beginning of the appendix).

3. After you exit PCONSOLE, install the ExtendNet card or PocketPrint-Server hardware.

4. Attach the network cables.

5. Turn on the power.

6. Run the PMAN utility provided on the Extended Systems Network Utilities diskette. An opening screen appears.

7. Highlight the printer network interface card and press Enter. A User Selections menu appears.

8. Select Configure the Printer Network Interface Card.

9. Select Configure for PSERVER mode.

10. Press the spacebar to display a list of file servers.

11. Select a file server either by accepting the default or by pressing Insert to bring up a list of available servers. Press Esc twice and enter the name of the print server.

12. Press Esc twice to save your changes. Once the NIC is reset, it will be logged in as the print server using the name you assigned.

You may also choose to configure the PMAN utility for RPRINTER mode. You can verify the printer number by looking at the list of PSERVER printers in PCONSOLE. When you assign a printer to a print server, NetWare 4.11

automatically assigns a printer number. This number can be verified by looking at the printer list under Print Server Information in PCONSOLE. Refer to the *Pocket PrintServer User's Guide* for information about using the PMAN utility for RPRINTER mode.

Hewlett-Packard JetDirect Network Boards

OU CAN CONFIGURE the JetDirect network board in your Hewlett-Packard printer to operate as its own print server or as a network printer serviced by PSERVER.NLM.

These instructions assume you are running JETAdmin for Windows. See the HP JetDirect Network Interface Configuration Guide for more information about using JETAdmin.

Note that JetDirect network boards manufactured before late 1992 use unencrypted passwords that NetWare 2.12 and later versions don't allow by default. These boards generate messages at the server console, unless you type:

```
SET ALLOW UNENCRYPTED PASSWORDS=ON
```

at the server console. You can also place this command in the AUTOEXEC.NCF file.

Queue Server Mode for HP JetDirect

Follow these steps to configure the JetDirect device in queue server mode:

1. Determine the bindery context (as described at the beginning of the appendix).

2. Log in to the network from a workstation as Supervisor and run JETAdmin.

3. Select the printer you want to configure from the list box.

4. Select Configuration. The Printer I/O Configuration screen appears.

5. Choose Queue Server and enter the print server's name in the Printer Name (Queue Server) field.

6. Select Add Queue. The Available Print Queues list appears.

7. Select a print queue from the list, or create a new queue, and then click on Close. The Printer I/O Configuration screen appears.

8. Type a description of the queue in the description field. The description will be available to users through JETPRINT.

9. Select Test Page to print a test page.

10. Click on Close to exit the Printer I/O Configuration screen.

11. Select Exit to exit JETAdmin.

Remote Printer Mode for HP JetDirect

Follow these steps to configure JetDirect in remote printer mode:

1. Determine the bindery context (as described at the beginning of the appendix).

2. At a DOS workstation, log in to the same NetWare server used in step 1 as user Admin, execute PCONSOLE (remain in NDS mode), and use the Quick Setup option (as described at the beginning of the appendix). Choose Other/Unknown from the Printer type field.

3. Save your changes (press F10) and exit PCONSOLE (press Esc).

4. Reboot the print server, and then run JETAdmin.

5. Select the printer you want to configure.

6. Select Configuration. The Printer I/O Configuration screen appears.

7. Choose Remote Printer and enter a name for the printer in the Printer Name field.

8. Select the print server's name, or enter a new name in the Print Server field.

9. Select the printer number assigned in PCONSOLE.

10. Type a description in the description field. This description will be available to Windows users in the JETPRINT utility.

11. Click on OK to exit the Printer I/O Configuration screen.

12. Select Exit to exit JETAdmin.

Intel Netport Express XL/EL

THIS SECTION PROVIDES instructions for setting up an Intel Netport Express print server under NetWare 4.11 Bindery Services. Testing of Netport Express XL and EL print servers with NetWare's Bindery Services has shown the products to work successfully. NPAdmin requires a few additional installation steps, as described below. Netport Manager sets up the XL or EL for NetWare Bindery Services without additional steps.

You must have Admin rights to configure an XL or EL on NetWare 4.11. If you are logged in to the NetWare 4.11 server as Admin but are not recognized as having Admin rights by Netport Manager or NPAdmin, your bindery context may not be at the root level. One solution is to create a user named Supervisor and give it Admin rights.

Follow these steps to configure a port as a print server using NPAdmin (XL only):

1. Select the Print Modes Setup option. If this option is grayed, you may need to specify a Remote Boot Load server.

2. Select Print Server mode.

3. Identify the appropriate file server in the File Servers to Service window.

To configure the port as a print server, you must define File Server 1 (the primary file server). You must set up one server at a time and define its port and queues before adding another file server to the list. Repeat the process as needed to configure the XL to service as many as eight file servers.

The XL's primary file server contains the list of the other file servers (2 through 8) that the XL services print jobs for. To select a file server from a list of available servers, press Insert, then highlight the desired server and press Enter. Press Enter until NPAdmin displays the Configure Port window.

4. Select the port you want to set up for the server identified in step 3. The Configure Port window uses check marks to indicate which ports you have configured during this session.

5. Select the queues you want the port to service. You can assign a total of 32 queues per print server. To see a list of available queues, press Insert.

6. Press F10 to accept the current server/port/queue settings in the Configure NetPort Port as Print Server window. Press Esc if you wish to back up to a previous window and change a setting.

7. Return to the main menu by highlighting Return to Main Menu and pressing Enter. When you return to the main menu, NetPort is automatically updated and reset.

8. Exit to DOS and run PCONSOLE.

9. Select Print Queues and delete the queue you created in NPAdmin by highlighting it and pressing Delete. Then re-create the queue with the same name by pressing Insert, typing in the queue name you just deleted, and pressing Enter (this allows you to associate a volume with the queue).

10. Press Insert at the Print Queues Volume box and select the volume you want for print services. Press Enter twice.

11. Select Highlight queue name by pressing Enter. The Print Queue Information box appears. Highlight Print Servers and press Enter.

12. Press Insert at the Print Servers box. Highlight and press F5 on each entry that matches the name of ID of the NetPort print server. Once the entries are marked, press Enter. Then exit to DOS.

13. Invoke NPAdmin from the DOS prompt. Reset the NetPort print server by highlighting Port-Status and pressing Enter. Select Reset NetPorts. Highlight the NetPort print server you just configured and press Enter. Then select Reset NetPort and press Enter.

14. View the results by choosing Port Status and then selecting the Check All Ports option. The two ports are then listed as print servers. Choose Port Status and then View NetPort Settings to view all information, including the queues selected (press the spacebar to see the list).

You are now ready to print.

Lexmark Products

EXMARK SUPPLIES TWO versions of its network printer adapters:

- The external version is the IBM 4033 LAN Connection for Printers and Plotters. This version provides attachments for one parallel device and one serial device. The 4033 requires a new PROM, which can be ordered from Lexmark for a nominal fee. The PROM was made available June 1, 1994.

- The internal version (INA) is available for the IBM 4039 family of laser printers. The INA requires a firmware level of 44 or above. INA level 44 firmware is available free of charge from Lexmark.

Both versions can operate in either print server (PSERVER) mode or remote printer (RPRINTER/NPRINTER) mode.

Contact the Lexmark Technical Support Center at (606) 232-3000 for more information.

Print Server Mode for Lexmark Adapters

Both Lexmark adapters require NetWare Bindery Services to operate as print servers. Determine the current context for Bindery Services by using the SET BINDERY CONTEXT command at the file server's console, as described at the beginning of this appendix. If no context is defined, use the SET BINDERY CONTEXT command to set up an Organizational Unit for Bindery Services. After setting the context for Bindery Services, configure the adapter as a print server using the PCONSOLE utility.

Both a print server and a print queue are required. The adapter does not require a Printer object, but Lexmark recommends defining one because the CAPTURE and NPRINT utilities can send jobs to a Printer object.

Follow these steps to set up the Lexmark adapter as a print server:

1. Use the CX command to change to the proper context for Bindery Services.

2. Start the PCONSOLE utility. Make sure the current context is the one with Bindery Services enabled. If the context is not correct, choose Set Current Context to change it.

3. Select Print Servers, press Insert, and enter the adapter name. If you are configuring a 4033, also create an entry with the name appended with _PAR or _SER to differentiate between a parallel and serial port.

4. Select the newly created print server.

5. Select Users to define users for the print server. Print server users can be located anywhere in the NDS tree.

6. Select Operators to define operators for the print server. Print server operators can be located anywhere in the NDS tree.

7. Make sure no password is enabled for the print server.

8. Select Print Queues and press Insert.

9. Enter the print queue name. PCONSOLE next prompts you for the print queue's volume name.

10. Enter a volume name. The volume can reside anywhere on the network.

11. Select the newly created print queue.

12. Select Users to define users for the print queue. Print queue users can be located anywhere on the network.

13. Select Operators to define operators for the print queue. Print queue operators can be located anywhere in the NDS tree.

14. Select Print Servers to define the print servers allowed to service entries in the print queue. Press Insert to bring up a list of defined print servers. Select all the print servers allowed to service jobs from this print queue.

For the 4033, select both the adapter name and the adapter name appended with _PAR or _SER. The appended names allow the 4033 to tell if the queue is to be serviced by the parallel port, the serial port, or both.

15. Select Printer, press Insert, and enter the printer name.

16. Select the newly created printer.

17. Go to the Print Queues Assigned entry and press Enter.

18. Press Insert and select the print queue created in the previous section. This completes the configuration of the adapter for PSERVER mode.

Remote Printer Mode for Lexmark Adapters

The Lexmark adapters support NPRINT mode and operate as remote printers under NDS. The Bindery Services feature is not required since no bindery-related calls are used. Therefore, the print server, printer, and print queues can be defined anywhere within the NDS tree.

To configure the adapter, follow these steps:

1. Start PCONSOLE, select Print Servers, and select the desired print server. This is the Novell print server (NLM, VAP, or EXE).

2. Select the Printers option. This brings up a list of printers serviced by the print server.

3. Press Insert to see a list of defined printers (within the current context). To create a new printer, press Insert again.

4. Enter the adapter name if you are using an INA. Enter the adapter name appended with _PAR or _SER (depending on whether you are using the parallel or serial port) if you are using a 4033. The printer now appears in the list of defined printers.

5. Select the newly defined printer to place it in the list of serviced printers.

6. Select the printer from the list of serviced printers.

7. Select the Configuration option.

8. Highlight the Location option and press Enter. Change Auto Load to Manual Load.

9. Select the Print Queues Assigned option and press Insert to view a list of defined print queues.

10. Select the print queue. Press Insert to define a new print queue, or select a previously defined print queue, or browse the tree for other print queues. This completes the configuration of the adapter under NDS for PSERVER mode.

Glossary of
Terms

ACCESS CONTROL LIST (ACL) A list that contains information about which other objects can access it. ACL is an attribute of every object in NDS. Trustees and the Inherited Rights Filter (IRF) are contained in the ACL.

ACROSS-THE-WIRE MIGRATION (AMU) METHOD A method of migrating file server data, trustee rights, and other information to a NetWare 4.11 server. The AMU method allows you to migrate from other network operating systems, such as LAN Manager and LAN Server, in addition to earlier versions of NetWare. A similar utility, known as BMIGRATE.EXE, allows you to migrate from Banyan VINES.

ADD SELF PROPERTY RIGHT (A) Grants a trustee the right to add or remove itself as a value of the attribute. This right is only used for attributes that contain object names as values. For example, the A right can be used for lists of group members or mailing lists.

ADMIN USER OBJECT A user object that is created during NetWare 4.11 installation. It has the Supervisor right to all objects, so it can be used to create your NDS tree. The Admin user can be renamed or deleted. Plan carefully. The bindery supervisor password is the same as the Admin object password when you initially create the Admin object, unless you are doing a bindery migration. In that case, the Supervisor will have the same password as it did in the bindery.

ALIAS OBJECT A leaf object that points to the original location of an object in the Directory. Aliases are used to point to other objects to provide easier access to those resources from different parts of the tree. Access to the Alias object, and the properties of the object to which it refers, requires the Read right to the Alias name and the Read right to the properties of the object it refers to.

ATTRIBUTE A term used interchangeably with *property* to signify a characteristic of an NDS object. Each type of object has certain attributes that hold information about the object. Attribute also refers to the characteristics of a directory or file that tell NetWare what to do with the directory, such as compress, migrate, purge, and so on.

BACKGROUND AUTHENTICATION The process by which a workstation is given access to a particular NetWare 4.11 server. Authentication uses a public key encryption process that encrypts password information before being sent across the network. The process is handled in the background; the user only needs to enter a password to continue.

BACKLINK A multivalued attribute used by NDS to maintain external references. An individual backlink identifies the locations of external references. The backlink attribute contains the name of the server that holds the external reference and the object ID of the object on that server.

BINDERY A network database found in versions of NetWare prior to NetWare 4.11. The bindery contains definitions for entities such as users, groups, and workgroups.

BINDERY CONTEXT The container(s) where a NetWare 4.11 server sees user objects. When a bindery-based NLM (NetWare Loadable Module) makes bindery calls to the server, the server searches for the objects located in its bindery context(s). You can specify up to 16 bindery contexts in NetWare 4.11.

BINDERY QUEUE OBJECT A leaf object that represents a queue placed in the Directory during a migration from NetWare 3.

BINDERY SERVICES A feature of NetWare 4.11 that allows bindery-based utilities and clients to coexist with NDS on the network.

BLOCK SUBALLOCATION The NetWare 4.11 disk process that allows files to share the same disk block. Block suballocation divides various disk blocks into 512-byte segments. Files needing these extra blocks can use them rather than wasting a whole new disk block to copy the remainder of a file. At most, the wasted disk space will be less than 512 bytes.

CHILD PARTITION A partition that is subordinate in the tree to another partition, called the parent partition.

CLIENT 32 FOR DOS/WINDOWS Novell's latest 32-bit workstation client for use with DOS and Windows 3.*x* versions.

CLIENT 32 FOR WINDOWS 95 Novell's latest 32-bit workstation client for use with the Windows 95 operating system.

COMMON NAME (CN) The naming attribute of an object, as displayed in the NDS tree. Currently, all noncontainer (leaf) objects are named by CN.

CONTAINER LOGIN SCRIPT A script containing drive mappings, printer assignments, and so on, for users that reside in a particular container. Every container can have a container login script. Users will not execute login scripts of other containers unless they are an object in that container.

CONTAINER OBJECT An object that holds or contains other objects. Container objects are used to logically organize all other objects in the NDS tree. The three types of container objects used are Country (C=), Organization (O=), and Organizational Unit (OU=). Locality (L=) is also a container object, but it is not currently being used.

CONTEXT The location of an object within its container in the NDS tree or its parent object name.

COUNTRY OBJECT A container object that resides above the Organization object(s) in your tree. The Country object can be used to further differentiate locations within a large, worldwide network.

CURRENT CONTEXT Your current location in the NDS tree.

CX A workstation utility that allows you to change your current context in the NDS tree.

C2 SECURITY A security mechanism based on U.S. Department of Defense (DOD) security specifications. Novell IntranetWare/4.11 is C2 security compliant when all the proper steps are taken with the servers and workstations.

DIRECTORY MAP OBJECT A leaf object that is used to point to a file directory on a particular NetWare volume. This object is useful in login scripts. If the location of an application moves, you can change the Directory Map object to point to the new directory rather than change the login script.

DIRECTORY TREE A hierarchical structure of objects in the NDS database, also called the *NDS tree*. The tree includes container objects that are used to organize the network and leaf objects that represent resources.

DIRECTORY TREE NAME A name of 1 to 32 characters assigned during installation of a new tree. The tree name is the [Root] object in NetWare 4.11.1 and previous releases. Future versions of the NetWare utilities may display the tree name.

DISTINGUISHED NAME The unique name of each object in an NDS tree. The object's distinguished name consists of the names of each object between itself and the [Root] object of the tree.

DSMAINT A utility found in the INSTALL.NLM that allows you to back up NDS files to have in case of server hardware failures or maintenance of servers' volumes where NDS must later be restored.

DSMIGRATE A migration utility found under the Tools menu of NWADMIN. This utility, licensed from Preferred Systems, allows you to model an NDS tree and migrate bindery information from NetWare 3 to IntranetWare/4.11.

DSREPAIR A NetWare Loadable Module (NLM) based utility that repairs and corrects problems in the NDS database. It is also used to view partition and time synchronization information.

EFFECTIVE RIGHTS The rights that an object can actually exercise to see or modify a particular directory, file, or object. An object's effective rights to a directory, file, or object are calculated by NetWare each time that object attempts an action.

EXTERNAL REFERENCE A pointer to an NDS object that is not found locally on the server. External references provide NDS with the ability to authenticate and reference objects that are not local to the server. They also maintain an object's lineage up the tree. The external references are stored on each NetWare 4.11 server in a separate NDS partition called the external reference partition. The data in this partition is not synchronized to other NetWare 4.11 servers.

FILE MIGRATION UTILITY A migration utility found under the Tools menu option found in NWAdmin that allows you to migrate file data from one server to another, typically used during a migration from NetWare 3 to IntranetWare/4.11.

GLOBAL LOGIN Allows users to log in to the network, rather than to individual servers, and gain access to all network resources.

GROUP OBJECT An object that contains a list of user object names. The Group object can be used across an entire tree. This object is used for users needing the same access rights to applications, print queues, and so on. Groups can be used to further differentiate rights within a container rather than creating another container to assign rights.

HEARTBEAT The interval at which time stamps are exchanged to see if synchronization is necessary if no update has occurred.

INHERITANCE The rights granted to a trustee by a trustee assignment and received at a lower level in the NDS tree. These rights apply to everything below the point where the trustee assignment is made, unless another explicit trustee assignment is made or the rights are blocked by an Inherited Rights Filter (IRF).

IN-PLACE MIGRATION METHOD A method for loading NetWare 4.11.1 on an existing hardware platform already running an earlier version of NetWare such as 4.02, 4.01, 3.1*x*, and so on. The In-Place method preserves existing passwords but does not allow you to change block size during installation.

INTRANETWARE Novell's latest generation of operating system, providing a full-service intranet platform and offering all the advantages of NetWare 4.11.

LEAF OBJECT An object that doesn't contain any other objects, also known as a *noncontainer object*. Leaf objects are located at the end of a branch in the NDS tree. Leaf objects are users, servers, printers, print queues, and so on.

LOCALITY (L) OBJECT A container object that will be used beneath the Organization object(s) in your NDS tree to further define locations. This object is present in the NetWare 4.11.1 schema, however it has not been implemented by the utilities.

LOGIN SCRIPT A script file containing commands that are used to set a workstation's environment. A login script can map drives, display messages, set environment variables, and execute programs or menus.

MASTER REPLICA The replica that contains a copy of partition information. During a partition operation, the master replica prevents other partition operations from being performed on read/write replicas in the partition.

NAME TYPE Distinguishes the type of object name in a fully distinguished name. For example, in CN=BOB.OU=ENG.O=WWW, the name types are CN, OU, and O.

NDSMANAGER A 32-bit Windows-based utility used to monitor and manage partitions and replicas. It is considered a replacement for the older Partition Manager utility found in previous versions of NWAdmin.

NDS TREE The term used to describe an NDS database structure, also called *Directory tree*. It is an inverted tree shape, with the [Root] object at the top, proceeding down with branches (containers) and leaf objects within containers.

NDPS The acronym used for NetWare Distributed Print Services, this is the ability to more closely manage and secure printers that are part of the NDS tree.

NETWARE DIRECTORY SERVICES (NDS) A global, distributed, replicated, special-purpose database that maintains information about resources on the network. NDS is based on the 1988 CCITT X.500 standard.

NONCONTAINER OBJECT An object that does not contain other objects, also called a *leaf* object. Examples of leaf objects are users, servers, and printers that are part of an Organizational Unit (OU) object.

OBJECT A logical representation of a network resource. Objects include users, groups, printers, volumes, computers, and other items that make up the NDS tree. Some objects represent physical entities; others represent logical entities, such as groups and print queues. An object is a structure in which information is stored. It can represent the actual entity on the network.

OBJECT ID A four-byte value that is assigned to each object that exists on a server. Object IDs are unique only on that server. The assignments of file system rights are maintained using the object IDs. The object IDs become the owners and trustees for the files and directories.

OBJECT RIGHTS Access rights to an object that are assigned to another object (which becomes a trustee of the object). Object rights do not affect properties or property rights, with the exception of the Supervisor object right, which also allows access to all property values.

ORGANIZATION (O) OBJECT A container object that helps organize other objects in the tree. You must have at least one Organization object. This object is usually your company name.

ORGANIZATIONAL ROLE (OR) OBJECT A leaf object that defines a position or role within an organization. The Organizational Role is assigned security access to perform certain functions. Individual users are then moved in as occupants to the role and receive all rights assigned to the role as long as they remain occupants.

ORGANIZATIONAL UNIT (OU) OBJECT A container object that is subordinate to the Organization object. The Organizational Unit is used to designate locations, workgroups, and departments within your tree structure.

PARENT PARTITION A partition that resides directly above another partition. It is a partition that has a boundary in the NDS tree above another partition.

PARTITION A logical division of the NDS object hierarchy. A partition forms a distinct unit of data in the NDS tree. It is used to store and replicate NDS information. Each partition consists of a container object, all objects contained in it, and data about those objects. Partitions do not generally include any information about the file system or the directories and files contained there. Directory Map objects do contain information about file paths.

PARTITION ROOT OBJECT The container object (usually an Organizational Unit) that defines the top or root of a partition. This partition root object has additional attributes that help NDS synchronize the data associated with the partition.

PARTITION TABLE The list on each NetWare 4.11 server that has NDS replicas stored on it. All NetWare 4.11 servers, even those without replicas, have a partition table. The partition table contains the partition name, partition type, partition state, and partition time stamp for each replica on the server.

PRIMARY TIME SERVER A time source server that synchronizes its time with at least one other Primary or Reference time server and provides time to Secondary time servers and to workstations, if needed. See also *Time synchronization.*

PRINT QUEUE A network directory that stores print jobs before being sent to the printer. A print server removes the print job from the print queue and sends it to the printer.

PRINT SERVER A server that takes print jobs from the print queue and sends them to a network printer. NetWare 4.11.1 servers run PSERVER.NLM and can service up to 255 printers.

PROFILE LOGIN SCRIPT An object that contains a login script to be executed only by users whose property specifies execution of the Profile. This script can be used for users needing a specialized set of login commands.

PROPERTY A characteristic of an NDS object, also known as an *attribute.* Some attributes of a user object, for example, are the name, phone number, fax number, and e-mail address. Each object has various associated properties.

[PUBLIC] TRUSTEE A special trustee that grants users access to objects, directories, or files. The trustee grants access to users who have only attached to a server. By default, each user is security equivalent to the [Public] trustee, which has been granted Browse rights. This allows each user to browse the NDS tree before logging in to a server. Be careful about assigning rights to this trustee.

QUEUE SERVER MODE A method for configuring NetWare printing that assigns queue(s) to a printer and a print server to a printer.

READ/WRITE REPLICA A type of replica that can be used to read or update NDS database information. Like a master replica, a read/write replica can initiate changes to objects. However, it cannot be used to create a new partition.

REFERENCE TIME SERVER A time source server that provides a time to which all other time servers can synchronize. This type of time server can be connected to an external time source to provide highly accurate time. See also *Time synchronization.*

RELATIVE DISTINGUISHED NAME (RDN) The leftmost name of the object relative to the current context set for the user.

REMOTE PRINTER MODE A method for configuring a network printer to be run from a network device, such as off a workstation or a server. You must load PSERVER.NLM on the server console in order to run a printer in remote printer mode. You must also configure the print server object as a bindery object in NetWare 4.11.

REPLICA A copy of an NDS database partition's information. For fault tolerance, keep at least two replicas of a partition in addition to the master replica.

[ROOT] OBJECT An object in the NDS tree that provides the highest access point in the tree. NetWare 4.11.1 utilities show the [Root] object at the top of the tree. The [Root] object is the name you gave the NDS tree (although the name is not shown by the NetWare utilities).

SECONDARY TIME SERVER A time server that obtains the time from a Single Reference, Primary, or Reference time server and can provide time to its clients. See also *Time synchronization.*

SECURITY EQUIVALENCE The concept of being equivalent in rights to another object. A user object that is made security equivalent to another object has all rights that the other object possesses. Security equivalence is not transitive. This means that if object A is equivalent to object B, and object B is equivalent to object C, object A is *not* equivalent to object C.

SERVICE ADVERTISING PROTOCOL (SAP) A protocol used by NetWare devices to advertise and query their services on an internetwork. Servers, printers, and other devices broadcast their services, allowing routers to create SAP tables that can keep other routers updated. Workstations can query the network to find a server by sending SAP request packets. SAP broadcasts are typically sent every 60 seconds. Time synchronization uses SAP broadcasts by default.

SINGLE REFERENCE TIME SERVER A time source that provides time to Secondary time servers and to clients. It is the sole source of time on the network. See also *Time synchronization.*

SUBORDINATE REFERENCE REPLICA An NDS replica that ties the parent partition with its child partition. A subordinate reference replica is created on servers where the parent partition is stored and the child partition is not on the same server. This type of replica contains only one object: the partition root object. Subordinate references are only visible when you use the NWAdmin (Partition Manager), PARTMGR, or DSREPAIR utility from the workstation. These replicas are managed completely by the system; they cannot be modified by a user or system administrator.

SYNCHRONIZATION The process of updating each replica of a partition after an addition, deletion, or modification to NDS. NDS replicas are automatically synchronized by the system without user or administrator intervention. Since the NDS replicas are distributed, the data is considered *loosely consistent.* This means that after an NDS object has been modified and before all the replicas with that object are synchronized, the data will be different on individual replicas.

TIME PROVIDER GROUP The method of using a Reference time server and two to seven Primary time servers to provide time to your network. A time provider group is used in lieu of a Single Reference server.

TIME STAMP A unique code that includes the time and identifies an event. It is reported by NDS at the time events occur, such as a password change or an object being renamed. NDS uses time stamps to establish event order, to record real-world times, and to set expiration dates. Time stamps are created using three values: whole seconds, event ID, and replica number. The seconds represent the time in seconds when the modification took place (total number of seconds since January 1, 1970). The event ID represents the number of events that occur within the same second. Every second, the event ID is reset to zero, which allows multiple changes to occur to the same object within the same second. The replica number uniquely identifies the replica within a partition.

TIME SYNCHRONIZATION A method of ensuring that all servers in an NDS tree report the same time. Time is synchronized by NetWare 4.11 every 10 minutes (by default). This parameter can be modified.

TRUSTEE ASSIGNMENTS The specific rights granted to an object for a file, directory, object, or property. When an object is granted access to any of the above, that object is made a trustee with those privileges.

VLM (VIRTUAL LOADABLE MODULE) A portion of the NetWare DOS Requester that is loaded through the VLM.EXE program. There are two types of VLMs: child and multiplexer VLMs. Child VLMs handle a particular type of functionality. A multiplexer VLM routes calls to the appropriate child VLM.

Index

Note to the Reader:

Page numbers in *italics* refer to figures or tables; page numbers in bold refer to primary discussions of the topic.

Symbols & Numbers

\# command, in login scripts, 118, 124
* (asterisk), in MONITOR.NLM utility, 121
\+ (plus), in object names, 51
= (equal sign), in object name, 37, 51
\ (backslash), in object name, 51
/ (forward slash), in object name, 51
. (period), in names, **41–42**
3Com Ethernet Card, workstation setup with, **402–403**

A

ABORT REMIRROR utility, *278*
access control list (ACL), 295, 300, 303–304, *304*, 428
accessing objects, in same context, 39
%ACCESS_SERVER login script variable, *369*
access speed, replicas and, 80
%ACCOUNT_BALANCE login script variable, *369*
accounting information, migration options for, *230*
account restrictions, default, migration options for, *230*
ACL (access control list), 295, 300, 303–304, *304*, 428
Across-the-Wire Migration (AMU) method,147, 154, 155–157, 221, 428
  for BMIGRATE, 394
  from 3.1*x* to 4.11, **227–239**, *227*
    for applications, 233–234
    bindery connection, 228–229
    information options, 229, *229–230*
    for login scripts, 231–232
    migrating system files, 230–231
    NetWare 3.*x* directories, 230
    passwords in, **232**
    printing, 232–233

migrating printing with, **270**
  quick tip, 212
  in test lab, 165
Add/Delete Self property rights, 301
additive licensing, **122**
Add Self Property right, 428
Admin User object, **21–23**, 299, 428
  importance of maintaining, 22
  location in tree design, 61
  quick tips, 16
  renaming, 22
administration. *See also* NetWare 4 management
  centralized or decentralized, 57, **67–69**
administratorscreating with security equivalence, **311–312**, *312*
  creating specialized, 316
  creating with trustee assignments, **309–310**, *311*
  securing roles with IRF, **317–318**
AFP NLM, 279
AFPCON NLM, 279
AHA1640.DSK file, 167, 169
Alias of an alias (-681) error, 359
Alias objects, **23–25**, *24*, 428
  granting and administering rights for, 24
  names for, 24, *24*
  quick tips, 16
  to set context, 119
  to set mobile user context, **135–136**, *136*
+ALL DSTRACE command parameter, 361
[All Properties], 301, 316
All referrals failed (-626) error, 351–352
%ALLOW UNLIMITED CREDIT login script variable, **369**
Ambiguous naming (-651) error, 355
AMU (Across-the-Wire Migration) method, 428. *See also* Across-the-Wire Migration (AMU) method
API (Application Program Interface), from Novell, 12
APICD.DSK file, 168